BOUNDLESS

BOUNDLESS

A WAYWARD ENTREPRENEUR'S
SEARCH FOR PEACE

GREG HOPKINSON

Published by Mountford Media & Publishing
PO Box 3987, Christchurch 8140
New Zealand
www.boundless.info

This edition published 2014

Designed, typeset and produced by Mary Egan Publishing
www.maryegan.co.nz
Printed in Singapore

ISBN 978-0-473-26073-6

PART ONE

The Meaning of Life?

Make money, retire young

ONE

That fucking bald bastard!

Detaching myself from the intensity of that thought, I'm aware I'm trapped in snow, unable to move, unable to breathe. My mouth and nose are packed full. Colours start evolving out of the darkness. I feel as if I'm being drawn, gently but powerfully, into deep, endless tranquility. I'm free-flowing into an unfolding stillness that is doubling back on itself and then turning inwards again, in a different dimension. It's indefinable, yet familiar, as if it's always been there.

So this is what it's like to die.

I become aware of my trapped arms and legs. Every part of my body is encased, as if in a block of concrete. My perspective glides beyond my body, as if it's not me watching.

Is Monica in here? No, she's alright. I saw her get out of the way. She'll be fine. Whoever said to use your arms in a swimming motion to create an air pocket around your face when you get caught in an avalanche has clearly never been buried in one.

I can't swim.

I can't even move a finger.

I drift deeper into peace. I am drawn, gently and easily, into rich dimensions of evolving bliss that expands inside me and outside me simultaneously. There seems to be no end to the fullness of this expansion.

The colours are soft and textured. There is no sense of orientation or motion.

The occasional thought starts floating through the stillness again. Are my skis still on? I hope not. My legs could break. The pole straps must be preventing me from moving my arms. I hope the others aren't caught. We'll be buggered if we're all in here. No, I'm sure Monica is out. Clifford could be in here though. I don't experience any real concern. There's no point – there's nothing to do. Deep calmness returns, drawing my attention into the tranquility. There is no movement, only silence and peace. Deep, deep peace.

I'm out. *I'm out!* Blow the snow out of your mouth. Ah, suck the oxygen in. Get it in. Get it in! Quickly, you might go under again. The avalanche is still moving. It's still happening! I'm under. It's like being dumped by a wave. I'm struggling to breathe.

Jeeesus! I hope I'm not going to get trapped.

No, I'm back out. I'm out. I have another chance.

Whoa, I'm on the leading face of the avalanche. It's coming to a halt. It's stopping.

Breathe. Breathe, mate.

Pumped full of adrenaline I struggle out of the snow and immediately attempt to activate the transceiver. I look up to the clumped snow lying above me on the ridge line. Ah, there's Monica. Thank Christ for that. I wave and she waves back. Thank God she's alright.

Clambering over the snow at the head of the slide, Bald Man clumsily tries to make his way down towards us. He looks OK. On the other side of the rubble I see the guide is OK too. Where's Clifford? He's still under somewhere.

How do I get this transceiver going? I fumble with the controls thinking, Christ, that training was useless.

Fifty metres away an orange ski boot breaks the surface, the heel kicking skyward. Looking at the transceiver I tell myself there's no need for this bloody thing. Just get over there and help Clifford get out. He's buried face-down under about a metre of snow but struggles out as I clamber towards him.

"Are you alright, mate?" I ask, as he kneels on the lumpy surface and brushes snow off his clothes.

"Yeah, I'm OK. Bald Man must have started this."

"Yeah, the little prick."

Monica comes over to us. I hug her with more enthusiasm than I've felt for a long time. I'm relieved she has made it through unscathed. She asks me if I'm OK.

"Yeah, I'm good. How are you?" I ask.

"Fine. But I thought you were gone. It was terrible."

"It's amazing we're all out, eh? That was a totally strange experience. I was fully aware of what was going on, but I was just so calm."

Indicating imminent retribution Clifford calls out, "Bald Man! Get down here!" Equally keen to get the little bastard I remove my gloves. Jonty, or Bald Man, as we call him, likes to compete with anyone he skies with.

When Jonty reaches us, he immediately braces for our attack. We both lunge at him. We wrestle him to the snow, attempting to pin his arms down, but he curls into the fetal position. Right now he's a decidedly irritating bald bastard. Looming over him, Clifford exclaims, "Bald Man, you started the lanche!"

"Piss off!"

"You're a menace," I say. But realising the futility of expecting him to show any remorse, I release my grip and allow him to get up.

Clearly pleased that he's made it down the mountain in one piece, Jonty starts to tell his own story.

"*Shiiiit!* I was traversing along and started my first turn when a crack opened up. As soon as the snow started sliding down the hill, my legs crumpled and I slid into a sitting position at the top of the slide. My head was high enough to allow me to see the whole thing unfold in front of me. Jesus, I had an armchair ride all the way down the hill. Man I was shitting myself! What a ride!"

"That explosion was the loudest noise I've ever heard. It gave me a real fright. But then as soon as I went under I fell into a super calm state. I was able to calmly assess what was happening to me. I knew I was in a lanche, but I had no idea which way was up, or whether I was facing up the hill or down," I say.

"There's nothing new in that, Arnie. You never know which way is up," Clifford says.

That's what he calls me: Arnie. The nickname reflects his jaundiced view that my personality is similar to Arnold Schwarzenegger's movie persona. Unfortunately, the name has stuck. I'd rather be called by the name my parents gave me: Greg.

Intent on continuing to tell the others what happened to me, I say, "I didn't experience any panic. I had only the odd random thought about Jonty starting it. The rest of the time I was amazed by how calm I was." I look at the others. "It was unbelievably peaceful, wasn't it?"

"It was something else, alright," Clifford agrees.

I get the impression that my experience was different from the others. I drift off, thinking about how I'd love to live life in a state of peace like that. Maybe I was in Heaven? But I didn't die.

"Hey Cliffy, you did religious studies at university. What's your understanding of Heaven?"

"You're not going religious on me are you?"

"No mate. I wonder if I just experienced Heaven," I respond.

"The only thing I ever read about Heaven was something that Christ said. He reckoned the Kingdom of Heaven was within. But I can't see how that works."

Whoomp, whoomp, whoomp, whoomp, whoomp. The chopper rapidly drowns out our voices as it comes in to land. The pilot looks relieved. He's seen the magnitude of the avalanche but has accounted for everyone. He gives the thumbs up. The engine whine alters and the rotor blades decelerate. The guide starts to make his way over to the pilot.

We all climb into the helicopter. As we ascend something catches my attention – a hawk, gliding over the avalanche, observing everything from a great height. I ponder my near-death experience for a moment. It really was as if I wasn't in my body. I was just observing it. It was like an infinite me observing my body's predicament. If my lungs had stopped working, I reckon that the peace and my ability to observe would have continued. The me who was observing wouldn't have died. Maybe there can be death only of the body. And again the thought occurs to me – if I can experience such peace under the snow, why can't I be peaceful out of the snow? Surely, becoming that supremely peaceful observer must be possible in real life.

TWO

Gold mining peaked twice in this country, in 1870 and 1906. It now appears the country is heading into another resurgence of gold exploration thanks to the use of modern technology, which has helped locate previously undiscovered deposits as well as deposits that would have been uneconomical to mine.

Marketing Matters, Issue No. 5, November 1988

It's a few months later and I'm employed as the operations manager of an alluvial gold dredge situated near the Grey River on the West Coast of New Zealand's South Island. An alluvial gold dredge is an earthmoving machine the size of a warehouse, mounted on a pontoon floating in a flooded quarry. Winches pull the dredge across the pond, allowing it to excavate the flooded face during the traverse. Water jets and gravity separate out the glittery stuff from the alluvial gravel. The washed gravels are then conveyed to the tailings at the rear of the dredge. The dredge's metal surfaces are constantly being abraded, eroded, knocked, torn, scratched, ripped, hammered and fractured. The noise is brutal.

As the operations manager my responsibilities involve the maintenance and operation of one of biggest earth-moving machines on the planet. The problem is that the dredge hasn't been fully commissioned yet. It incorporates a bunch of unproven technologies that the manufacturer is scrambling to sort out while we attempt to recover gold. I've been called out to some major cock-ups. Whenever anything goes wrong, it's big.

In fact it was something big going wrong that got me into this game in the first place. I'm here because I lost all of our money (and more) in the share market crash of October 1987. I'd done well keeping out of the nonsense leading up to the crash, despite most of my mates making a small fortune. But one week before the crash greed got the better of me. I punted 100 grand on three cowboy companies. They all went belly up on Black Tuesday. But being the market sage that I was, I proclaimed to my mates that it was just a technical correction, so I went back in and bought more. The problem was fourfold: the market didn't know shit, I knew even less, the companies were driven by crooks, and I didn't tell Monica until it was too late. The companies went south even further than the market's drop of 60 per cent, and Monica and I went down with them. We had to sell the new car and mortgage the previously debt-free holiday house.

A week after the share market convulsion, while driving to work in the station wagon I'd bought for a grand, I came to a stop at a set of traffic lights. In a new BMW in front of me sat an old flatmate of mine. In his mirror he could see me behind him, and he was jiggling up and down, laughing and pointing at me. His jeering persisted long after the lights turned green, and for the first time in a long while I felt the intense discomfort of ridicule. More important, I saw the vindictiveness of humanity. Some people just have no compassion. In the last conversation I'd had with that prick he'd said his long-term ambition was politics.

A mate of Jonty's was another one who just couldn't stop cackling like a hyena at my despair and financial ruin. The icing on the cake was when the $1000 station wagon was stolen. The cops found it on the south coast. Jonty's mate was the one who gave me a lift, and by the time I got there all that was left was a hub cap and half a dozen wheel nuts. The car hadn't been insured. I've never seen anyone so gleeful about someone else's demise as Jonty's mate. He was even more scornful than the future politician.

So. Monica and I are now living in the recently mortgaged holiday house. It's been a couple of years since we got married. We were together for three years before I slipped the gold band on her finger. But I'm not sure the marriage has lived up to either of our expectations. I'd hoped the intimacy between us would grow, but it hasn't. Not for me anyway. I've never asked Monica how it is for her. I don't seem to be able to open up. I just keep things to myself. I wish I wasn't so reticent. It makes me feel like I'm not completely honest with her.

Don't get me wrong – I love so many things about her. There's an almost Latin quality to her. It's not just her olive skin and full dark hair. It's her adventurous style that sets her apart.

But the thing I like most about her is that she's solid. She's down-to-earth and she cares about people. She's always there when you need her. Others appreciate that about her too. She's a charge nurse in the surgical ward at the local hospital. Her colleagues love working with her, not just because she's so likeable but because she's capable and efficient, and she can manage dicey situations under pressure.

She's got a group of friends she's had since school and they're close. They get together a lot. We both enjoy the space that socialising with our own friends provides. But I can be a bit judgemental about her from time to time. To be honest, I'm probably more judgemental of her than I realise. She loses her confidence when I have trouble accepting her as she is. I wish I wasn't so critical, but I just can't seem to help myself sometimes.

I often describe myself as tormented, but the reality is my life is abundant. Take our house, for example. It was built by my father, my brothers and my mates – all as a gift. I was in awe of them. I still can't figure out why they were so generous. I love the house. Monica and I flow easily here. And the money side of things is sorting itself out. But despite things looking pretty good on the outside, the torment is never far away. One day I'm upbeat, the next I'm down. The thing that puzzles me is I don't seem to have any control over when I'm happy and when I'm not. Sometimes my frustration over an unexpected incident, or someone's behaviour, can be really intense. And then it disappears and I'm happily cruising along for a week or two, until the torment takes over again. It's hard to put a finger on it, but I often have a yearning for something I haven't got, and that creates a sense of unease in me and in those around me.

That's where drinking heavily or smoking marijuana helps. It allows me to relax and have some fun. I feel so much more articulate and unrestrained when I've got a few beers on board, especially when I'm with my mates. Having a group of good boys gives me a sense of belonging.

I grew up on the West Coast with about 25,000 others. The rainforest, the rivers and the black sand beaches are often pounded by big weather systems ranging in from the Antarctic. But in between those low pressure fronts it's absolutely magical. It's where I'm living now. Despite half a dozen generations separating us from the genes of the people who came from all over the world in search of gold in the 1860s, we still don't have much time for authority.

At school I always had a runny nose and an unrivalled inability to catch a ball of any shape. I was also the smallest boy in every year. These weren't necessarily the greatest physical attributes you can have when you're surrounded by wayward boys. So I compensated by being mischievous. As incongruous as it sounds, I was drawn to the rough diamonds at school – and there were plenty of them. We derived much pleasure from pushing the envelope of acceptable behaviour. I loved my mates and I loved being at school.

I lost my virginity at 14 to a girl who knew what she was doing. All I knew was I had to do it, otherwise I'd become a social leper. At 15 I was drinking heavily every weekend in country pubs. I left the West Coast to be educated as a mechanical engineer at Canterbury University, a career choice that confuses me to this day.

Despite my bemusement at the marginal vocational guidance I received, I enjoy the heavy engineering game. The energy of big rotating gear and the robustness of the blokes appeal to me. A spade is a spade and the boys get on with the job and do what needs to be done.

As an engineer I can quickly understand the mechanics of a process system, but I'm technically limited. I struggle to persevere with the necessary discipline to complete detailed mathematical calculations, mainly because I have insufficient focus. However, I appear to be good at project management. I can readily visualise results and I inspire people from all walks of life to achieve some big outcomes under onerous circumstances. I love the challenge – it doesn't matter how big the project or what the industry, I'm keen to give it a go. And so far, I have been able to guide every project to completion on time and on budget.

But sometimes I feel scared, usually just before I drive in the gates to work. There's always some issue to resolve and it invariably involves conflict. There's always someone pissing me off, someone pushing my buttons.

I haven't been sleeping well. That's why I was awake when the phone rang half an hour earlier. Picking up the phone beside my bed I saw it was 4.20 am.

"Arnie, we're sinking," an alarmed voice informed me. "The dredge is sinking!"

"What's happened?"

"The stacker conveyor has been dragging across the tailings. It's picked up gravel and carried it back on to the dredge. The aft is nearly under. She's going down."

"If you've stopped bringing more gravel onto the dredge why is the waterline still rising?"

"We think there's a hatch open below the waterline."

"Is everyone alright?"

"Yeah, we're all OK."

"OK, I'll be there in 30 minutes."

They say one thing all miners have in common is that we're optimists. Some say we're dreamers, but for me right now this is nothing less than a fucking nightmare. As I drive into the mine site I see the conveyor is positioned low and the rear of the dredge is listing. The deck of the pontoon is normally chest height above the water level, but now water is lapping the aft deck. I fire up the tender and motor across the pond to the dredge, which looms over me. The rain drives hard from the south. The absence of the growling and squealing of the buckets, gravel surging in the rotating screen and the clatter of stones falling onto the tailings is eerie. It feels forlorn.

I make my way to the back to get an update. The electric lights form harsh shadows on the deck and highlight the rain. As I stride along in my steel-capped boots I make eye contact with one of the dredge operators. He flinches.

I raise my left hand to acknowledge him then ask, "Do you know where Colin is?"

Before he can respond I see Colin, the maintenance supervisor, at the rear.

Because construction of the dredge is still incomplete the 20-odd compartments comprising the pontoon remain connected by a series of unsealed conduits the diameter of a soccer ball. Colin and I begin checking the hatches on the deck of the pontoon. When we open the first hatch adjacent to the flooded compartment we see it's flooded too. Moving forward we open more hatches and each compartment is flooded. Not until we get near the bow of the dredge do we find a dry compartment.

I say, "OK, so the priority is to stop the flow into the rear hatch. While we try to solve that problem, we need to pump water out of these compartments at a faster rate than it's coming in." Colin nods, and we get to work.

By nine o'clock the water flow is under control. The bulkhead hatch is covered and the sump pumps are running. The dredge should be operational sometime today, before dark. I've got enough time to get home, have a shower, put on a suit and drive back to town for the board meeting at one.

In the shower the dread kicks in. Oh, Jesus. How are we going to get on top of this operation? It's so precarious. We must be getting close to going broke. My gut feels tight. Come on mate, focus on the positives. We've just saved the dredge from a watery grave. But I'm buggered if I know how we're ever going to get on top of that cutter-wheel system. Maybe we should remove it. Yeah, like Dave Alexander is going to give up on his cutter-wheel innovation. Although the shareholding structure of the operation is a 50:50 joint venture between the publicly listed Aussie goldmining outfit and Dave, he approaches the operation as if he owns it all.

So here we are in the board meeting. Dave's son is here. He has the dual role of mine manager and project manager for the dredge construction. He and I get on well. He's an inspirational, can-do sort of a bloke. It's never *if* we do something; it's *when* we do something. Doubt never creeps in.

Well, if it does, he never shows it.

As he says, "It's infinitely more powerful to focus on what you want, rather than focusing on what you don't want. If you're a proponent of world peace, join a peace movement rather than joining an anti-war movement. If you want happiness, then focus on what makes you happy rather than what makes you unhappy."

It's such a refreshing approach. Anything seems possible and we achieve so much. He appreciates what I do and that gives me a lot of confidence. For now, he's my mentor and I'm enjoying learning from him.

The chairman asks me to kick off with my presentation. I try to make it sound positive. I support my description of the dredge's performance with a summary of the production logs. "We've been hit by a succession of major events that have hammered production, but the unreliability of the cutter-wheel system has been the primary maintenance issue. It accounts for 50 per cent of downtime."

A heated discussion erupts, but in the end the chairman concludes, "At some stage we may need to closely assess the viability of the cutter wheel in the greywacke gravels."

Dave gets angry. "The dredge won't be viable without the cutter wheel, especially with gold prices the way they are."

The chairman nods resignedly, then turns to me and asks with a frown, "What was the cause of today's event?"

Oh dear, here we go. I attempt to cobble together a plausible synopsis of the morning's debacle. The chairman puffs his cheeks as he blows air across the table. "Do you have any feel for when operations will settle down to a more stable mode of production?"

I'd love to be able to say when, mate, but I can't. My mantra used to be "Give me the unshakeable fact", but it's impossible to have a hunch let alone a fact in this game. "It's difficult to say. At the moment the operation is so variable it's impossible to predict anything."

The chairman nods his head but seems bewildered. "Oh well, you'll just have to keep pressing on."

Next the mineralogist is invited to give his presentation. "Recent drill results suggest the ground we're moving into is leaner than expected. This indicates that the original gold assays were salted."

Salted. Great. It's common knowledge around these parts that prior to the Great Depression entrepreneurs had a habit of overstating or "salting" drill results, a strategy that increased the success of raising capital back in London. On this property the Depression arrived before the capital and the mining licence lapsed. Dave picked it up five years ago.

Then out of the blue the mineralogist pulls a spectacular stunt. He produces a gold ingot out of his briefcase. It's the first gold we've recovered from the mine and the bar is the size of half a pound of butter. With his mouth agape Dave lunges for it. He is absolutely beside himself. He appears mesmerised as he fondles and caresses the metal in his hand. Then after what seems like a lifetime he uses the back of his hand to wipe the dribble from his distorted mouth. It's definitely gold fever. I thought he was driven by the challenge of developing new dredging technology, plus owning half of the mine would've provided a handy income for him. But no, it's gold fever. He can hardly sit still as his body jiggles about.

Taken aback by Dave's response I look on, feeling increasingly uncomfortable as he continues to make love to the ingot. He's quite oblivious to the fact that we are all staring at him. I think, 'That'll keep him going for another month or two'.

A few weeks later I'm in my office. It's Wednesday, a day dedicated every week to preventive maintenance. I ponder how we seem to be doing a lot of pushing and shoving in this game: we don't seem to be going with the flow. Then the door opens and Colin bursts in.

"John's dead. The pump wear ring collapsed on him."

I'm stunned. I can't comprehend what I've just been told. "How did that happen?" I ask as I stand up from my seat.

"The wear ring was being manoeuvred by the overhead crane and the lifting eye failed. The ring fell onto John. The ambulance and local doctor have been called."

I pick up my helmet and place it on my head. As I follow Colin to his utility truck I have an image of the two-tonne steel doughnut, the diameter of my ceiling at home, teetering at the point where it rested on the riverbed and then falling onto John. In between our edgy exchanges as we drive along the road leading to the dredge I think about John. He was such a lively, likeable character. He was forever excited. His joy and enthusiasm were almost frightening. How could this happen? He was only 19 and he loved his job on the site more than anyone else.

Our vehicle comes to a halt about 20 metres from the accident. I make my way to where John is lying. Two coats have been placed over his lifeless body. There's nothing to do, I'm told, but wait until the ambulance gets here.

Five of us stand looking nowhere in particular and feeling utterly helpless.

It's surreal. How could this happen?

Four days later. It seems as if the mining industry is full of sayings and one of them is: "A good mine makes a good mine manager". In other words, gold in the ground compensates for the odd cock-up and poor management. Who knows, there may well have been enough gold in our ground, but unfortunately we didn't uncover it quickly enough to offset the fundamental flaws in the operation. The ongoing repair work consumed too much money and too much of our attention. Plus we were skinny on relevant dredging experience.

So, we've gone broke. It's my job to get everyone together and tell them they no longer have a job. There are no surprises: everyone knows that failure is imminent when a mine isn't producing mineral. After the meeting I talk to a couple of the supervisors about the events of the last four days.

One confesses to me, "The mine closing will be a double blow for John's parents. It's like your son has been killed in war and then four days later the war is over."

I'm taken aback by this analogy. Before I can respond the other bloke says, "Look, when your number's up, your number's up."

I'm even more disturbed by what he has just said. What does that mean? The conversation comes to an awkward finish. I'm left feeling numb and unsettled.

The strange thing is that John is dead, but his personality and essence remain alive for me. I can describe him perfectly, yet I'd have difficulty describing his physical features. I wonder if he's having the same experience that I had in the avalanche.

That night at home I demolish the best part of a bottle of whisky. I'm 30 but I know what 60 feels like. When there are about three fingers of Laphroaig left in the bottle, tears begin to pour down my cheeks. I start sobbing uncontrollably. The tears sting my eyes. I wipe the moisture from my face with the palm of my right hand. I'll be fine, but what about some of the others? There have been hard yards put in by some of the guys and there has been too much grief along the way. There aren't many jobs around and some of them might have to leave town. I start thinking about John and his family again.

Maybe it's time for us to leave too. Monica comes into the room and tells me to stop drinking and go to bed.

I find out at work the next day that we can pay wages and holiday pay after all, because sufficient cash has been held in reserve by our corporate lawyers. I've got no idea why they've had it, but all that matters is that there's enough to look after the boys.

In a taxi on the way to pick up the money the driver turns to me suddenly and confides, "Driving a taxi pays the bills, but my passion is reading palms. There's no money in it, but I love it."

"That right?" I say dully. "How long have you been reading palms?"

"Nearly 20 years."

"Huh."

"I can read yours if you like."

What, so he'll tell me I'm going to make lots of money, live happily with my beautiful wife and have lots of gorgeous children? Unexpectedly I find myself saying, "That's very generous. I've never been interested in having my palm read, but yeah, that would be great. Thank you."

I don't know why I say that, but here we go.

After pulling up outside the building that houses our lawyer's offices, the driver turns around and takes my hands and observes each one in turn. He appears stunned.

"I have never seen anything like this before. Honestly, this is incredible. The lines strongly indicate you are about to have a major change in your life and travel a completely different path. It's as if you have a specific task to complete."

"Is that right?"

"Your life is going to be one of great adventure. You will achieve what few others have."

"That sounds interesting. I've got no idea how that might happen, but there you go. Thanks for that." I pay the fare and offer him a gratuity for the knowledge. He declines. After seeing the lawyers I return home with the money in my briefcase, pleased I've made it back without being accosted and robbed by some baddie. I'm especially pleased we'll be able to send the guys on their way with a few shekels in their pockets.

The next day I go to a hairdresser and tell her I want my collar-length hair cut all over with a number one blade. She says, "Are you sure?"

"Yes, I'm sure," I respond.

As she turns to get support from one of her colleagues, she says, "I don't feel comfortable cutting it that short."

"I definitely want a number one cut on the sides and top. Don't worry, it's OK," I say. As the clipper starts effortlessly cutting a swathe through my thick hair I feel the stigma of this episode of my life being cleansed. Although my image in the mirror looks harsh, internally I feel a huge revival.

I have to say that after a couple of years in the alluvial goldmining game, it appears to be a bit like life – totally unpredictable and continually changing. All you can do is roll with the punches. And that's exactly what I'm doing. I've been retained by the receiver at the mine. They think I might have knowledge that could prove useful to a potential buyer of the assets. I'm not so sure. But in the interim they've got me doing security work, just keeping an eye on things at night and making sure no one gets in to vandalise the place.

The down time is giving me a chance to recover. I'd been close to burn-out. Ever since the avalanche I've kept thinking about how to live a happier, less stressful life. I've begun to think the best way to do it is to make a shit load of money and retire early. Maybe that's what the palm reader meant. Bugger this working for someone else. The trouble is, I've got no idea how I'm going to do it.

THREE

It's November 1989, late spring, the time of year when it can rain long and hard. I like the rain, though: the calmness, the shades of grey and the purity of it all. It soothes me and slows me down. What I love most about rain on the West Coast is that it often falls without wind. There's so much comfort in the rattle of a downpour on a corrugated iron roof, especially if there are a few flames dancing around in the fireplace. Yep, that's what I like. It doesn't matter if I'm feeling a bit down or not, the rain makes whatever's going on feel alright.

I'm watching the six o'clock news. Well, not really. I'm drifting off into a little commentary in my head about the standard of it. Our news is dross – stories of insignificant events cobbled together with opinion, completely devoid of fact and delivered in bite-size bursts by shiny people. It has to be the most sensationalised reporting you'd find anywhere. I reckon our news is one of the reasons we're a nation of depressed bastards. I lash out at the television screen. "Give us a break! You're supposed to be the umbilical cord connecting us to the rest of world! It's a responsibility, mate!"

They seldom appreciate or recognise what we do, either as individuals or as a collective. They just hammer us down. Sometimes I wonder how they get away with it.

I say to Monica, "Look at this prick. He earns a shit-load. You just wait, I bet he'll end up on the Queen's Honours list in a few years' time."

25

Glancing out of the window I'm drawn to the purple and grey mountains shimmering on the surface of the lake. I focus on the reflected colours: the shapes and movement of light captivate me. Instantly I feel calm and relaxed. My attention moves to the green foliage on the black-trunked trees in the foreground. I love the stillness and peace.

I'm about to turn the television off when my attention is drawn to the most amazing footage. "Monica look, there are people coming through the Iron Curtain in Berlin! People are coming through a gap in the wall." I'm stunned as the events unfold in front of me. A New Zealand journalist is trying to interview someone, but no one is interested in talking to him. Why would they be? They've probably been dreaming of this moment for a lifetime and the last thing they'd want to do is yak to some journalist about it.

He's got the attention of an old woman. She hasn't even had a chance to see what it's like on the western side and yet she's got the humility to stop and talk. Shit, life's been hard for her. Struggling with emotion, she seems bewildered that someone from as far away as New Zealand is interested in her plight. She looks as if a lifetime of fear is at last beginning to dissolve.

My throat is uncomfortable. It's difficult to swallow. I'm trying to contain the distress. Monica has come into the room and I turn my head so she can't see my face. I don't want to cry in front of her. The weight of emotion overpowers me. I swallow hard and tears start dribbling down my cheeks. The feeling continues for a minute or so. I have no idea what that's about. Sadness, I guess. Sadness for what this woman has lost, for all those years of an unfulfilled life. It's as if I am physically in the presence of this unknown woman. As my distress subsides I wipe away the tears from my cheeks. What was I experiencing? Why was I so overcome? After all, I don't even know this woman.

Monica, also wiping her face, says, "How amazing was that. Don't you just feel for her?"

"Shit, yeah," I respond, stunned by the significance of what's happening right now, not only for this particular pensioner but also for Berlin and the Eastern Bloc and the whole world. Even though I live on the other side of the planet, the Iron Curtain has been a harsh reality for as long as I can remember.

I've always believed that there were many ways in which the Wall was a symbol of fear and repression, but it would've been cool to visit Germany before this happened. West Berlin always seemed like a party town. I'm excited suddenly about what might exist on the other side.

"Man, there must be some business opportunities behind that wall!"

From the time I was a kid I knew I was going to do something big, and this could be it. I could do something big in the Eastern Bloc! I spend the rest of the evening devising ways to raise money. I have absolutely no idea how to go about getting there and making contacts, but it doesn't matter. As my grandmother used to say: where there's a will there's a way.

Later I lie in bed unable to sleep. I realise that I'm forever bombarded with an endless stream of thoughts. But to be honest, I'm sick of all this thinking. Sometimes it feels as if I'm walking around in a bubble, caught up in an ongoing dialogue in my head, and the world around me seems like a foggy backdrop.

It's August 1990 and I'm still living on the West Coast. It's nine months since the corroding Iron Curtain finally fell. To be fair, I've been a bit ambivalent about getting in there. It's funny, because I'm forever taking the piss out of Clifford for being traumatised by his ongoing inability to make a decision. But I've been thinking about it lately and I realise that I too have trouble with big decisions. I investigate so many possible paths that I become muddled. One minute one particular way forward seems ideal, the next minute another solution pops up. I worry every hypothetical outcome to death. And once a decision has been made, I berate myself for making the wrong call. It's so exhausting.

I always feel as though my current difficult situation – whatever it is – results from a series of flawed choices that keep leading me down the wrong path. In the end I've just got to make a decision so I can get on with life. So over the last few days Monica and I have revisited the idea of doing business in the Soviet Union.

We're sitting in our living room. Monica is reading a book.

"You'll be interested in this," she says.

"Yeah?"

"It's a quote from Goethe about commitment. I'll read it to you if you want."

"OK," I say, thinking, "How does she come across this stuff?"

> The key to success in any endeavour is commitment; when we commit 100 per cent to a goal it's as if the universe lines up to support our intent 100 per cent. Inconceivable material outcomes and synchronicities are presented to help us in achieving the outcome.
>
> But sometimes we say we are committed to doing or achieving something but a filament of doubt holds us back. This subtle apprehension, or opportunity to use the "back door", detracts from our focus, and diminishes the energy and intensity we have available to complete the task. In these cases we really aren't committed 100 per cent and, unfortunately 95 per cent is about as good as 0 per cent. It just doesn't work. Whatever we do, we need to play big and commit.

I think about this for a moment and realise this has been my experience in so many situations in my life, but I've been in a phase recently where I haven't really committed to a clear goal. I say, "OK. Are you on for getting into the Soviet Union to do business?"

Monica says, "Yeah, why not? Let's do it."

I say, "OK, let's get in there somehow."

An hour later the phone rings and a voice says, "Hi Greg, my name is Merv Johns. I'm the managing director of Ashfield, a subsidiary of a global commodity trading company. Someone suggested I call you because you have the relevant experience for an aspect of our business that is growing quickly."

Merv explains that he's impressed by my role as the on-site project manager of the construction of an abattoir two years earlier. He goes on to say that the link between New Zealand butter and the Soviet market has been a long one, and that Ashfield sells huge quantities to the Soviets. Ashfield has signed contracts for the construction of five food-processing plants in the past 12 months and they need someone on the ground in Russia and Kazakhstan to co-ordinate the construction of their abattoirs. There could be an opportunity for me to join the team and head to Russia. Am I interested?

Absolutely!

He suggests that I fly to Wellington to meet him. If the visit is successful I would travel to Russia to get an understanding of how things work, plus it would give the Ashfield guys a chance to see if I was the man for them or not.

I get off the phone. "Can you believe this? That theory about commitment really works," I say to Monica, assuming she has overhead me. She shakes her head in disbelief as I tell her about the possibility.

Two days later I'm on my way to meet Merv at his office in central Wellington. I catch a taxi in from the airport, find the building, make my way past the secretaries and am shown into his office.

Standing up, Merv thrusts his oversized hand out in greeting. He's a big boy, with a belly even bigger than mine. This bloke has lived hard. He looks about 55, but I know he's about 35. He's wearing a well-tailored shirt, probably cut from Egyptian cotton, with cuffed sleeves buttoned together with cufflinks, dark suit trousers and shiny slip-on black brogues. Slip-on brogues at work? And that moustache. It's been a while since I've had much to do with anyone with a moustache, but Merv has got one hanging over his top lip. Mate, moustaches went out 10 years ago! Where've you been?

After shaking my hand he invites me to take a seat. As I do so I glance at the framed photograph on the wall behind him. It's of a naked woman crouched on all fours in a car that looks like a 1940s Ford. The car is parked in front of austere gardens that lead to a huge, gothic-looking structure built from stone. The scene is slightly disorienting. This isn't my idea of the Soviet Union, or of what a Russian girl would look like, or of what the CEO of a company like this would have hanging on his wall.

He explains how, in the past couple of years, the business has moved into a number of remote regions in Russia, effectively pioneering direct trade with local regional governments and state production facilities. To do this Merv had side-stepped and displaced the centrally controlled state trade organisations. He's been doing deals with the general directors of coal mines, steel mills, oil-producing entities, copper mines and the huge state farms.

When he finishes he says, "So, have you brought the boring stuff like your CV?"

"Ah, I had it sent by courier on Monday."

"Tell me about yourself."

Clearly he hasn't read it. I give him my well-oiled patter, moderating any propensity I have to embellish my own importance. I tell him how since graduating with a degree in mechanical engineering I've been driven to grow my management capability and engineering knowledge. I love challenges, but the thing I love most is overcoming them.

"Engineering is one thing, but working and living with the Soviets is an altogether different thing," Merv says, looking down at a gold pen he is rotating clockwise and anticlockwise in his right hand. "It definitely has its challenges. The Russian is like a child. Give him a lolly and very quickly he wants the whole bag."

Merv looks at me.

"Are you married? Do you have children?"

"Married without children. But my wife is prepared to go anywhere."

"The job we have in mind would make it difficult for a partner to live in Russia. As the projects coordinator your responsibility will include supporting five construction sites and supervising the site managers. Although the job is based in Moscow, the role will require continual travel. You'll probably get back to your Moscow apartment for only three or four days a month. There's also not much support in Moscow for the wives of foreign businessmen."

This catches me by surprise. "So the role is a single man's job?"

"Is that a problem for you?"

"No, not at all," I assure him. I hope Monica can fit into this equation somehow. God knows how, but I'll have to make it work.

"Do you drink?"

"I enjoy the odd drink." Mate, I can drink as much as the next bloke, especially you, ya fat bastard.

"Good. It's a necessary part of the job. The Russians enjoy drinking. If you aren't prepared to participate or keep up, then you're not serious. It's their way of getting to know us. It's an opportunity to see who we are, whether we are trustworthy and if they want to do business with us. In the end, people want to do business with people they like."

"Sounds great to me." Drinking to excess has in fact been an integral aspect of my adult life. These Russians won't be a problem. Full of enthusiasm, I say, "I've been interested in working in Russia since the collapse of the Iron Curtain and this sounds like a very exciting business."

"It has its moments."

I don't know what that means and he doesn't seem inclined to explain. Merv has a huge presence, but he's a trader and one thing traders have in common is that they're born poker players.

After less than 20 minutes the meeting comes to an end. I stand up and point to the picture on the wall. "That's an interesting photo."

Turning to view the scene, Merv says, "Yes, it was taken by Lord Snowdon. The building in the background is the Moscow University and the car is an iconic symbol for the Communist élite – it's a Chaika. It was probably taken in the 1960s, about 10 years after the building was constructed. It's a fine depiction of the complexity of Russia."

A taxi is called and I bid farewell to the man with the moustache. My dreams of greatness are on the cusp of being either fulfilled or dashed. I'd love the challenge of this job. It'd be a chance to play big in the world arena and develop some super-sized skills. Plus I'm keen for the early retirement this could provide and, hand in hand with retirement, the elusive peace and contentment I want.

Two days later the phone rings.

"Hi, it's Merv here. I've had time to consider your suitability and, assuming you're still interested, I'd like to take you with me to Russia. Next Friday I'm flying over there for 10 days. It would be great if you were able to come with me."

"Fantastic! That's great news."

"Excellent. It probably won't be much use to you, but I'll get someone to fax the itinerary to you."

Two days later the fax squeals and chugs out a copy of the itinerary. With the help of *The Reader's Digest Great World Atlas*, purchased by my old man in 1965, Monica and I follow the circuit of unpronounceable cities and regions. The most remote region is the Altai, bordered by Kazakhstan, Mongolia and China. Then I read up about what's going on in the Soviet Union. Gorbachev is restructuring the political and economic system with an initiative called Perestroika, and for the first time since the establishment of socialism nearly 70 years ago he has introduced openness, or Glasnost. From what I can gather, the changes are unfolding rapidly and randomly. There appears to be no clear direction or idea where it will all end. As with change anywhere, it's inducing fear and uncertainty. He and George Bush (Senior) had announced recently that the Cold War was over. Shit, during a visit to the Pope, Gorbachev even acknowledged the importance of spirituality in people's lives.

FOUR

After leaving from Auckland, Merv and I fly to Russia via Tokyo. The plane sets down at Sheremetyevo International Airport, 29 kilometres north-west of central Moscow. As we commence moving into the airport I'm pumped up by a couple of Bloody Marys and the Sex Pistols hammering away in my headphones. Ah, the Pistols. They're a great band.

We are ushered downstairs into a poorly lit concourse housing a series of booths, staffed by uniformed immigration officers. The ceiling is low, much lower than in any other airport I've been in. It's congested down here and some of the waiting passengers are crowded up the stairs. The available light is restricted by copper tubes of varying lengths hanging from the ceiling. The tarnished surface of each tube is coated with dust and grime. The space feels claustrophobic and uncertain.

There's always tension when people line up to gain access to a country, but the people here are more edgy than usual. It feels as if the place has been designed to induce a feeling of vulnerability. The air is drenched with the odour of fear and close confinement. There isn't much chatter. I want to talk, but there's no point. What am I going to say? Maybe, "This looks grim. A few extra lights and a clean-up would do wonders, wouldn't it?" Nah, I'm not going to say anything. I'll just be patient and try to look calm and hope I'm better at it than everyone else.

Bolstered by the knowledge that they control every visitor's ability to have a seamless entry (or not), the immigration officers are taking an inordinate amount of time inspecting passports. I'm bored enough to think there's something slightly erotic about the way that officer is wearing her tight-fitting uniform and reviewing, in a slack yet arrogant way, every jittery traveller entering her booth. She makes me think of a black widow. Her wanton disregard for those lining up is amplified by their palpable uneasiness. The blokes are young and scruffy, but they too display a kind of indifference and lack of respect for the importance of their work.

Finally, after an hour and a half I'm in a booth, a structure flooded with fluorescent light and fitted with a mirror that allows the immigration officer to see the back of your body. I have no idea why. Maybe it's to see if I'm hiding something, or maybe it's just another method of intimidation. I greet the boy behind the screen. He reluctantly acknowledges me with a nod of his head as if to say, "What do you want?" He opens my travel documents and slowly and grudgingly studies my photograph. Then, with his detached gaze, he inspects my face. He repeats the action a second time in an overtly exaggerated manner, as if he might have missed my nose the first time. Why is this all taking so long? Merv didn't indicate there'd be any problem getting in.

As he is about to return my passport he asks in stilted English if I have any cigarettes for him. It's such an unlikely question I'm thrown into confusion. I pull myself together and apologetically inform him that I don't smoke. He contemptuously slams the rubber stamp down onto my passport and passes my travel documents back to me.

I regroup with Merv in the baggage claim area, relieved that one hurdle is behind me, but also aware the journey hasn't really kicked off yet. We collect our bags and begin negotiating our way through the melee towards the customs inspection area. The place is predominantly populated with blokes, many wearing baggy track pants cut from cheap synthetic fabric and dark, over-sized leather jackets. Most of them are shod in an assortment of rubber-soled shoes, tan slip-ons with zips, or sports shoes from some other era. Keen to display my discerning taste in footwear and my recently acquired geographical knowledge of the Soviet Union, I raise my eyebrows in the general direction of a group of travellers and say to Merv, "What a fine array of shoes. They look as though they've been stitched together by a Moldavian cobbler."

Merv smiles. "Yeah. That may not be too far from the truth. This place is so rigidly controlled the left shoe was probably made in Moldavia and the right one in Estonia. The two separate shoes would have been paired up in Moscow before being distributed throughout the Soviet Union."

"Seriously?"

"Yep. It's how the economy has been structured. It forces all 15 countries of the Soviet Union to remain together. They can't function without each other. All roads lead to and from Moscow. The distribution of all manufactured and consumer goods is controlled by Moscow. And that's why we're here. We can build an abattoir in no time compared to the Soviets because we can source all the requirements from one place."

Looking around, I'm attracted by some stunningly beautiful women moving through this sea of badly dressed men and ordinariness and apprehension. It's such a surprise. Beautiful Russian women? How could that be? Russian women look like shot-putters, don't they? Far out. Not only are they completely unlike anything I expected, they are also a stark contrast to the men. They are so elegantly dressed and radiate an overt sexuality.

As we queue to have our luggage inspected a group of Asian passengers suddenly tosses a dozen bags over a glazed security wall to some men waiting on the other side. The blokes on the outside snatch the bags and run. There's a hell of a racket as Russian security officers pursue the perpetrators through the concourse. It's difficult to see what happens next, whether they've pulled off their stunt or not. Man, this is loose. I'm beginning to feel disoriented.

We make our way through the doors separating customs from the Russian motherland and find Merv's man dressed in a grey business shirt and black trousers. He has dark, collar-length hair. Merv hugs him and then introduces him as Lukhum. Merv had informed me that the Moscow office employed a character in his twenties who was responsible for supporting the project work. Lukhum is Georgian, and he is renowned for keeping the details of his background private. It had been suggested that he is good mates with a few mafia types, but Merv said you could never really know.

Shaking my hand, Lukhum welcomes me to Moscow. He exudes a warm but street-wise confidence. He allays any concern I might have had about finding our way around. I'm pleased he's here and very relieved that he speaks English. Then he enquires whether Merv has remembered to bring the latest editions of *MAD* and *Skydiving*. Lukhum's face lights up when Merv removes the magazines from his briefcase and hands them to him.

"I have everything in place for your trip," Lukhum says. "The three of us will be flying out tonight at midnight." He offers to carry the heaviest bag and we head out the main entrance. As we exit we are enveloped in a haze of combustion by-products discharged by inefficient Aeroflot jets, exhaust fumes pumped from a fleet of motley Ladas, Nivas and Volgas, all idling in unauthorised parking positions, and black, sooty diesel smoke belching from lines of stationary buses. Penetrating this effluvia are the screams of the Tupolev jet engines from the other side of the terminal building. It's clear I'm entering a country in decay. But most noticeable is the anticipation of change that permeates the place.

Lukhum has paid an airport attendant to look after the V8 Chevy van while he was inside. It's parked illegally in one of the non-existent parking positions directly outside the arrivals hall. Lukhum slides open the side access door to reveal four oversized seats, each the size of a La-Z-Boy recliner. Lukhum informs us there isn't anything else like it on the streets of Moscow. In his thick accent he informs me that the Chevy is called the Pussy Wagon.

Behind the wheel he cranks the Pussy Wagon into action. He negotiates his way out of the airport and then weaves in and out of the line of cars making their way along the road leading into town. As we race through the silver-birch forest on the outer reaches of Moscow it's becoming clear Lukhum is acutely aware of the location of the traffic police stations. Like something out of a 1950s black-and-white movie set in the Cold War, regularly spaced shabby, flat-roofed, brick buildings are manned by uniformed police equipped with poorly maintained Ladas and strange radar technology. He slows down to the 80 km/h speed limit as we approach each station, then immediately accelerates to 150 km/h after passing it.

We leave the countryside and begin driving through rows of high-rise apartments. They are constructed from grey, pre-cast concrete panels and fitted with timber-framed windows and interlinked ochre-coloured balconies. Most have an unfinished, unkempt look. Some balconies are fitted with windows that appear to have been installed by half-arsed do-it-yourselfers. The Soviet Union I imagined was different. I had no real idea what to expect, but these buildings are so not it.

"These apartment buildings were first built in the Khrushchev era," Lukhum informs me, "and this style of architecture and construction has continued throughout the Soviet Union ever since. It's not to my liking, but it's where many people live."

I look at the grassless areas of earth leading up to the concreted entrance ways. "I suppose it's cheap and easy," I manage to say, aware that it's altogether too easy to see fault in anything new. Plus, it isn't good form to openly mock aspects of someone else's country. Shit, don't New Zealanders get really sensitive if someone says anything even slightly derogatory about our precious little homeland?

Lukhum says, "Soon we will be in a more appealing part of Moscow, the central district. The architecture there is of the Stalin era."

As we drive closer to the city the urban scenery takes on a more established appearance. The streets are four-lane avenues, called prospekts, and they are bounded on each side by imposing apartment buildings. Typically five to 10 storeys high, they are constructed from brick, stone and plaster. The earthy brick and stone walls support plastered façades. Variations of cream predominate, but occasionally some striking colours break the monotony: there are lime green, lemon, ochre, sky blue, oxidised-copper green, chalky pinks and teal. But whenever we have to slow down or stop, I see it's all under attack: flaking paint, cracked plaster, missing patches of façade, disconnected downpipes, window frames that need putty replacement and timber repairs.

Shop frontages are identified with matter-of-fact signage in blue Cyrillic letters on dirty white squares. Retail and product branding appear to be non-existent. Many ground-floor windows and doors are fitted with robust metal security grilles, and grime coats every surface. But this inner segment of Moscow boasts formidable architecture. It looks resolute in the face of all odds.

After continuing in silence for a while I say to no one in particular, "There are bugger-all cars using this avenue. It's as if the city had been planned and built for a future that never eventuated."

"People can't afford cars," Lukhum says. "Besides, we have very efficient subway and trolley bus systems. Here is Yuri Gagarin," he suddenly says, pointing to a muscular cosmonaut mounted on a titanium-fluted spire the size of a rocket.

To a pre-pubescent kid the US space programme was awesome. But NASA seemed like a whole army of people, whereas old Yuri, with his improvised missile technology bolted together and supported by a wish and a prayer, appeared to do it all on his own. And here he is – one of my all-time heroes and most certainly one of the greatest Soviet heroes of the Cold War, towering 15 storeys high in front of me, glistening in the dull autumn sunset.

"That has to be one of the most impressive sculptures I've ever seen," I enthuse. "It's easy to imagine just how excited the people here must have been when he orbited the Earth."

Lukhum says, "There's a word in Russian, devai, which means 'Let's go'. It became a very common part of our vocabulary after Gagarin said it moments before lift-off. Let's do it, regardless of the outcome."

I have some vague recollection that Yuri came to grief early in his life. "What happened to Yuri? Didn't he die in a car accident?" I ask.

"He died in an aircraft crash," Lukhum replies. "It was a fighter jet crash."

There's silence, and then Merv looks at me and says, "Although there was some suggestion that his body was never recovered."

We pull up outside an apartment building, which turns out to be where Lukhum lives. As we make our way into the lobby the reek of decaying food washes over us. Apparently the landing on each floor is fitted with a tube to take away domestic waste, but then the waste is discharged near the entrance of the building. As we enter the lift I try to appear relaxed as I wonder what the hell we are doing here.

I walk into Lukhum's living room. A portrait of Brezhnev is mounted on the wall, but it has a few additions. Hanging from his forehead and dangling over his left eye is a knitted penis cover, and pinned to his chest is a metal medal. Above the portrait, the light fitting is draped with an American flag. "Rebellious times," I laugh. "Where did you get the medal?"

"From a broke military officer," Lukhum nonchalantly responds.

It is soon clear we are here for no other reason than to kill time. Six hours after arriving at Sheremetyevo it's time to leave for Domodedovo, Moscow's busiest domestic airport. We will be flying to the city of Barnaul, which is situated on the Ob River in the West Siberian Plain. It's 10 at night and it has started drizzling. We leave the high-rises of Moscow and slip into the darkness of rural farmland and forest. I notice the vehicles on the road are driving with only their park lights on.

"Full beam is a prohibited activity," Lukhum says. I don't ask why. Maybe it's a hangover from the Cold War. Maybe the Soviets are still paranoid about a US invasion. Or maybe it's about conserving energy. Whatever, it adds to the mystery of the place.

We approach a badly damaged Lada. The driver's door is folded around the front mud guard and the driver is slumped over the steering wheel. She doesn't look well. On the verge of the road stand four people. There is no sense of urgency. I look at Lukhum. "She must be dead. Do you think they're waiting for an ambulance?" He shrugs his shoulders. Why haven't they covered her with a blanket or clothing? The scene is saturated with a profound sense of helplessness. Lukhum continues to drive on. Why hasn't he stopped to help?

We arrive at Domodedovo. The Chevy is even more obvious at this airport, especially since Lukhum has just bribed two security guards to get into the zone restricted to authorised vehicles. He steers us over to an access stairway that leads to the departure lounge. The scream of Aeroflot jets landing and taking off is punishing. The entire area is filled with chaos. It's difficult to think straight, so we just carry our bags and follow our leader.

Thirty minutes pass before the Aeroflot air hostess gives us the go-ahead to commence boarding. Lukhum, Merv and I take ownership of three seats clustered together. We are soon accosted by a disgruntled old man in a military uniform who wants his assigned seat. Like half the elderly blokes I've seen so far, his chest is adorned with medals and service badges. In an unwavering tone Lukhum suggests in Russian that he needs to find an alternative.

I sit back in the seat. The seat back reclines fully into the passenger behind me. I can't believe it. I pull it back into the upright position and try again. No luck. I turn to Merv. "I've drawn a short straw, mate. The seat back support mechanism is buggered."

Lukhum stands and with his indescribable presence demands attention from the hostess. She's indifferent. "Chto delat?" she says as she puckers her lips and rotates the palms of her hands upwards. What to do?

What *am* I to do? Nothing. Sit upright or lean forward. "Don't worry," Lukhum says, "there's a spare seat over there." He points to the row behind us. "Take it."

I do what he says. As the plane accelerates down the runway and lifts off, a violent vibration originating from the starboard wing starts radiating throughout the plane. What *is* that? An imbalanced turbine rotor? Has the landing gear malfunctioned? Is this normal? No-one else seems too concerned. Either this is a standard characteristic of the Tupolev 154 or all these punters are well rehearsed at hiding their anxiety. Lukhum is reading his *MAD* magazine. That's good enough for me. What can I do anyway? After an inordinate amount of time the intense juddering subsides.

About an hour into the flight the hostess makes her way down the aisle disdainfully handing out meals. Maybe "Do not communicate with passengers" is a non-negotiable in this job. Despite some apprehension I eat the offerings and then slide into a fitful slumber for a couple of hours, waking up just in time for our descent. The downward trajectory is very slow. It takes another hour before we rejoin mother earth with the most gentle touchdown you could imagine.

I stand to disembark. "You may as well stay seated," Merv says. "We have to wait for the most important people on the plane to leave."

"Who's that?"

"The flight and cabin crew." Adorned with uniforms more suited to the airforce, this prestigious group departs first, allowing the rest of us to sit in awe of their greatness. After they've left we have to wait for those in the rear cabin to disembark.

Lukhum turns round to talk to me. "The centre of gravity of the loaded plane is located behind the wings. If the passengers in the forward cabin bailed first, the nose of the plane would tip up and the plane's tail would hit the ground."

Why? I think. Maybe the location of the loaded plane's centre of gravity in the air enhances the aircraft's ability to fly. There must be some good reason. Mustn't there?

When we're finally allowed off, Lukhum guides us into the VIP lounge. We are introduced to a woman called Tatiana. She shakes my hand. Her dark hair is perfectly cut and placed and her olive complexion is highlighted by her red lipstick. She's wearing a short black skirt and high heels. I love legs, and hers are perfect. Everything about her is delicate and sweet. Cooing at me in the most divine voice, she informs me that she's more than happy to help us with whatever we need. I'm mesmerised. Tatiana is one of the sultriest creatures I've ever met.

When I ask her about herself, she informs me in broken English that she recently gave up her career as a doctor to work in the VIP lounge, a facility that had previously been available only to party officials and government functionaries. She explains that the money and conditions are better. She says her only regret is that she learnt German instead of English at school. I'm not sure that it matters.

Lukhum, Merv and I begin breakfast. It consists of black tea, boiled eggs, salami and coleslaw, all of it prepared by Tatiana. I feel uplifted and privileged to be eating a meal prepared by Tatiana. The conversation meanders, but ultimately leads to nuclear armaments.

Lukhum asks me, "Grigori, do you know what the Semipalatinsk Polygon is?"

I try to concentrate but I can't help surreptitiously snatching glances of Tatiana as often as I can. I want to make a connection with her. Feeling addled trying to focus on two completely separate things, I wonder if it's a clever geometrical structure or a secret facility in a spy movie, or even the title of a Solzhenitsyn book.

"Ah, no, I don't."

"The Semipalatinsk Polygon is the site where nuclear bombs were tested."

I can't keep my eyes off Tatiana's beautifully sculpted hips and waist.

"The last test was just three years ago. Initially the tests were discharged above ground, but in the final years the bombs were detonated below ground. They even used nuclear bombs to create water reservoirs . . ."

I'm excited. I love her balance of sexuality and refinement.

". . . crush ore in open-cast mines, and create underground storage for toxic waste."

It's impossible to pay attention to the conversation. All I want is Tatiana.

"What was that, Grigori?" asks Lukhum.

"Huh?"

"I thought you said something."

"Oh, seriously?"

"Ser'eznye. Ita Pravda."

It's true. I nod my head and scan the room, but with a sinking feeling I realise Tatiana has left. I sigh and try to focus on the conversation.

"There's a lake near Semipalatinsk that was created by detonating a nuclear device. The locals call it Atomic Lake."

"Nev-er-roy-atno," is all I can manage. Un-be-liev-able.

Then we're on our way again. Lukhum leads us from the VIP lounge out to a helicopter, a Vertolet, distinctive because of its bulbous nose, car-sized landing wheels and exhaust-stained fuselage. We're introduced to the flight crew. The MIL Mi-8 requires a pilot, a navigator and an engineer. Entering the cabin I'm surprised to see comfortable padded lounge chairs, carpeted flooring, walls lined with wood panelling and double-glazed windows – it's a flying lounge. We settle in and the boys crank up the engine. The drooping blades elevate as they rotate, and cautiously the helicopter rises about 100 metres above the deck, then commences moving forward. It's a very systematic approach to helicopter flying and I feel safe.

We fly out over a settlement of dachas, each with its own garden plot. Lukhum explains how traditional Russian dachas are small cottages constructed from rough-sawn timber or logs. They are an integral aspect of Russian life, offering refuge from city living because many families live in small, one-bed-room apartments. The dacha garden provides a source of fresh vegetables during summer and the opportunity to preserve vegetables for the winter months. A well-located dacha can give access to swimming in nearby rivers or to social outings in the nearby woods. Lukhum adds that the dacha also allows the continuation of the Russian connection to the land and that's important.

Lukhum gives us a sketchy overview of what he has organised. Apparently the primary objective of the helicopter is to collect a group of Austrian hunters who have just completed a guided hunting trip in the Altai mountain range. We will disembark at the hunters' camp and wait while the hunting group is flown back to Barnaul. The Vertolet will then return to collect us and we will continue our journey to Ongudai. Given the number of aircraft parked at the end of the tarmac at Barnaul, you'd think we could have flown directly to Ongudai. But no.

Soon we drop into a clearing adjacent to a log hut. We are greeted by the guides – two wiry characters clad in khaki military clothing, dusty and stained from hunting. One has a roguish grin and badly chaffed hands, the other has greasy hair and fingers heavily stained with nicotine. After shaking our hands they go off and fetch the Austrians. Not wanting the Austrians to know what we're up to we're economical with our words. The tourists reciprocate, and after about 10 minutes of mutually cagey behaviour the Austrians depart with Lukhum in the Vertolet.

Hang on! What's he doing in the chopper leaving us here without an interpreter? What are we going to do now? I ask Merv why Lukhum left.

"He said he needs to finalise some arrangements back at the airport. You never know what he's up to. There are always smoke and mirrors at play here. But you'll soon get used to it."

Will I? I hope so.

It's midday and I'm somewhere – God knows where – in the southern Siberian mountains with no means of conversing with our hosts and no clue when Lukhum is going to return. Great.

The guides generously offer us some venison casserole. The meal is dished up using military-style utensils. Before we start eating, the bloke with the big grin suggests it's time for a chut chut – a small drink. A three-finger shot of vodka is poured for each of us. He offers us a toast, and we follow his lead, draining the glass in one action. I grimace as the vodka goes down my throat. Then we all tuck into the casserole, communicating our appreciation for their hospitality with gesticulations. Very soon Merv prepares for another toast, filling up the glasses from a half-litre bottle of vodka. He delivers his few words of pidgin Russian. They seem to get it.

I love these rustic encounters. If you let your guard down and become open to anything, then truly great interactions can take place. Even without a shared language it's easy to communicate appreciation and gratitude for what's being given. It can be communicated with humour and body language. I really appreciate being here with these random characters. Yeah, this is the life I'm after.

We each drink four shots of vodka, everyone taking a turn to toast. My insides feel warm. I feel as though I'm on the cusp of something exciting. Realising that my euphoria is probably induced by the combined effects of vodka and jet lag, I withdraw to a comfortable spot on the ground outside the hut. It's not a bad day, cool but sunny. Stretching out on my back with my jumper rolled up under my head I close my eyes. I'm told heavy vodka consumption delivers one to a state of bliss for 10 short minutes, then you feel like shit for the next 24 hours.

I don't know how long I've been out for, but the clatter of the returning chopper wakes me in a hurry. Hovering directly high above us, the Vertolet maintains its altitude and position instead of coming in to land. "What's going on?" I ask Merv.

"I'd say Lukhum is getting ready to practise a dive."

A figure suddenly lunges out the side of the chopper. He free dives until the parachute opens, forcefully arresting his fall and allowing him to circle just once above us before he lands on his feet in the clearing. He immediately recovers the parachute and commences packing it, simultaneously calling out instructions for us to get ready to board the Mi-8 as it comes into land. We bid farewell to our hosts, hugging them like great mates, and scramble into the helicopter.

Our journey continues over hilly terrain covered in alpine grasses and clusters of trees, and valleys sparsely stocked with cattle and deer and etched with clear rivers. The occasional gravel road runs alongside a braided river, connecting one small settlement with another. "How the hell did you end up doing business out here?" I ask Merv.

He explains that he was doing business in the Soviet Union long before Perestroika was initiated in the mid-1980s, but it was around that time that he first arrived on the scene in the Altai. One of the few products capable of generating hard currency here is deer velvet, cut from the deer's head before it matures into antler. Some Asians use it as an aphrodisiac, he says. It must do wonders for those dysfunctional cocks, because they buy a shit-load of it.

Before Ashfield arrived, a Soviet ministry had the sole responsibility for selling the velvet to Koreans traders. He says it's always difficult to know exactly what goes on in Soviet ministries, but what he does know is that velvet of this quality fetched US$1000 per kilogram last year and the local state farms received only a fraction of that. Now Merv and the regional prime minister have usurped the boys in the Moscow ministry. It means the local boys get a better return and Ashfield gets a generous clip of the ticket. Not only that, but along the way Merv hopes to get his hands on some local deer genetics.

I wonder how you could do that without pissing someone off.

At the head of the valley, the pilot changes course, gently swinging the

Vertolet right into a smaller valley. Up ahead is an incongruous sight: a pristine white, newly constructed food-processing building nestled into the foot hills of this incredibly remote mountain range. The Vertolet lands.

I'm keen to meet the New Zealanders working on the site and to see how the construction is going. I hope it'll provide me with something familiar within this disorienting Russian paradigm.

The boys on site are pleased to see us. We have mail from home plus we are fresh New Zealand faces. I chat with all the tradesmen. They appear to be capable characters. They are enjoying it here but missing home. It strikes me how the camaraderie between construction people is unique. I love the way in which a process facility unfolds from a single desire to build something, and how everyone works together to achieve that goal. Every day more hydraulic lines and water pipes appear. Machines are installed and flat surfaces are created. People take pride in their work, and it's always easy for others to appreciate good workmanship. Recognition of such craft is an uplifting thing. As I look around the process facility I realise that I'm familiar with much of the equipment. I appreciate its simplicity and robustness. I know it works well and that it is absolutely appropriate for this environment. The straight lines of the wall surfaces, pipelines, electrical cable trays, duct work and the mechanical process equipment in this facility are a clear indicator of good workmanship.

After a couple of hours we all walk back to the accommodation for the evening meal and a few beers. As I start talking to a couple of the guys it becomes apparent that progress is being hampered by a delay in the delivery of construction equipment shipped from New Zealand via Nakhodka in the Far East. The delays are being exacerbated by the lack of crucial support from the local administration. No one knows why. The evening perks up as the frustration of the non-deliveries is displaced by the boys regaling us with their adventures.

Yet later in bed I feel restless and unable to sleep. It's probably induced by alcohol, excitement and jet lag.

I grumble my way into the new day. We eat breakfast, during which I mutter a few words in response to any comments from Merv or Lukhum.

We bid farewell to our compatriots and saunter up to the Vertolet. The three flight crew look about as shagged as I feel. The pilot looks as if he has slept in his uniform.

The whine of the jet engine drills into my cranium as I stare out of the scratched window. I feel like shit. I feel helpless. A couple of hours interacting with people is enjoyable, but most of the time I just want to be by myself. Here, I'm fully immersed in being with people I don't know, and I've got another 10 days to go. I feel as if I have to be continually on my guard.

We fly on to Gorny Altai to meet the prime minister of the local government and his deputies. When we touch down at our destination I scramble out of the Vertolet feeling very uncomfortable. My bladder is inconveniently giving me problems. Our host hasn't arrived, so, anxious to relieve myself, I stride over to the public toilet. It's a shack knocked together from rough-sawn timber planks, just to the right of the terminal building. I enter the shed and I'm confronted by an acrid blast. The smell of urine is so intense it feels like I've hit an invisible wall.

Far out! I'm standing in front of a conically shaped pile of faeces about half a metre high and a metre in diameter. A timber beam is positioned over the pile of crap. In order to sit on it I would need to hoist myself above the mountain of excrement, then I'd have to drop my load in front of anyone else using the facilities.

Bugger that. There's no way I'd ever have a crap here. Two Russian boys are having a leak in a makeshift urinal mounted on one of the walls. I have to wait in line to use the urinal. No-one else seems fazed. The boy in front of me peels off and the receptacle is now available. It's caked in filth, the residue from the ablutions of tens of thousands of vodka drinkers. My eyes are stinging. Breathing is difficult, but my bladder is distended beyond belief, so I grit my teeth and get the job done.

I try to regain my composure as I walk over to where Lukhum and Merv are engaged in an animated encounter with a character wearing a suit and tie. There is much laughter and physical embracing. I am immediately introduced to the Functionary. He has a name, but I forget it as soon as we're introduced. From then on he's just the Functionary.

After we shake hands the Functionary says, "Grigori, I hope you aren't as naughty as Merv. He leads us into too much mischief when he's with us."

"No, no. I'm a good boy."

The Functionary, or apparatchik, as the Bolsheviks call his profession, is an amiable character in his early fifties. He has an oversized stomach and apparently an oversized influence on the affairs of the region. His Volga is parked directly in front of the airport and soon we are being chauffeur-driven along a poorly maintained sealed road, past horse-drawn agricultural trailers, tractors and trucks, and chocolate-coloured log houses that have been sunk into the ground to provide winter insulation.

We arrive at the office building of the regional administration. The Functionary leads us into his office. It's a large office by Western standards and a portrait of Lenin is mounted on the wall. We are invited to sit at a table in front of the large desk. The Functionary lifts the receiver on one of the three phones and orders some chai. Then he makes another call on a different phone.

The tea is delivered with a bowl of individually wrapped Russian chocolates. Biting into a chocolate it's clear they have been crafted from quality cocoa. Lukhum says that one of the advantages of the Soviet support of socialist third-world countries has been chocolate and cigars. But then everyone thinks their country makes the best chocolate, don't they?

"OK," the Functionary announces. "We should leave here in 10 minutes. We are going to the Communist Party official's dacha and Kolosov will meet us there."

Merv reminds me that Kolosov is the regional prime minister.

Set in on the banks of the Katun River, the dacha looks like a boutique lodge. In the lobby there's a portrait of Mikhail Gorbachev (minus the birth mark) and an intensely earnest portrait of Lenin. In some misguided gesture the dacha has been renamed Kiwi Lodge. Merv has agreed to fund the refurbishment of the building as part of his commitment to his relationship with the prime minister. In fact, the new fit-out has already started. Some of the materials and appliances, including a large refrigerator and chest freezer, have been shipped all the way from New Zealand.

We sit outside in an area near the river in the late afternoon sun. The Functionary busies himself constructing a fire and skewering pieces of lamb that have been marinated in a big glass jar of brine, mustard seeds and fennel. Communication between the group flows more easily after we are joined by Vlad, an interpreter employed by Ashfield during the construction season. The prime minister arrives just as the fire settles down to hot embers. By now it's dark. The Functionary commences cooking the shishlick or shish kebab. A woman who acts as caretaker of the dacha with her husband brings a selection of salads and breads from the kitchen.

Puffing his chest out, the prime minister declares it's time for a chut chut. He half fills our five-ounce glasses with vodka and proposes a toast to welcome Merv back. Then he drains his glass and we follow suit. I follow the lead of the others by quickly swallowing a glass of mineral water and eating something off my plate. Within a few minutes Merv encourages everyone to fill their glasses again. I also refill my glass of mineral water in preparation. Merv stands up and makes a toast, reciprocating the welcome, saying it really is a pleasure to be here again, enjoying good relations with the locals and engaging in serious business activities.

The toasts keep coming throughout the evening – only alcoholics drink without toasting, they tell me. Vodka is followed by Georgian cognac. Would I like some Moldavian champagne? Why not? In the absence of guidance from Merv, I respond in the affirmative.

Like old school mates on the piss together, the Functionary starts wrestling Merv. Then, grinning playfully, he offers neat alcohol. The drinking procedure is explained. There's one hundred per cent alcohol in one cup and water in another. We drink half a cup of water from the left hand, swallow the full cup of home-distilled alcohol in the right hand, and immediately follow this with the remaining half cup of water.

Merv, shaking his head in discouragement and repeatedly telling the Functionary he doesn't want any of it, is informed that we all must partic-ipate. Since he is a good friend and leader of the visitors he must set the example. An experienced drinker is aware of the need for self-preservation, which generally involves consuming only one form of alcoholic beverage in one sitting. Only the novice or the seriously hardened drinker mixes his drinks. Or, as in my own case, the stupid and cavalier. I eagerly consume the full glass of firewater. I notice the prime minister doesn't participate, but it would be inappropriate for me to challenge him.

I'm quickly beginning to realise I was deluded in thinking that my ability to drink ample volumes of ale would stand me in good stead for this onslaught. I'm losing control. My surroundings are blurred and my head is beginning to spin. I don't really know what I'm saying or what others are saying to me. I decide it's time for bed.

When I wake up in the morning I'm pleased to have finally had a good sleep. I get dressed and find the Functionary waiting for us in the dining room. The angst-ridden caretaker of the lodge and his subservient wife have prepared breakfast for us. It's identical to last night's meal and vodka is on the menu again. I'm always up for a hair of the dog, but this morning the taste of the vodka repels me.

Apparently the caretaker is someone who drinks without toasting. His wife enjoys the odd vodka too. I recall his erratic behaviour from last night. He continually scolded and bullied his wife as they served us. Now his sullen demeanour and gruffness are accentuated by the quietness in the room.

After another shot of vodka, breakfast is cleared away and we settle in for a meeting to discuss the progress on existing sites and, more importantly, the new proposals for additional meat processing plants. Vlad starts translating and soon I see how skilled he is as a professional interpreter. It's as if he doesn't exist. Functioning as a conduit between Merv and his counterpart, Vlad gesticulates at exactly the same point in the delivery as Merv.

The meeting is adjourned and the morose caretaker is soon asked to serve lunch. It's the same as breakfast.

Later I ask Merv: "Is Vlad available to be my full-time translator?"

"Sure. You need someone like him. Vlad is more than just an interpreter. He'll be able to give you a sense of how things function in the Russian organisations we're dealing with. Besides, you'll be continually travelling and you'll need someone like him as your right-hand man with you pretty much all the time."

"What's his background?" I ask.

"From what I can discover, he was employed as a translator in a scientific facility, so from an engineering perspective he's technically very capable. But what is very unique about him is that he has quickly proved his worth translating in contract negotiations and social situations."

We arrive in the hinterland of Russian heavy industry, Novotroitsk. Mining and steel-making dominate the landscape of this southern Ural city. Novotroitsk exists to house workers and to provide an infrastructure for the nearby steel-making plant. Inspired by Uncle Joe Stalin, this facility consists of sprawling process halls that house numerous furnaces. Its chimney stacks feed huge plumes of iron oxide particles into the rust-coloured cloud smothering the city. Shunting yards laced with overhead pylons and cables and crowded with wagons laden with scrap steel and pig iron add to the general impression of decrepitude. In the developed world steel mills like this would have long been retired and replaced by more efficient facilities.

Everything in this town is covered in a layer of grit and red dust. The dust is so prevalent that even double-casement windows need to be taped up in the summer months to prevent dust seeping into the apartments and coating everything. Here in Novotroitsk the average male lives to only 53 years. Not only does the vodka hammer any chances of longevity, but the fine dust takes its toll on the lungs. In this environment the food-processing plant, with its white exterior cladding, no doubt looks like a star gate to another universe.

In the late afternoon we are led along a railway shunting yard full of train-loads of old tanks and other military hardware that has been scrapped in compliance with agreements reached with the Yanks. Overhead cranes deliver the redundant components of the Cold War to blast furnaces. We are ushered through a nondescript door into a canteen, equipped with a dining room, banya (sauna) and plunge pool.

Here we are entertained by the men responsible for purchasing the meat-processing plant. Vlad is translating. We enter the banya naked, except for towels wrapped around our waists. It's not exactly like business meetings back home, but what the hell.

Not long after entering the banya, the project manager offers to exfoliate my back, gesturing that I should lie on my stomach while he performs the task. I'm told that beating one's skin with a branch of birch soaked in water is an effective way to increase circulation and remove dead skin, but this bastard beats me with such intensity it feels like he's drawing blood. It stings like buggery. I wonder if it's supposed to be like this? Suddenly I don't care either way. I sit up, indicating that's enough. I'm not sure what it was all about, but I feel as if the prick has just attacked me. We leave the banya and dive into a cool plunge pool. My skin stings.

The dining-room table is laden with food and beverages. The meal commences with a toast from the project manager. He holds up his glass and declaims, "As my counterpart in this project, I would like to toast you, Grigori. Like me, you are a young man with much to prove. My desire is that you not only fulfil your own expectations, but ours also. This project is an important investment by us. It will be a facility to provide premium-quality meat products for the people of our city. It will also be a showcase for your business. I toast to our productive engagement. As the recipient of this toast, I invite you to drink to the bottom. This is the custom in Russia."

I need to let this boy know I'm up to the challenge. I immediately accept the toast. The smell is intense, like commercial cleaning fluid. As I drain the vodka the harsh taste of the alcohol burns my lips and the inside of my cheeks. My tongue feels numb. The alcohol lingers in the back of my throat with a slight aftertaste of aniseed. The inside of my guts burns. I'm pleased I packed some antacid. I reach for a bottle of mineral water and drink the water slowly.

Continuing to lay down a challenge, the project manager says, "Grigori, we Russian engineers pride ourselves on our tenacity. As project manager from the Russian side, it is my responsibility to ensure you deliver all that is promised."

This boy could be a handful. I respond, "I'm looking forward to the two of us working closely together. It will be through our mutual co-operation that we both bring the project to fruition in the agreed timeframe."

"You're right, so we need to be good boys to each other."

As the evening progresses the project manager reveals that during his recent visit to New Zealand he was initially skeptical of what the country had to offer, but he soon concluded that our democracy had delivered true socialism, much more in line with what Soviet communism had promised.

"There's a well-known joke that indicates one aspect of our style of socialism. It's a question and answer joke," the project manager says to me. "When the final stage of socialism is built, will there still be thefts and pilfering?"

I smile. "I don't know, will there?"

"No, because everything will have already been pilfered."

We have a toast to what Perestroika could deliver.

One of the other Bolsheviks adds, "There's another joke that's also a good representation of our experiment with socialism. It's called the seven paradoxes of the socialist state. Nobody works, but the plan is fulfilled. The plan is fulfilled, but the shelves in the stores are empty. The shelves are empty, but nobody starves. Nobody starves, but everybody is unhappy. Everybody is unhappy, but nobody complains. Nobody complains, but the jails are full."

After the meal Merv and I stagger out of the social facility and almost collide with a locomotive that is shunting wagons loaded with billets of pig iron. The blocks of iron glow orange in the darkness, barely five metres from where I stand. Banging and creaking as they move at less than walking pace past us, the wagons and their radiant cargo make the whole scene seem completely surreal. The heavy vodka consumption and the ongoing pace of travel add to my sense of disorientation.

"This is unbelievable, mate," I say to Merv, as I shield my face from the heat with the palm of my right hand. "What a bizarre place to entertain the boys."

"Yep, this place sure is different."

"Hey, how do you find that project guy to deal with? He beat the shit out of me in the sauna with that bloody birch branch."

Merv laughs. "Initially he comes across as a tough nut, but he's OK to deal with. He can be very exacting and dogged, but you'll find he generally yields. They all do."

"He seems like a competitive bastard."

"Yeah he is, but so are you, mate. You'll be a good match."

I think to myself that I've never considered myself to be competitive. Ambitious, yes, but not really competitive. But maybe I am.

The next morning we inspect the construction site. The locals have commenced earthworks and foundation form work. As we're walking around, the project manager suddenly picks up a crowbar and gestures that he's going to throw it at me. He holds it horizontally in both hands and hurls it. Like I say, if there's one consistent failure in my life it's being unable to catch things. I brace myself. I have to perform here. I try to focus as the bar flies at me. I catch it in both hands. I caught it! But hang on – it's light as plastic.

The project manager and his mates are pissing themselves with laughter. "What is this?" I ask.

"Titanium."

The bloody thing is made from titanium! Although I'm jubilant that I've just caught a projectile for the first time in my life, I can't believe that an economy can be so distorted that rare metals are put to such humble uses.

"Shit. Let's get a container load of these together and see if there's a market in the West," I say to Merv. "The metal has got to be worth way more than the crowbar."

"Nah. Bigger fish to fry," Merv says.

Back in Moscow, as we drive I see long queues of women lined up behind trucks with enclosed canvas canopies. "What are they queuing for?" I ask.

"Food. Vegetables and meat," Lukhum says.

Jesus, that looks like a highly inefficient way of going about your day.

"There is a joke," Lukhum tells me, "and it goes like this: what is the most permanent feature of our socialist economy? The answer: temporary shortages."

Another joke. The Russians certainly know how to take the piss out of themselves.

On the trip this totally incomprehensible world has hammered at me from every direction. The unpredictability of the people and the half-arsed way they do everything is completely unsettling. The saving grace seems to be their stoical approach to life and their sense of humour. Later, I share my confusions with Lukhum.

He responds, "The Russian poet Tyutchev said, 'Don't try to understand it, just feel it.' This is the only approach."

We soon arrive at the head office located on the 11th floor of the prestigious World Trade Centre, a modern high-rise office structure built by Armand Hammer, the wealthy American of Russian-Jewish heritage. I'm introduced to the people here. One of these is the very dapper Popov, who is conspicuous by his clear disdain of the idea of me being considered for a job here. He grudgingly shakes my hand and grunts when I am introduced.

After an hour of uncomfortably milling around the office Lukhum indicates it's time to go to Sheremetyevo for the trip home. As we drive I think about what I want from the job. My primary focus is to help the construction guys to build the facilities. I'm also excited by the adventure. I want to learn how things are done so that I can establish my own business. I want to be a serious man and I want to make sufficient filthy lucre so that Monica and I can retire and enjoy life. But ultimately I want to be happy. Everything I've done in my life has prepared me for this challenge. If I'm not ready now, I never will be.

FIVE

It's now April 1991 and I'm still living on the West Coast. For reasons known only to him, it takes Merv six months to call me and give me the nod. He confirms that he wants me to live and work in Russia as a single man. Monica and I decide that the best bet will be for her to live in London. The one concession is that I will return to London every month for a four-day weekend and spend time with her. It'll also give me an opportunity to catch up with some of my mates, including Jonty, who have recently moved to the "Smoke".

Monica and I endure the long flight to the UK and immediately begin looking for a flat while still coping with jet lag. We find one in the first week down the road from Jonty's place in Camden Town. A week later I fly to Moscow to meet Merv.

That night Merv tells me that nobody seems to know exactly what Lukhum did before working for Ashfield. You never know, he may have been KGB or, even better, he still is. But apparently he is a magician when it comes to negotiating his way around the Russian labyrinth, which appears real and daunting one moment but gone the next.

"How did you get hold of him?" I enquire.

"Popov knew him."

The next day I'm in the office trying to fit in – as you do in a new job. Popov is blustering his way around the office. He bullies anyone who dares move into his sphere. I've got no idea what he does, other than keep the doors open at the central government agency that buys the primary commodities from us. I've worked and socialised with some arrogant bastards in my time, but Popov takes it to a whole new level.

During the Brezhnev era he lived in Africa and London, functioning as a trader for some Soviet ministry. He's had a privileged life, and like the rest of the guys in the office he's a member of the Communist Party. He's impeccably dressed in what must be a Saville Row tailored suit and shirt and he's wearing handmade brogues. They look good but I still feel confident in my Loakes.

I decide I have to get on with him somehow, so I try to make small talk with the arrogant prick. "It's great that Gorbachev has received the Nobel Peace Prize, isn't it?" I say, trying to find some common ground. Wrong move.

Popov blasts air from his lips and distorts his face in disgust, "No! It's a mistake, a huge mistake. What he has done is unforgivable. Everything we have worked for is being destroyed."

"What about Perestroika and Glasnost? You've got freedom here now."

"It will never work," Popov retorts. "We need strong leadership and structure. Not a free-for-all. Communism provided for all, not just a few. We had the highest educational levels in the world. There was housing and health care for everyone. Look how it is now. The planes can't even fly. Pensioners aren't receiving their pensions and people are queuing for food. All this has happened in no time at all. Perestroika isn't working. Nor will it ever work."

"Huh," is all I can manage. I didn't feel comfortable with the bastard the first time we met, but I'm somewhat surprised by his vitriolic response. I really don't think we're going to get on. Then two of the others join in, confirming their support of Popov's views.

"Inflation is currently three per cent per week here," one of them says. "And our productivity is down by more than 10 per cent in the last six months. State workers are three months behind in their wages, and many people are going to work but sitting all day doing nothing."

"Well, Gorbachev is a hero in the West," I counter. "What he's done has changed the whole dynamic of the world in a positive way. People are no longer obsessed with the Cold War. It's as if there has been a collective release of stress."

Popov nods his head abruptly, as if to say that may be well and good for the West but not for the Russians. "This Nobel Peace Prize is a joke. Maybe Gorbachev should move to Scandinavia. He'll be more welcome there. Let *them* be impressed by him."

Vlad, who is now acting full time as our interpreter, and Merv and I, are leaving Moscow tomorrow to visit the construction sites. Given this aggressive reception I can't wait. I decide the best bet is for me to keep as far away from Popov as possible. First stop is Sovetskaya.

Petr Brandt is the state farm director here, and he's a member of the Soviet Union People's Committee, or what we would refer to as a member of parliament. He's an eccentric bastard, strutting around as if he's the central character in an opera. He's also in the minority. His passport states he is German. He's proud of his origins, but also very self-conscious. Understandably, since history demonstrates that wayward minorities can be given short shrift here. But even if he's a mad bastard, he appears to make prudent staff choices.

One of these is Boris Ivanovich, who appears to be the most senior of Petr Brandt's deputies. He will be leading the social activities that night, which will inevitably involve endless toasting. I think about how equal participation is such a wonderful aspect of the evening meal. It is expected that everyone joins in the toasting (although, to be fair, the girls aren't expected to drink). For the socially reticent, as I can be from time to time, toasting ensures full participation in the friendly banter and the opportunity to step outside one's comfort zone. The results can be enlivening. Wisdom, intelligence and humour can be discovered. Toasting also minimises the likelihood of a social gathering becoming dominated by an extrovert keen to control a group of less garrulous friends, and there's not much chance of awkward silences.

For me, it's such a structured approach to appreciating other people.

It's a chance to commend someone for the support they've given, to thank the host for his generosity and hospitality, to appreciate the capability of an interpreter or the charm and beauty of a hostess. We all want to be witty and engaging, so between toasts I patch together a rough skeleton of what I want to say, then when it's my turn I step forward and deliver. Everyone listens attentively. If the translator is on top of his game, it's possible to weave a subtle theme into the toast. If the translator is a novice, the communication needs to be simple and direct. Either way, whatever is communicated in a toast can help to build trust and respect.

Then I remember the complete obliteration caused by toasting on my last trip and decide to ask Merv if he has any tips for me on how to drink vodka.

He says, "Etiquette requires whoever is toasting to drink all the contents of the glass. The recipient is also expected to drink to the bottom. Those on the periphery can get away with half a glass. So full participation in the evening's events requires a few tricks. Always take an ample swig of mineral water, and eating dairy or fatty foods beforehand provides a lining for the stomach. Usually there's plenty of sour cream or kefir. The choices of tipple are generally vodka or Georgian cognac. If you are really unlucky there may be only Polish vodka. To overcome the brutal assault on the old olfactory system, I learnt a trick a few years ago."

Using his left hand to depict the action of holding a piece of bread, Merv continues. "Before you drink, get hold of a piece of dark brown bread, place it over your nostrils, inhale deeply through the bread and exhale out your mouth. As soon as you've completely exhaled, drop the contents of the glass into your mouth and swallow it immediately. The smell of the yeast in the bread masks the vodka fumes."

"I'm keen to use that one," I say.

"OK, you get used to the harshness of vodka and the instant rush that follows knocking it back. But let's be clear, there is simply no way you can do business in Russia without alcohol being an intrinsic part of each stage of the business process."

"Do all Russian blokes drink?" I ask.

"It is very rare to meet someone who doesn't. Vodka consumption is endemic in Russia. It accounts for a considerable proportion of the deaths of working-age citizens."

"Seriously?"

"The real trick though, is to retain focus right through until the end. If you have consumed admirably and you are still standing, then such an approach gains respect. That is the sign of a serious man," he concludes.

And that's what I want to be – a serious man.

Now Boris Ivanovich tilts his head to allow the smoke from the cigarette to drift away from his eyes. It's a proper cigarette, with a filter. Not one of those cheap things, half tobacco and half cardboard tube. Squinting, he flicks the tops from four bottles of mineral water using an opener that has been placed on the table by Almira, the head chef and this evening's waitress. She's been doing this job for a long time and she's good at it. She has strategically positioned half-litre bottles of vodka on the table near Boris Ivanovich – four with orange labels and two with lime green labels.

"Looks like it could be another big night," Merv quietly cautions me.

Lifting his eyebrows, Boris Ivanovich asks, "Chto, Merv?"

Vlad translates, "What's that, Merv?"

Merv points to the vodka. "This looks like trouble."

With an unrestrained smile, Boris Ivanovich says, "We are always pleased to have you here, so why not celebrate your stay with a chut chut or two?"

Just back from a holiday in Hawaii, Merv is wearing one of those T-shirts proclaiming, "I survived Hawaii". This particular garment is made even more distinctive by the large pocket sewn on the left-hand side.

I want to say to him, "That's a handy pocket you've got there Merv. Do you use it to carry your lunch to work?" I wonder how it is that some people have absolutely no taste.

"I would like to welcome you all to Sovetskaya," says Boris. "Much has been achieved in your absence. Our winter is over and it's spring. We Soviets may sleep heavily in the winter, but once the days grow longer we're people of action. The containers were delivered here from the Bulaeva railway yards last week. We look forward to opening these containers with you tomorrow. Naturally we are very interested to see what treasures may lie inside. We have dreamed about having our own meat plant for years, so this truly is an exciting time for us. This toast is to you, for helping to make our dream come true."

We all drink to the bottom.

As the most senior member of our team, Merv responds, "It's great to be back. It's pleasing to see work has commenced on the construction of the foundations and floor. We are also pleased that everything is on track so we can begin to install our equipment. The reward for us is the chance to socialise with you, and so this toast is to our joint working relationship and friendship." We all drink.

Almira sets some food on the table. It's a sausage the size of a woman's forearm, composed of a dark, coarse meat, held together by an intestinal casing, probably removed from a cow, and tied at each end with fine twine.

"Do you like horse meat?" asks Boris Ivanovich.

Horse? There's no way I'm eating horse. I've never heard of anyone eating horse before. It'd be like eating dog. "I didn't realise horse meat was edible," I blurt out.

Boris Ivanovich looks slightly affronted. "Absolutna. It's a local delicacy. Please, have some."

Cautiously chewing the horse meat I manage to indicate that I like the taste of it but not necessarily the idea. Trying to avoid any further discussion about the food I say, "Boris, I'm interested to know why you are called Boris Ivanovich rather than just Boris."

"We are generally known by both Christian names. My first name is Boris. My middle name, or patronymic name, is Ivanovich. Ivanovich identifies that I am the son of Ivan. Russian middle names end in either -ovich or -evich for males, and for females the middle name ends in -ovna or -evna."

I nod, still chewing reluctantly on the horse meat. Gradually our exchanges become more random and boisterous. Vlad is still on his game translating and he is still in good enough shape to filter out any inappropriate behaviour – thankfully, otherwise someone could easily take offence. If there's ever a perpetrator of offensive behaviour, it's me.

Suddenly Boris Ivanovich slaps his hand on the table. "I have a joke to tell. An Englishman, an American and a Russian are sitting around a table chatting, and they are asked, 'What is the one thing you fear more than anything?' The American responds, 'Driving down a steep hill and the brakes on my car fail and the car plunges over the edge of a cliff.' The Englishman says, 'Being required to play Russian roulette and when it is my turn the chamber is loaded with a bullet.' The Russian says, 'When I am drinking vodka with my friends and someone has put water in my glass.'"

Fuelled by vodka the camaraderie escalates. Vlad continues translating throughout the changing dynamic. He seems to be doing a good job, but I really wouldn't know. The dialogue is generally flowing freely and he doesn't seem to be missing a beat. He's the only one here interpreting and he's currently about one-and-a-half courses behind the rest of us. I didn't realise how intense translating is, and how time consuming.

Merv stands in an ungainly manner and launches into an erratic delivery. "It's time to toast our hostess. Almira, you have obviously worked very hard preparing this food for us. It's stunning. Your abundant selection of food is so flavoursome and well presented, it's like an extension of you." Raising his glass to chin level, Merv biffs the contents over his shoulder and sits down.

There's an uproar. Boris Ivanovich refills Merv's glass and insists that he drink it. Despite being heavily intoxicated, Merv downs the vodka. Then he suddenly rises from his chair and bolts out the door. Soon after, looking dishevelled and walking slightly erratically, he returns to the table. His Hawaiian shirt pocket is dripping wet.

Taking his place, he grins at everyone. "I didn't make it to the toilet. I didn't want to vomit on the floor, so I pulled my pocket open and targeted the gaping pouch. I captured most of it!"

The response from everyone is overwhelming delight. You can see it in their faces. They have challenged our leader and he has consumed all that has been expected of him, but they have won. Boris Ivanovich looks victorious. "Let us make this drink the last of the evening, or as we say, 'Let this be the walking stick'." I drink to that.

In the morning I notice Vlad is talking to some woman who looks like a cleaning lady. I fell asleep on the couch in the living area last night. The room was warm, so I draped a couple of blankets over me. I couldn't be bothered going to my bedroom. Vlad tells me this woman thinks I'm a Russian. It would only be a Russian who would fall asleep in his clothes in the lounge after drinking heavily. She was concerned that a local had snuck into the accommodation reserved for foreign guests. He has assured her that I am not Russian. Wherever I go they tell me I look like and behave like a Russian. Right now I feel as crook as a Russian dog.

After breakfast Merv and I bid farewell. He is returning to Moscow ahead of me. Vlad and I will stay here to open the shipping containers. I'm just as eager to open the first container as anyone. At the site I greet Boris and shake his hand. "Boris Ivanovich. Kak dela?" How are you?

"Normalno," he responds with a loud voice.

I think normalno is an understatement, because he's smiling. I unlock the padlock on the container and open the door. I step back as the sound of steel sliding on steel rushes at me from the darkness within. I catch a glimpse of the source of the sound: a beam the length of the container is hurtling towards me, accelerating as it slides down from chest height to the ground. The end of the beam smacks into my right foot. Initially I feel nothing except dismay at how poorly the container has been packed. Then the pain hits me! *Jeeesusss*! It feels like someone has thrust a red-hot poker into the top of my foot.

Reeling around while trying to hold my right foot off the ground I feel overwhelmed with nausea. Vlad rushes forward to help me as I struggle to sit on the dusty ground. "How could this happen!" I growl. "Those useless bastards must have closed the door with a forklift. It's the only way you could jam all that shit in there."

The flood of anger intensifies. I can't control myself. The frustration is intense. I say through gritted teeth, "I've never broken a bone in my body in my whole fucking life. And here I am, at the beginning of my time in the Soviet Union, with a broken fucking foot!" With my face screwed up like an empty can of coke I try to visualise the last-minute shoving and grunting that went on prior to trucking the container to the port in New Zealand. "I can't believe this."

"We will take you to the hospital immediately," Vlad says. He and Boris Ivanovich help me into the front seat of the yellow Volga sedan. My mind is racing. I have to complete a circuit of the construction sites every month. That's what I'm here for. I can still do it.

I *have* to do it.

We start driving through vast unfenced fields of grass and recently germinated crops. The fields flow around islands of birch forest. It's difficult to think how I can function here with this injury. It feels bad. I need to think about something other than how I'm going to do my job. And I need to stop trying to find someone to blame.

But I can't.

The frustration continues for at least another 20 minutes. Then I haul myself out of my silent tirade of contempt at the unknown container packer and try to focus on the countryside.

"It's great to see the forests have been retained around here," I comment to Boris Ivanovich.

"One of the benefits of the trees is that they provide a habitat for mushrooms. We have a love affair with mushroom hunting, you know. It's a Russian tradition for families to gather mushrooms in summer and autumn. The knowledge of what mushrooms to pick and how to prepare them has been passed down from one generation to the next. They've always been a part of our culture. In times gone by, poor people living in the countryside substituted meat with mushrooms."

My mind wants to go charging back to the internal dialogue about my foot but I continue the conversation. It takes a lot of determination, but I do it. I start thinking about what it was like for Vlad last night. I could tell it was bloody hard work for him keeping up with eating and interpreting the conversation, especially near the end of the night. From now on I'll use two translators in social situations. Vlad can keep an eye on things and I'll get one of the construction site translators to look after the social conversations. That way I'll be well armed.

Shortly we reach the town of Bulaeva and pull into the hospital car park. Vlad helps me out of the car, through the entrance of the hospital and along the corridor to a waiting room. It's full. People are standing in the corridor.

Vlad and I remain in the hallway as Boris Ivanovich goes off to look for the chief medical officer. He soon returns with him. Boris has a relaxed chat with the doctor and then gives him four packets of Rothmans cigarettes. Smiling in appreciation, the doctor puts the fags in his coat pocket and amicably pats Boris on the shoulder. This means that now I am at the head of the queue.

Within minutes I'm being wheeled into an X-ray theatre on a trolley. The theatre must have been constructed around the time of the invention of the X-ray. It's half the size of a tennis court and fitted with a solitary device resembling a huge X-ray gun. The wall at the end of the room is lined with lead and the dark brown ceiling is sagging. The radiographer is in her forties. She looks intelligent. She's not bad to look at either. She gestures, indicating that I should remove my ankle-high leather boots and my jeans. Thankfully I can leave on my Y-fronts and new cuffed shirt. It's chilly and dark in here, but the blue and white stripe of the shirt fabric makes me feel clean and calm.

The radiographer swings around and places a heavy lead blanket over my Y-fronts. Christ! Monica and I want children. I ask her in one of the few phrases I have learnt, "Chto delat?" What should I do?

She responds, "There's nothing to do."

It's probably futile but I cup my hands around my gonads to provide more protection. The radiographer has just positioned the X-ray device in the general direction of my foot. She buggers off towards the doorway in the lead-lined wall at the far end of the cavern. The control cubicle is so far away you'd think a thermonuclear reaction is about to take place. Shit, my purpose in life is to continue the family name. That's what we are here for – to have children, look after them, nurture them, provide guidance and then worry and stress about supporting them. This torching could interrupt all of that.

There's a dull vibration and the room reverberates. There's not much I can do but hold on tight. God only knows if I'll ever have children after this. My ability to produce sperm is probably being well and truly annihilated. I slowly look around the room with a sense of surrender. The giving in, the acceptance of what has happened, makes me feel relaxed.

The X-ray reveals that I have three fractures and each one is a clean break. The radiographer pushes me out of the nuking room into the corridor and quickly catches the attention of a nurse. My foot is soon plastered and I shuffle out of the Bulaeva hospital on a pair of wooden crutches that must date from before the Great Patriotic War.

We return to the state farm. "Grigori, would you like to go to the banya?" Boris Ivanovich asks. "You don't have to have a sauna or a plunge in the pool, but we can put a plastic bag over your foot and you can take a shower if you would like. Almira will bring some food over. Would you like to do that?"

"OK." I feel slightly confused by the day's events as Vlad and Boris accompany me to the banya. After my shower a thought occurs to me and I ask Vlad, "Is this banya available for the whole community?"

"In remote towns and villages there is often no domestic hot water, so everyone has a sauna and shower in the communal banya once a week," Vlad responds. "They are assigned a specific attendance time."

"Only once a week?"

"Yes. Once a week is normal for most people. There are benefits from not washing more frequently in the winter. The skin oil provides a layer of thermal insulation and helps with immunity. If people living in cold conditions wash frequently, the layer of oil doesn't get a chance to form."

That explains the male body odour.

We sit down for our meal. While we eat, Boris Ivanovich shares another of his jokes.

"A patient sees a doctor. The doctor says, 'This medicine is for insomnia, this one is for nervous break-down, and this one is for depression.'

The patient thanks the doctor very much and asks, 'Do you have any other medicine besides vodka?' " He looks at me, grinning. "So Grigori, the best remedy for you is rest and some medicinal vodka."

The next day Boris Ivanovich has his driver take Vlad and me to the airport. After 20 minutes Vlad successfully negotiates with the truculent Aeroflot ticket agent for two tickets to Moscow. He tells me it cost an arm and a leg to bribe the "incorrigible" woman.

We touch down, and as I make my way to the baggage reclaim area at Moscow's Domodedovo Airport Lukhum greets me and points at my foot.

"Grigori, what have you been doing? Trying to kick-start the construction down there."

"You'd think so, wouldn't ya? Lukhum, I'll need you to collect me and bring me home each day from the office. Will that be OK?"

"Of course."

"I'll need you to do my shopping at Stockmann's too. I'll give you a power of attorney to use my credit card."

"Not a problem, Grigori. Anything you need, I will be able to do for you."

Although it's a practical place for me to shop, Stockmann's is a symbol of the division between Russians and foreigners. I've never seen Russians shopping for themselves in there, because it's too expensive.

Lukhum parks the car outside my flat and helps me in with my black Samsonite suitcase. The apartment building is like many others around here – a big-boned, two-storey structure built before the revolution. The peach-coloured exterior is interrupted with bold window joinery painted white. The heavy double front door is always locked. The ground-floor windows have white security bars, welded from steel reinforcing rods. There must be much more crime around here than I'm aware of. Why would you have steel bars on your living-room window when you live in the socialist capital of the world?

I live upstairs in a large one-bedroom flat that is accessible by stairs and an open cage lift. The lift isn't working. I hop up the stairs on one foot using the crutches only for balance. By the time I get to my floor I feel like a complete cripple. As I enter the front door of the flat I'm greeted by the reek of harsh cleaning chemicals. The cleaning lady must have been in. I struggle to open the small window at head height in the hope it will air the place. Then I make my way to the plush tan lounge chair, placing the crutches alongside me.

I lift my encased foot onto a stool. It's comfortable, but the space feels lifeless. Numbly, I stare at the large, glass-fronted book case positioned in front of me. It's packed with books, but they're no good to me. They're all written in Cyrillic. Still, I can never sit still long enough to read anyway. I haven't got the patience.

I really don't have any connection with this apartment. I'm juxtaposed into someone else's life. And for that matter, I have nothing in common with the Russians in the office either. They're wary of me. Any interaction is superficial and they're so guarded. Actually, they look as though they distrust each other, especially Popov. He's continually dismissive of me and what I'm doing. *Bastard*. His conceited attitude makes everyone edgy. He must be good at his job, otherwise why would you employ someone like that?

The heaviness of disappointment settles on me. I'm not going to be able to function freely here with this foot. If there's one thing I can't cope with, it's incompetence. I ponder once again the image of someone forcing the container shut with a forklift. Surely they must have been aware that the gear would fall out when the door was opened?

I look around the room. I'm here in Russia by myself with a broken foot. A feeling of isolation joins the feeling of disappointment. A sudden deep depression starts pulling me down. I haven't felt like this for a while and I wish I didn't feel like it now.

I want to cry, but I don't.

Come on mate, pick yourself up. You've always dreamed of doing something like this. Get on with it. Monica is probably just as lonely as you are. She's probably wondering what this hunger for success is all about.

I call Monica in London the next day. She sounds lonely too, but I feel considerably cheered up when she tells me she is very keen to visit Moscow soon. "There is a couple of things I would love to do while I'm there," she says enthusiastically. "From the time I was a little girl learning ballet, I've always wanted to see a ballet performed at the Bolshoi Theatre. And I think it would be great to sample some caviar."

At least I can arrange that.

Later that week I'm at the airport when I suddenly see Monica's face in the crowd. She shakes her head as she makes her way towards me standing on my mid-century crutches. I'm so pleased to see her. We hug each other awkwardly. Lukhum greets Monica with his friendly smile and a heavy accent. He leads us to the car, carrying her bag and making sure there is a pathway available for my hobbling.

"That's an interesting plaster you've got there," she says nodding at the appendage on the end of my leg. "When we get back to London I'll take you to an outpatient clinic and have your foot re-plastered."

I feel comforted. "Sounds like a plan to me. How has it been for you over the last month?"

"Lonely," she replies. "I've really only got Mary around the corner and she's just as lonely as I am."

I didn't really think she could be lonely in London, but now she mentions it, it's easy to understand. Get up, go to work as a personal nurse for some ra-ra in Hampstead, come home, have a couple of glasses of bubbles, have a meal and go to bed. The only break from the grind, apart from the half bottle of Veuve every evening, is the weekly trip to Harvey Nicks to spend the money she's been making. I've been too tied up in my own problems to consider hers.

She continues, "The landlady has been giving me gyp as well. The hot water doesn't run properly – it takes an hour to fill the bath. I've called her about it four times and she just fobs me off. She sent around one of her dodgy boyfriends the other day to have a look, but it felt like he was just there to intimidate me."

"Shall I get Jonty's lawyer mate on to her?"

"God no. She's got a nasty streak and I think that would only inflame her."

"Jesus. I'll have a word to her when I get back to London."

"That would be helpful."

As we drive into the city my mind strays off into business.

"What are you thinking about?" Monica asks me.

Feeling as if I've been caught out I say, "Oh, nothing of any consequence." God this bloody thinking is a distraction. Monica gets sick of me being in my own little world. I need to be more focused on her while she's here. But I can't help it sometimes. I try to focus my attention on Monica.

Lukhum drives up to the security guard stationed at the entrance to the apartment's car park. They exchange a few words and he drives past the two-and-a-half-metre-high gates made from welded steel bar.

As we get out of the car Monica looks up at the 10-storey apartment building. I hope she'll be alright here. It's Merv's flat and normally only used when he visits Moscow. I don't think I'll tell her about the mysterious history of the place. An Englishman who had previously lived in the flat was found dead in the car park. The Moscow police claimed he'd fallen out of the window. You'd have to be intent on jumping out of a window in this place – they're all double casement and positioned about a metre off the floor.

"So, here we are," I say as Lukhum opens the front door to the apartment for Monica.

I confirm the arrangements for tonight with Lukhum. He departs. Monica enters and eagerly explores the place. "It's much more spacious than the flat I've been living in," I tell her. "A Finnish outfit knocked it into shape."

"I like it," she says.

"It's a bit of an oasis," I respond. I look at her. "I'm pleased you're here."

"I've been looking forward to it," she says.

The doorbell rings. Struggling to use one of the few words in my sparse quiver of Russian, I greet Lukhum. We get in the car. It feels slightly odd having Monica with me. I try to overcome the unease by talking about superficial things we are driving past. Lukhum takes us to Red Square. We approach on foot from the St Basil's end. The pastel-coloured cream spirals of the church look like something from another planet. We move towards the other end of the square, past the red-brown walls protecting the mustard-coloured buildings of the Kremlin. We continue towards the polished brown-and-grey granite cubic structure that is Lenin's mausoleum.

"This is the structure the old Communist geezers like Brezhnev used to stand on during the May Day military parades," I tell her.

The mausoleum looks like a contemporary version of an ancient temple. The power and the intrigue of the place are accentuated by the floodlighting. The black granite pelmet to the entrance to the Communist sacred site is engraved with the name "Lenin" in large Cyrillic letters.

"I've never been inside, but Lenin's preserved body is on display." As we get closer I feel reluctant to walk too close.

Monica asks, "Is Lenin's body really in there?"

"Apparently."

"Bizarre."

"I guess he's still the face of Communism, and they use his body to remind people what it's all about. Who knows?"

Lenin might be one of the most recognisable people in the world after Christ. It strikes me that the idea and the image of both men have been used in ways that wouldn't please either of them. Their images and names are used as a reminder that we are all here to be controlled by one dominating apparatus or another.

Lukhum drives us home as we sit silently in the back.

The next day he takes us for a drive around the city. Our first stop is the huge structure of Moscow University. I remember the photo in Merv's office of the beautiful naked woman in the Chaika – this is where it was taken. It looks like a bleak, neo-gothic rendition of a wedding cake, topped with spires.

"This is one of Stalin's high rises that are called the Seven Sisters," Lukhum says.

"Shit, there's some stone in that," I say. Grimacing slightly as I look at the fortress-like structure I add, "It's like something from Gotham City."

"The University was built by about 14,000 German prisoners of war. It was finished in the 1950s."

Monica is just as incredulous as I am. "German prisoners of war – in the 1950s?"

"Yes. They were incarcerated and set to hard labour until the mid-1950s."

"You're joking?" I respond.

"Nyet."

Far out! Now I know what Merv meant when he said that Lord Snowdon's photograph was an example of the enigma of the place.

A few nights later we go to the ballet. The Bolshoi Theatre is imposing, and it's obviously a place of significance because it's the only building in town that seems to be getting a lick of paint at the moment. Everything else is languishing. Monica and I weave our way through the scaffolding into the foyer, where we rent some opera binoculars as Lukhum has recommended. Then an usher leads us to our dress circle seats. The hum of conversation dies away as the musicians take their place in the pit. The conductor calls the orchestra to order and they begin. Then the vast curtains open, revealing the ballet dancers.

Viewing the ballerinas through the binoculars I'm in awe. They are absolutely gorgeous. In their lovely tutus with skintight bodices they look like supermodels. Like radiant princesses, they weave their sensuous and precise dance of love across the stage. The whole thing is just so wonderful. I love it. I'm uplifted by a feeling of excitement and pure joy. It's as if the ballet performers, the orchestra, the audience, Monica and I, and even the very bones of the theatre, are all as one. Tchaikovsky's music enlivens me, one moment delicately and ever so lightly lifting me up and the next dramatically overpowering me. I don't want it to stop.

At the end I wander out to the foyer still feeling overwhelmed. The entire performance has been so incongruous, such a startling contrast to the disorganised, undisciplined, nearly chaotic level of activity that exists outside the theatre.

"This has to be one of the most vivid examples of the contrasts in Russia," I say to Monica.

The following day at the office I'm excited about sharing my experience of the Bolshoi Ballet with everyone.

"I am pleased you enjoyed *Swan Lake*," Popov says. "It is my favourite too. I have seen it 68 times, and I have seen *Nut Cracker* 59 times."

"You're joking!" I say, dumbfounded.

"Pravda. It is true. I love the ballet, and so do many, many Russians. For those who can afford it, ballet, opera and theatre are the most common forms of entertainment. If you go to lesser-known theatres you will find second-tier ballet troupes perform *Swan Lake* and *Nut Cracker*. The performances are still world-class, though, and you will find that a large proportion of the audience is made up of many grandparents with grandchildren."

So beneath the huff and puff and the aloof veneer of the typical Moscow resident lies a heart drawn to beauty. There is, after all, a soft inner core to the harshness that prevails in this city.

The next experience on Monica's list is Russian caviar. As usual I need help from Lukhum with this. He takes us in the Merc to a Khrushchev-era apartment building. The Merc stands out like the proverbial dog's balls in this neighbourhood and the foreign business number plates are a dead giveaway.

"What do you think's going on?" Monica asks nervously as we wait outside for Lukhum. "I'm not comfortable with this."

I feel at ease with this dodgy carry-on, so I attempt to allay her fears. "It'll be fine. It's the way things are done here. He shouldn't be long."

Lukhum has ordered six kilograms of Beluga caviar for us. It's not an official transaction but I have no interest in asking any questions. It's a safe bet that we are buying merchandise that has been pilfered from somewhere. He's told me a bit about the product. The bigger the eggs, the higher the quality, and he has assured me this stuff will be the best. I enjoy most delicacies, but what I enjoy most is sharing them with others. This should be more than enough to share around. Anyway, at $50 a kilogram it's not a huge punt.

After 10 minutes Lukhum confidently strides across the muddy car park carrying two plastic bags. Smiling with satisfaction and pride at pulling the deal off, he opens one of the bags to reveal a stack of round metal tins, each the diameter of a large side plate and about five centimetres deep. I'm excited.

When we get back to the flat I follow Lukhum's instructions, gingerly opening the blue-labelled lid of one can. Like hundreds of light grey pearls, veiled in the finest oil, the fish eggs glisten in the subdued light of the apartment. Placing the tin in a bowl of ice, I scoop out the first little clump of eggs with the mother of pearl spoon that Lukhum has lent me. He has instructed us not to use silver or stainless steel – apparently metal taints the delicate flavour. Gently wiping the eggs off the spoon with my lips and slowly pushing them against the roof of my mouth with my tongue, the soft skin of the pearls bursts, leaving a creamy taste with a faint hint of salt.

I get a bottle of Monica's favourite champagne out of the fridge and we make a toast to decadence. Monica and I give each other the thumbs up as we continue savouring the caviar. We experiment with different combinations. We try caviar on blini (a buckwheat pancake), caviar with butter and blini, and caviar with nothing other than butter.

The next day Lukhum knocks on the door to take us to the airport for our departure to the "Smoke". He takes Monica's bag and leads us down to the parked car. Sitting on the driver's seat is a book he has been reading. "What's that you're reading?" I ask him.

"A short story by Chekhov. Have you read any of his work, Grigori?"

"No I haven't."

"The book I am reading is called 'The Black Monk'. I've just read a very interesting passage about death. Would you like me to read it to you?"

"Sure. Go for it."

Lukhum starts reading:

"You mentioned Eternal Truth . . . But is that within men's reach, do they need it if there's no such thing as eternal life?"

"There is eternal life," the monk said.

"But what is the purpose of eternal life?" asked Kovrin.

The monk responds, "Like any other kind of life – pleasure."

I nod at Lukhum indicating my gratitude for him reading it to me.

"Do you believe in life after death, Grigori?" he asks.

"I do, actually. I've had a near-death experience and most definitely I had a sense that there was no end to the experience of life even after my body dies."

We get through customs inspection with three kilograms of Beluga stored in glass jars and onto our British Airways flight. After take-off I start reading an article titled "The fastest route to happiness" in a magazine someone has left in the pouch in front of me. It quotes research recently undertaken on what makes people happy. The three most important ingredients are: a sense of belonging to a community, service and a sense of personal growth. I read on. Money comes in at number eight.

I slouch slightly as I discharge a stream of air between my closed lips. At the moment I don't experience any sense of community. I'm on my own in Russia. Seeing my mates in London will give me some respite from that. In recent times I've thought that doing service for the community was admirable but not necessary. I've been following the advice I read in an autobiography by a CEO of a hugely successful multi-national business. He was adamant that it is much better to provide a good environment for your staff than to diffuse your focus doing service elsewhere. I adopted his approach about five years ago.

As for growing, well, I'm learning and up-skilling in how to do business in the USSR, but I'm definitely not growing on the personal front. I'm probably regressing. I've heard before that money isn't the source of happiness. Really? I think that's questionable. Money has to make you happy, otherwise why would humanity pursue it so vigorously?

The day after Monica and I get back to the "Smoke" I have the cast removed from my foot. It's still tender but I can walk on it. That Saturday we convene a Beluga and Stolichnaya (a kind of vodka) party in our Harmood Street flat. As we wait for our mates to arrive I feel wired. I always get a bit manic prior to the first few people arriving when I'm throwing a party. Parties are lucky dips, really. You never have any control over how they'll go and that makes me anxious.

I flick on the television. An old James Bond movie is about to start. Here's James skiing down a slope in some arctic landscape, chased by a bunch of Russian geezers clad in white winter military clothing. In true style he escapes onto a waiting luxury submarine, and he's being welcomed by a sultry KGB agent who seductively offers the nonchalant Bond a glass of Stolichnaya and a small plate of Beluga caviar. I miss her name, but it was probably something like Pussy Galore.

"Yes!" I say, turning to Monica and punching the air with my fist. "What a perfect introduction to our night." The party goes well and it's the wee small hours before the last guest disappears.

The following afternoon Monica and I go into the city. As we stroll along I take the time to enjoy my new purchases. I always feel particularly pleased with a fine pair of shoes that fit well, but my first pair of Church's brogues makes me feel really special. I'm also chuffed with a new double-cuffed shirt, cut and sewn in Saville Row. We visit Harrods' Food Hall and Monica calls me over to a display area and points at the Beluga caviar.

"Far out," I say. A 56-gram jar of Beluga costs nearly 200 quid. Let me see, that's close to £3500 a kilogram. Shit! We purchased more than £20,000 worth for just US$300. And last night a dozen of us got through about 5000 quids' worth. "Makes you wonder who makes the money, eh?" I say.

Soon it's our last night in London, and it's a good opportunity to discuss the way forward with our living arrangements. We both agree that it wouldn't be much fun for Monica living in Moscow full time. Let's wait and see what happens.

SIX

Vlad and I fly from Moscow to southern Siberia on 23 July 1991. After we land I change my watch to the local time. It's 6pm here in Barnaul, but the airport clock, like all airports, displays Moscow time: 2pm. We get a ride into the city. The car is driven by a casual driver making a few rubles on the side.

Pylons appear to be an essential part of the cityscape. Everywhere I look they are supporting inadequate street lighting, poorly maintained electric trolley-bus cables, large clocks displaying the wrong time, and loud speakers for communicating instructions. Vlad and I enter the restaurant in a cavernous space on the ground floor of a hotel just as the band finishes a Beatles song.

"Vlad, why is it that just about every second restaurant I go into has a cover band playing the Beatles. Is this a coincidence?"

"No, it's not a coincidence. Many people would say that the Beatles inspired a cultural revolution that ultimately undermined Communism. You know that Gorbachev said that the Beatles were the single most important reason for the end of the Cold War?"

Incredulous, I say, "Seriously? How did they have such an impact?"

"At the time many young people were tired of the fear that existed in their lives because of state control. The state feared what the Beatles might bring, so officially their music was banned. But the Beatles gave us the courage to overcome our fear." Pausing for a moment, and then continuing to speak quietly, he says, "The Beatles also allowed us to see that we had something in common with people in the West. We realised that we were all passionate about the same thing."

"So the Beatles were really a catalyst for people to create a different life?" I say.

Vlad says, "Yes they were. And if you look around it appears to have worked. Imagine how great it would be if everyone in the world could create a different, less fearful world."

"Yeah." I pause for a moment and then say, "There's no point even thinking about it, Vlad. I don't think it's possible. It could never happen."

On the way out of the restaurant I walk past the open door of the kitchen. There, sitting near the entrance, are four 40-litre milk cans without lids. I glance inside and see they are full of vodka. What a find! A few vodkas for the boys on the construction sites would be a real treat. I negotiate with the restaurant manager and we quickly strike a deal. I think I've got a bargain, but the other bloke looks like he's just won Lotto.

The following morning Vlad and I are off to Ongudai. We've got one of the milk cans with us, plus some telecommunications gear that I'm also pretty chuffed about. During my stay in Moscow I've been negotiating to gain access to the Satnav satellite communications system. Unbelievably, I've pulled it off. We've got the first two Satnav satellite dishes registered to anyone outside of the military. The suffixes of the two registration codes are 001 and 002. Admittedly they cost an arm and a leg, but hey, if it means the guys on site can keep in contact with me in Moscow and with the office in Wellington, then the units have got to be good.

We've chartered a helicopter, this one flown by just one pilot. He is a thick-set character in his forties who looks like he's had more than his fair share of vodka and salami. As he undertakes the mandatory checks prior to kicking the engine into action I realise how complacent I've become. This machine is as rough as guts, but it really doesn't bother me.

We've been in the air about an hour and now we're trapped. The cloud layer below masks any sight of land, although I know that not far beneath my backside are the foothills of the Altai Mountains. The pilot is incessantly demanding a response from ground control.

"Ongudai. Ongudai. Ongudai. Ongudai. Ongudai. Ongudai," he chants as he frantically flicks the toggle switches to gain access to different frequencies on the overhead radio. Then the same chant on a new frequency, "Ongudai. Ongudai. Ongudai. Ongudai. Ongudai." Now he tries another location, "Abai. Abai. Abai. Abai. Abai. Abai."

No response.

We're too remote, and chances are whoever is responsible for air safety in these parts isn't even at work. People aren't fronting up to work because they're not getting paid. The air controller is probably on the piss. If he's not on the piss, he's probably shagging one of his female workmates or organising to get something done for nothing.

The pilot's demand for attention is becoming more fevered. "Koksa. Koksa. Koksa. Koksa. Koksa."

We've been sitting here in this same location, trapped by a floor of cloud, for close to 30 minutes. The bloke behind the controls is perspiring profusely, his shoulders are elevated and his hand actions are erratic. Well, it'll be interesting to see if we've got enough fuel to sit this out. I couldn't give a shit. There's nothing for me to do. No point getting wound up. It's misguided, but I really feel it's inconceivable that I could come to grief. Maybe I'm just cocky or I think I'm too important to die. The saying "Don't stress the things you can't change" reinforces my ease.

I remove the camera from my bag. "Hey Vlad, can you take a photo of me and the pilot?"

Vlad fumbles around trying to take a photo. Shit, he's useless sometimes. "Look through the view finder here and click this button," I instruct.

He clicks and I grab the camera back off him. I don't know how many permutations of place names and radio frequencies the pilot has cycled through but no one has responded. Awash with perspiration, the pilot is completely unaware that I've now got the camera lens about 30 centimetres away from his tortured face. The shutter captures the image. If I make it out I'll have a reminder of the event.

Miraculously the clouds part directly in front of us, leaving an opening the size of about half a football field. Below, maybe 100 metres, is the top of a mountain. The pilot slumps in relief, then seizes the opportunity to descend through this tube of clear sky, directing the machine down the side of the mountain into the valley below. He looks at me and gives the thumbs up. Despite the earlier bravado I'm very pleased. When we land I tell the pilot he did well getting us out of that hairy situation and he responds, almost disparagingly, "Normalno."

"Whatever," I think, in response to his typically Russian off-hand response to a razor-thin escape from catastrophe.

The site manager is here to meet us. Looking at the aluminium milk can he says with a wry smile, "That should provide a refreshing change." Then looking decidedly disgruntled he scowls, "Look, I had to send four guys to Novosibirsk for a 10-day holiday. There was nothing for them to do here."

Christ! What a waste of time and money sending tradesmen more than halfway around the world to build a meat plant and having them end up on holiday during the short summer construction period. He informs me the locals are unable to supply the essential building materials, such as acetylene for gas welding and electricity for construction work.

"Every Monday is Acetylene Monday," the site manager says. "They keep promising the acetylene will be here on Monday. Four Acetylene Mondays have passed with no sign of action. Progress on the site has nearly ground to a halt. The final shipment of containers of construction materials hasn't shown up either."

Feeling decidedly impotent in my support for this site, I say, "OK, I'll visit the Functionary and see if he can shake things up."

"Have you not heard what happened to him?" he says.

"No."

"He died four days ago. First, I was told it was a heart attack, then I heard he drowned in the Kartun River. There's some suggestion of foul play."

I pause momentarily then respond, "Seriously?"

"Yep."

"He was recently employed as the general manager of a joint venture that Merv has established. They've been trying to develop a private deer farm," I add.

"Who was his partner in the joint venture?" the site manager asks.

"I don't know for sure. Maybe the prime minister."

"Interesting," he responds.

I show him the Satnav computer and dish, hoping to placate him. He's understandably pleased. It makes me feel as if I've been at least partially effective.

The first person I see as we walk over to the construction site is one of the electricians. He sports a Mohican. "Hey! How ya doin?" I call out.

"Good!" he calls out from the top of a ladder. "What have you done with those bloody containers?"

Here we go. He steps down from the ladder and comes over to shake my hand. His two mates come over as well. One boy's head has been completely shaved, including his eyebrows. The other has a band of hair running between his ears. He points to the medieval monk, "This is Latitude." Then he looks at the bald boy with no eyebrows. "This is Attitude. My new name is Longitude."

"Clearly you've had a few beers."

"Yeah, Grolsch," he responds.

"Grolsch? I've never heard of it," I say.

"Well, that's what arrived in the last delivery."

That evening the pilot shakes his head in disgust as 20 of us start drinking vodka ladled directly from the milk can. I'm not sure if it is repugnance at us drinking without toasting or whether it is mixing the vodka with orange juice as we're doing, but I don't care.

Then things start to become a bit crazy.

Longitude hurls abuse at me. "You're *useless*. You should've had the containers on site long before this. What've you been doing?"

I feel uncomfortable under this attack. My stomach tightens. I want to lash out at him, but it would be inappropriate for me to do so. I try to appease him, but he continues on with his gnarly behaviour. I decide to terminate the encounter and begin talking to one of the other, more sober characters. Five minutes later I surreptitiously check the level of the vodka can. It's half empty. They've all got more than half a litre of vodka on board. Thankfully the site manager says enough is enough.

In the end the pilot didn't need much encouragement to join in. In fact I think he drank more than his fair share. The next morning we're about to take off in the helicopter. The pilot looks like shit. He says it was the orange juice that made him crook.

I return to Moscow and Lukhum picks me up at the airport.

"Hey, the guys on site were pleased you got the cigarettes and beer to them last week," I tell him.

"Oh, Grigori, that was so funny. Getting 250 dozen cans of beer wasn't easy. We had to buy it from about 10 kiosks, and Grolsch was the only brand available. You should have seen the Pussy Wagon. It was packed full. When we got to the airport we tried to get the beer on as accompanied baggage, but there was no way they were going to let us do that. So I insisted on speaking to the airport manager. At the start he wanted nothing to do with me, but when I suggested he could have some beer he opened up. In the end we agreed on 10 dozen cans."

"Ten dozen cans!" I respond, thinking how ridiculous this was.

Lukhum pushes on, "As soon as we agreed, he telephoned Barnaul and told them that one tonne of mail would have to be removed from the plane because sophisticated technology from New Zealand was urgently required in Barnaul."

"Unbelievable." I love this place. "Well done, Lukhum."

He beams with pride and responds, "Thank you, Grigori." As he drives me back to my apartment he enquires about progress on the construction sites.

"Progress in the Altai is very slow," I say, quietly, as I look out the side window of the Merc. "Too slow. The problem is the shipping containers. No one knows where they are. They arrived in the Far East about a month ago, but no one has heard of them since. And the locals aren't supporting us. There are always delays."

"Maybe this is normalno for the Altai," Lukhum says.

I drift off. The Altai sites are nearly grinding to a halt. Interestingly, the containers have been delivered to the other construction sites in Kazakhstan and the southern Urals, so I have to wonder what's going on. I'm jolted out of my ruminations by the sight of four trams trundling past us. Two are painted gold with a blue camel emblazoned on the side, exactly like the cigarette packet, and two have a white twist snaking across the red sides of the trams, rendering them as Cola cans.

"Can you believe that?" I exclaim. "I've only been gone three weeks and look!" I point at the yellow and red intruders. "Three weeks ago there was no advertising here. None. And now look!"

"I know Grigori, I know," Lukhum replies. "But wait. See what is here."

He gestures at the image of a cowboy smoking a fag on what must be the biggest billboard I've ever seen. Marlborough cigarettes! "A cowboy in Moscow!" I shake my head at how brazen this cultural attack is. "Those stupid Americans." And now that I think about it, "Those stupid Moscow officials," for letting this happen.

I'm aggrieved. The bland, dull Soviet cityscape is being transformed in front of my eyes. I liked the old Moscow. It was a different world and I want it back. Three weeks ago there was no such thing as a brand, or even the concept of a brand. Now there's a cowboy towering over Leninsky Prospekt with a fag hanging out of his mouth and a hat on his head more suited to Wyoming. And, God, now that my eyes have been opened, just look at the number of Mercs and BMWs on the road. Lukhum points out a red Ferrari driving in the opposite direction. Where is all this money coming from? The rate of change is completely incomprehensible.

"Vlad, we need to find these bloody Ust Koksa and Ongudai containers," I say, as soon as I walk into the office the next morning. "Who knows whether they've even left the port yet? I want you to go to Nakhodka to find them."

"Of course I'll go. It needs to be resolved."

If feels as if the fuckability factor has definitely kicked in. If something can be fucked up, it will be. I get Vlad to call one of the dead Functionary's colleagues. But all he can say is, "Normalno". There's nothing wrong.

"There's nothing wrong?" I ask. "What did he have to say about the Functionary's death?"

Shrugging his shoulders and puckering his lips Vlad says, "It was an unfortunate accident."

All I can do is shake my head. Vlad organises his trip to Nahodka in the Far East near Japan. It is seven time zones from Moscow.

That night I go alone to a place called Night Flight. I've been told it's a nightclub geared specifically for boys and girls to meet each other. It's a large lounge bar heavily populated with absolutely beautiful women, all of them looking like models. I'm one of about a dozen blokes here. There's no chance of getting rejected by any of the women. Every single gorgeous one of them is available and keen – for a modest fee.

A new girl walks in. Her thick auburn hair falls below her shoulders. Her tanned thighs are exposed above black, knee-high boots. Her short halter-neck dress, patterned with black-and-white checks, reveals her olive cleavage. She has fine fingers with painted red nails. I'm mesmerised by her gestures as she speaks with the other girls. Looking around the room she makes eye contact with me.

She smiles.

A jolt of adrenaline surges through me. I respond with a strained smile. I feel excited and nervous. I can't stop looking at her. She looks intelligent and confident, but she also exudes warmth.

I've never had sex with a prostitute. I've never wanted to. Until now the thought of it repulsed me. I could never understand how a girl would want to sell her most intimate self for a few shekels.

She's walking over.

Tightness grips my chest and stomach. I stand up and greet her.

"Ochen preartna," she says in an alluring voice.

I'm excited, but composed enough to respond, "Kak dela?"

"I am very well, thank you," she replies in English with a sultry Russian accent. "My name is Anna. What is your name?"

"Grigori. That's a lovely dress you're wearing," I reply.

"Thank you. You flatter me. You have a Russian name but where are you from?"

"I'm from New Zealand. Where are you from?" I say.

"I am from Khabarovsk. It's in the Far East of Russia."

"Ah, I've never been there, but our business has an office there."

She says, "Really? In such a place as Khabarovsk?"

I nod. "The funny thing is that our office is in the Communist Party Building in the middle of the city."

"You must be well connected," she replies.

"Not me, but the guy I work with is." Enough of this banter. I want to have fun. "So, are you available for the night?"

"Of course," she says. "Do you have somewhere we can go?"

"No, I don't." I don't want to take her back to my flat.

Reluctantly she suggests we go to her place.

I shouldn't be doing this. It's not right. I have Monica. She'd be gutted. But this woman is just too beautiful.

"How much will it cost for the whole night?"

"One hundred dollars."

One hundred dollars is a small price to pay for a night with this delightful woman. I agree to the price. She takes my hand and leads me over to the cloak room to collect our coats. Her hand feels lovely in mine. Her skin is so smooth and warm. I look at her and she responds by raising her eyebrows slightly.

"You seem like a good man," she says.

"I am a good man," I reply, though I guess that depends on the terms of reference. Right now my wife would think, quite rightly, that I wasn't a good man at all. I hold her coat so she can ease into it.

She thanks me, "Spasibo."

I feel a combination of excitement and satisfaction that I'm going to spend some time with her. Exhaling I calmly say, "OK, let's go. We'll need a taxi."

After a long taxi drive into the outskirts of Moscow we arrive at a nondescript apartment block. As we enter, the smell reminds me of the entrance lobby of every high-rise apartment building I've walked into in Russia. On the lift I see the too-familiar sight: "Nyet Rabotet".

"We need to use the stairs. The lift is not working," Anna informs me.

I feel uncertain as we go up into the darkness of the second and third floors. The lights aren't working on these landings. You'd think someone would put a new bulb in, wouldn't you? We continue on up to the fourth floor. The light is working here.

Anna unlocks the security door fabricated from sheet steel. Then she unlocks a second door and we enter the small hall. The tiny bathroom is on the right, just before the kitchen. It's a one-bedroom place.

Later, basking in post-coital contentment, I ask, "Why are you working as a prostitute?"

"I do it for money, of course. I'm studying at university. Things are so expensive now, it is necessary. The money gives me a good lifestyle."

"Huh. What're you studying?"

"I am completing a master's degree in psychology."

I wonder what on earth she could do with such a qualification in the rapidly decaying Russian economy.

"Interesting subject. Do you enjoy it?"

I have this theory that all psychologists are drawn to the profession primarily to study their own madness.

"Da. That's why I am completing a master's degree."

"Fair enough. What do you want to do once you graduate?"

"I have no idea."

"Do you have a boyfriend?"

"Nyet. Getting a man is not a problem for me. I like Russian men, but they don't make good partners. They are chauvinistic. They behave like spoilt brats."

I say, "I know what you mean. I see it all the time, especially in Moscow."

"Many men have been brought up by single mothers, and Russian mothers dote on their children, especially their sons. They smother them. When boys become men they expect their girlfriends and wives to fuss over them and spoil them just as their mothers have." She pauses briefly. "They have bad habits, too. They drink too much, and when they are drunk they behave irresponsibly. You must see it in business – not many of them are loyal. They often have more than one girlfriend at a time. What is the word? They are . . . prom-is-cu-ous. Even after they are married."

She gets up, totally comfortable with her naked body.

"But it's always the woman who chooses the man. You know, the woman is the one to open the gate, so to speak," I say.

"That's true. But what is your point?"

"For a man to be prom-is-cu-ous, there needs to be a prom-is-cu-ous woman allowing him to have sex." Casting my attention over her perfectly shaped legs, I'm still intrigued she doesn't have a man. I could be her man. "What is it that you want in a man?"

"I want a man to be strong. I want him to provide for me and our family so that I can look after our children and him. It is for the man to make money and the wife to create a warm, loving home. Of course I want my man to be masculine. We love it when they are strong and they can lead. But I need a man who will be completely attentive, not one who will sleep around or abuse me."

She flicks her hair. "And of course, I will look after myself. I will keep in shape and look sexy." She playfully spanks her supremely cute arse with her hand, then she jiggles her hips and pouts.

"Krasivyi devushka. You're beautiful, you know," I tell her.

"Spasibo," she responds with an affectionate smile.

Jesus, I like this woman. Getting up from the bed I hold her face and kiss her succulently on the lips. She looks even more sultry as I pull away. She likes me as much as I like her. "I'm leaving Moscow tomorrow but I'll be back in three weeks. Would you like to go for a meal in a restaurant when I return?"

"I would like to see you again, but restaurants don't interest me. I prefer to walk in the countryside. I don't like the city. Life here in Moscow is very stressful now. But I would like to see you. Come and stay with me. I will give you my telephone number." Running her hands over my chest, she leans in and kisses me. "Thank you for being so strong. You are a good man for a Russian girl."

I prepare to leave. Everything about her is perfect. She's everything I've ever wanted in a woman. She writes her phone number on a piece of paper and gives it to me. We hail a car. She kisses me on the lips and says, "Spokoini nochi."

"Do svidaniya." Goodbye.

I return to my flat feeling full and light. But when I exit the lift on the ninth floor I walk over to the garbage chute. I lift the lid and throw the piece of paper with Anna's phone number down the tube. Never go back, mate. I unlock both doors of the flat and enter. I shut the doors again and take my boots off, placing them on the wooden shoe rack. I hang my black overcoat on the hanger above the rack.

A sense of loss suddenly consumes me. That woman was perfect for me. I'd love to share my life with her. I visualise her youthful flesh, the divine shape of her hips and the curve of her arse. Her luxuriant hair. The connection we had, the talk of wanting peace and simplicity. But it's impossible. I'm married to a fine woman who is completely dedicated to me. The melancholy is joined by a flood of guilt. I cover my mouth with my hand. Ah Jesus, how could I have done it?

It's done, mate, it's done. There's no going back. Now you have to hide it. Forever. As I think this I realise the framework of my life has just shifted. It has become much less stable. I'm no longer a man of my word. The commitment I made to Monica has been destroyed. Encounters with girls will be easier from now on. I'm in a new paradigm. It's the new drug. Life has just become a lot more complicated.

Standing up and looking out at the series of partially lit apartment buildings I staunchly commit to putting this encounter with the exquisite Anna behind me. It's done and there's nothing to do but get on with life. I need to focus on doing a good job here and being a doubly good husband.

But a week later I still can't get Anna out of my head. One moment I feel as though I'm in love, the next I'm overcome with a sense of loss. Then guilt and remorse kick in. I'm infatuated with her, but I still love Monica.

I'm tormented to buggery. It's easy to fantasise about making love to Anna, the memory is so vivid. I'd committed to putting this behind me but I can't stop the intoxication. Christ, I only spent a few hours with the girl and it's like I've lost the love of my life. But it's a waste of time.

I can't get in contact with her.

She's gone.

SEVEN

It's now 22 August 1991. A short time ago I arrived in our Moscow office to be informed by Irina, the secretary, that one of our drivers – thankfully not Lukhum – is now a hero of the Russian Motherland. Tanks and military personnel were parked outside the Russian White House, as they call it, while our new hero, armed with a Kalashnikov, was inside helping Yeltsin defend the building from a small group of influential Communists attempting a coup against Gorbachev.

I'd suspected Irina had been shagging the driver for some time. She had become increasingly smug. In the end she must have inspired him to take up arms. What a gloriously masculine thing for a Muscovite male to do for his devushka. I doubt he would have had it in him if she hadn't waved her arse in front of him. Fortunately for Russia and our driver, the military didn't have the passion or fortitude to defend Communism any longer. Outside, another one of our drivers tossed Molotov cocktails at a tank.

By the time I got into the area where all the action had taken place the streets were quiet. A burnt-out trolley bus and a mountain of flowers marking the spot where someone had died were all that remained. The world is in limbo. What now? Within days Yeltsin fills the void. The 70-year experiment is over. Soviet Communism exists no more.

On 24 August I'm in the Moscow office and the phone rings. Lukhum answers it. "Grigori, it's Vlad for you."

"Ah, I see the washing department is in full action," Popov comments. He cynically claims we achieve nothing other than washing our clothes, and refers to Vlad and me as the washing department. I have no interest in grappling with him. There's no point. Like Vlad, I'm an outsider. It's as if the Muscovites think they are a nation of superior beings. I take the receiver.

"Grigori, you'll be pleased to know I have located the missing containers," Vlad says. "They had been loaded onto railway wagons, but for some unknown reason they were off-loaded onto a railway siding just north of Nakhodka."

"Really? That's odd." I pause, slightly confused, and then say, "Molodets." Well done.

"I've instructed the freight forwarding manager to have them reloaded onto a train and railed to Biysk."

"Good. Did you have any trouble with the guy you're dealing with?"

"No. He's been very helpful."

That evening Lukhum drives me home past the Bolshoi Theatre and on to Dzerzhinsky Square, the home of the Lubianka, the KGB building. A crowd is animated as the statue of Felix Dzerzhinsky, the first director of the KGB, is dismantled.

I figure Vlad will resolve the container situation, so a week after the coup I take a trip alone to the Urals. I will return from Orsk via Samara and back to Moscow. Because of its strategic significance, Samara was a closed city until only recently. It's a centre for the manufacture of weapons, missiles and aircraft. Apparently factories are still disguised with made-up names and registration numbers.

This isn't the first time I've flown by myself. I enjoy travelling alone, but I have to be alert. I can't afford to miss a beat, otherwise I might end up on the wrong plane or miss a flight altogether. I can't even decipher the Cyrillic alphabet. But even when I'm vulnerable it all seems to work out. People step forward to help me, or I notice something critically important just at the right moment. Actually, solo travel without the ability to communicate verbally becomes an exercise in observing what's going on around the place and why, noticing the way individuals interact with each other. And when

I think about it, it's also an exercise in observing how I myself behave. I notice within that observation that I remain calm.

The last time I was a lone punter I sat next to a young woman, and within minutes of take-off she had her arm inside mine. I didn't know what the hell was going on – whether she was keen for a shag or whether she was just after a bit of comfort. I did nothing. I just let her leave her arm there. It was nice.

Now I'm standing in the departure hall at Orsk doing my observation thing. My attention always moves to the good-looking women. After a cursory assessment I hone in on the most appealing woman here. She's cute. We've made eye contact and she's smiling at me. My heart's cranking up and my chest is tightening.

I want to explore as much about her as I can from this distance, but I need to control myself. I casually look around the room then slowly bring my gaze back to her. She's looking somewhere else. I wonder if she's doing the same thing as me – attempting to be cool and calm. Then she looks at me, with a piercing, prolonged gaze. My heart is thumping against my ribs but it doesn't distract me. I can't keep my eyes off her. I look fixedly at her, not in an intimidating way, but in a way that lets her know I'm keen. She's running her hand through her hair. It's as if there's no one else in this airport concourse. She glances away, as if to tease me, and then we make eye contact again. This time it's like a huge magnetic field pulling at me.

Suddenly a flight announcement. "Orsk . . . Samara . . ." People begin trundling towards the exit. I hang back, watching as my new lover momentarily hovers before joining the other passengers who are jostling their way through the door. Then I go down the stairs and follow the group out onto the tarmac, keeping my attention on the delicious one. Her dress billows with the exaggerated sway of her splendid hips.

I don't want to make it obvious, but I'm sure she wants me to catch up with her. I stretch my stride beyond its natural rhythm. I want to intercept her before she makes it to the plane. She's looking over her shoulder. With the confidence of a girl in control, she makes eye contact again, this time acknowledging me with a radiant smile and an expression of openness.

She slows to an amble. As I catch her, she abruptly turns to me with an expectant look and the most wonderful smile. I gesture that I'd like to lift her bag into the baggage compartment for her.

"Spasibo," she murmurs, in the most alluring voice.

We exchange some words, but I have trouble saying very much. She has a go at English. She's not fluent, but it's good enough. The Aeroflot hostess says something and the people mingling around the base of the stairway immediately start boarding the plane. Reluctantly we board. I'm seated about 10 rows behind her. I can think of nothing other than the delicious one for the duration of the flight.

As I disembark from the cabin at Orsk she looks wantonly up at me from the bottom of the stairs. *Jeesuss*. We idle over to collect our bags from the rear compartment. I lift her bag and carry it. She leads me to the end of a long queue in the arrivals hall. It's crowded. It appears we have to queue for another boarding pass to Moscow. People press against each other as a defence against others pushing in. The tension between us is palpable. I'm completely captivated. If I don't make a move now I never will. We'll be in Moscow and this will be nothing other than a memory.

Gently I press myself against her backside and place the palms of my hands on her hips. They are firm and tender. The layers of light fabric separating us act like graphite, and her dress offers no resistance to my fine woollen trousers. I move unimpeded against her. Lifting her heels, she moves her hips and buttocks up against my front. I keep steady. She deliberately lowers her heels. Again she lifts. Momentarily, I hold her up, then lower her, allowing her heels to rest on the floor again. She lifts back up. I press ever so slightly against her. Bending my head forward, I kiss her neck with the soft pad of my lips, then I nip her earlobe.

She turns around, brushing her breasts against my arm and then leaning them into my chest. She says something I can't hear. I'm too excited. We're both exhilarated. We continue touching each other, but more gently, as we move with the queue. Only now do I notice we are surrounded by people. But I don't care.

After an indescribable period the intensity dwindles, transmuting into a mellow warmth. Slowly, the desire to get to know each other leads into conversation. Her name is Katya. She tells me she grew up in Orsk and her family still lives here. She is studying chemical engineering in Moscow. Her vocation is understandable. Her home is in the heart of the Russian heavy engineering hinterland.

I don't have the words or the desire to complicate our connection, but I want to bathe in this bliss as long as possible. We get on the plane. This time we sit together. She tells me how she cried with joy when she saw the image of Yeltsin standing on the tank outside the White House – it had been a profound moment for her.

I respond with "Neveroyatno." Unbelievable. The image has given people the belief that freedom is possible.

Does she want to meet in Moscow later in the week? Absolutna. Does she have a telephone number? Yes. She gives it to me. We disembark at Sheremetyevo domestic airport.

"Do svidaniya," I say, bidding her farewell as she walks on from where Lukhum waits to greet me.

Lukhum looks at me, slightly startled, aware that something has happened between me and the girl in the polka-dot dress.

A few days later and the restaurant we are in is packed full of locals. When I dined here six months ago, there were just four people in the restaurant – all foreigners. At that time the idea that Russians could afford to eat here was inconceivable. It's the same at Stockmann's. These days more Russians shop there than foreigners.

A couple sit at the table alongside us. The man's girlfriend appears not to notice his body odour. Maybe she puts up with it because the money is so good. Then again, Russian men often smell and the women don't seem to mind. But this boy's pong is particularly strong.

His girlfriend's black-ribbed woollen top highlights her blonde hair. It's tucked back in a bun and held in place by a simple diamante studded clip. Her legs are crossed and she wears black boots with high heels. She playfully engages him – her fine, well-groomed fingers gesture with ease and grace. Sweat forms on his brow. His head is lowered, and with his elbows sticking out, he grapples with the spaghetti. A gold Rolex dominates his left wrist. At another table a girl gets up from her seat and moves over to her partner, kissing him tenderly on the lips, then returns to her seat. She continues to reel her man in with her sultry gaze.

I'm here with Katya. She really is beautiful. More beautiful than any other woman here. I'm very fond of her. I love her freshness and vitality, and her alluring ways. She's luxuriant in every respect. The band takes a break and Katya tells me in deliciously broken English, "If you want a Russian princess, I am available."

Katya suspects I'm a bad boy. Her appeal is enhanced by an ample intellect, but not too much. I would feel intimidated by a woman with more intellect than me. I want to fall in love with her, but I can't. It's impractical for me to be with her. She's stunning in every possible way, but I remind myself I have other priorities. I'm married and I desire success in business. She'd be too much of a distraction. A woman like this would need a lot of attention, and this particular princess would want a man like me to provide abundantly. I feel deflated and despondent.

A heaviness settles over me. A sense of loss. Again.

I don't want the complication of a proper relationship. I could do with the companionship and the intimacy, but I'm married to a good woman.

I again look around the room at the other diners. What I really want is love, unbroken love. I feel I deserve it. Not this continual void inside.

Two weeks later I discover that the containers still haven't arrived at their destination in Biysk, in southern Siberia. "Once the containers are loaded on the wagons, how long does it take to rail them from Nakhodka to Biysk?" I ask Vlad on the phone.

"Maybe five days."

"Well, keep in touch with the station master and the Functionary's offsider. If they haven't arrived by the end of the week, you'll need to do something."

I'm buggered if I know what's going on here, but whatever it is we need to get to the bottom of it.

In the meantime I go on a quick trip to St Petersburg. Until recently it was called Leningrad, but it reverted to St Petersburg in June this year. A friend has taken me to meet her mother and sister, who live in a communal apartment. Before the revolution this would have been the residence of a wealthy family, but now it accommodates 65 people, who all share bathroom, toilet and kitchen amenities. As I walk down the three flights of stairs people are milling around in the kitchens on the landings. Getting privacy here would be tough.

My friend says, "Can you imagine living here with three generations of your wife's family and only these paper-thin walls separating you?"

"Ah, no." How the hell could you ever have an undetected shag?

"Resentment permeates places like this," she says in a hushed voice.

"What do you mean?" I ask, like a dumb bastard.

"Jealousy for the food you may have or the benefits your job provides or the partner you may have."

I get it. It's easy to visualise the tension and complexities that could fester in this environment, easy to imagine all the innuendos and the fantasies about shagging your neighbour's wife. But, interestingly, my friend's elderly mother looks happy enough.

"Are there many apartments like this?" I ask her.

"About 750,000 people still live in communal apartments in St Petersburg."

As we walk out to the street my friend points out a sign on the other side of the road, which instructs people to beware of shelling. The reminders of the Great Patriotic War remain. "During the Nazi siege of Leningrad, one million out of the two million people who lived here died." She looks at me as if that experience is woven into the very fabric of her being. And yet she would have been born just after the war.

"It amazes me how people can survive in a completely annihilated environment like that. How do they do it?" I ask.

"Hope. We have a saying. Hope is the last thing you lose."

"I guess that's right." If anyone knows about hope it has to be the eternally down-trodden Russian.

"We still cling to hope. Hope that things will get easier, hope that one day there will be no fear, hope that the grace of God will flow in our favour. We all hope that one day we will experience endless love and peace and joy."

Startled, I realise that's exactly what I want. As I gaze around the street I realise not only how resilient the Russians are but also how determined humanity is to survive and to cling to the hope we will all "live life in love".

My friend is gorgeous in every way. I love her a lot. Her first husband was a dissident who died falling from a balcony in a public place. It was reported that he was in a drunken stupor. The only problem with the story is that she said he didn't drink. Her new husband arrives in his Mercedes. He is conspicuous by the car and his age – he is at least 15 years younger than she is. He's probably a good man, but I think he's lucky to have her.

He suggests I come with him to visit the St Petersburg Stock Exchange. He explains that the stock exchange opened for business in August last year and that already the number of businesses listed there is growing very quickly.

It's October 1991. As we walk into the building I'm amazed at what a relaxed and amateurish operation it is. Most of the blokes are aimlessly standing around in jeans and casual clothing chatting with each other. My friend's husband tries to convince me to buy shares in a number of businesses that he knows well – they have proven to be good investments for him. But how the hell would you know what was going on inside these businesses, let alone what's going on here? It would be worse than investing in the crooks back home. The starting point of a capital market is surely a precarious thing. Not for me, mate. I want my money for retirement and peace.

As I leave he offers me a chance to be involved in business with him. His parting words are, "It's up to you."

For once I think I'll stick to what I know: five-fifths of fuck all.

I take the overnight train from St Petersburg to Moscow, downing some blue bombers to induce some rapid eye movement. When I arrive Vlad gives me the unwelcome news that the containers still haven't arrived. This definitely feels like the fuckability factor at play. I realise that from now on

I need to be perpetually prepared for things to go wrong at any moment.

"I'm sorry to tell you this Vlad, but you're gonna have to go back to the Far East again. This time, when you find those containers, stay with the bloody things until they're loaded, and personally view the train leave the siding. I don't care if it takes two weeks. You need to be there to ensure they leave unimpeded."

"OK, Grigori. I understand."

"And take plenty of money with you."

I've got no idea who we've crossed, but it appears they are closely monitoring our activity and they've got the ability to pull strings. I wait to hear from Vlad.

The next day I'm scratching around with some paperwork in the Moscow office when Popov struts in. He's been on a 10-day holiday in Yugoslavia.

"We'd just arrived in Dubrovnik and fighting broke out between the bloody Croatians and the Serbs," he says, clearly very pleased with himself. He complains scathingly about the tourists who fled within the first two days of fighting. "The guns kept ringing out, and the only tourists remaining were Russians and Germans, the two peoples familiar with war and conflict," he chuckles.

"Were you under threat?" Lukhum asks.

"Nyet." His mouth stretches into a snarl. "We were fine. We had no interest in leaving – we kept drinking and eating. It didn't faze us."

Popov tells us that he and his wife stayed for another week, thoroughly enjoying the anarchy. Then he launches into an analysis.

"People in the West think that a democracy is suited to everyone. Fucking democracy created this war. It would never have happened under Communism. Russia is like Yugoslavia – it comprises so many different cultures and ethnic groups with conflicting interests that without control we could end up in a bloodbath. Autocratic leadership is needed here to ensure stability."

For once I agree with him. It would be a wonderful thing if the world could live in a democracy, but right now some people are just so self-centred that without some semblance of a benevolent autocratic state many people would go without. Unfortunately, that's what's missing here at the moment with Yeltsin's "democracy". The plundering by a few is driving millions into poverty.

I get a phone call. "The containers are exactly where they were last time I was here. They haven't moved," Vlad tells me, as I strain to hear his voice on the scratchy phone line.

"What happened to that guy you were dealing with?"

"He's here."

"What's he got to say for himself?"

"Not much. He said he received instructions from Biysk that they were not ready to accept the containers. The instruction was very clear – the containers need to remain here."

"You're joking!"

"No, I'm not. He has shown me a telex from the station master at Biysk instructing him what to do with the shipment."

I close one eye and grimace. "OK. You need to do whatever is required to get those containers moving. And you need to stay there until you see the arse end of the last container leave that railway yard."

"Grigori, I know what I have to do."

"I know you do, Vlad, but this time we need to be more tenacious. Keep me updated. Shishleeva." Good luck.

I've never been comfortable with the deer velvet trade. When you think about it, Merv has bypassed Andropov in Moscow, who was selling the Altai deer velvet for a handsome profit. The hard currency we are deriving from the sale of deer velvet is paying for the Altai meat plants we're building. The missing containers are packed full of construction materials for those meat plants. To make things even more interesting, Merv has got a scientist trying to funnel the deer genetics out of there in the form of frozen embryos. I'm sure he has the full support of the local deer farmer directors for this activity. Yeah, right. If there's one way to hit Merv in the pocket, it would be to stall progress on the construction sites. Who knows? If the money is right, or if a favour is owed, then anyone could do it.

But the next update from Vlad is a positive one.

"Grigori," he says excitedly, "the containers are on their way."

"Great. Well done."

"I will fly from here to Barnaul, then make my way to Biysk."

"OK. You need to remain focused on this task until the gear actually arrives on the sites."

"Of course. I'll call you when I get to Biysk."

The next day Vlad calls me while I'm in the office and the news isn't good. "Grigori," he says, "I'm here with the station manager at Biysk."

"Good."

"Last week he received instructions to unload the containers at a remote location 2000 kilometres from here. It appears the instruction came from our Moscow office."

Instantly I zero in on the statement, "*Our* office?" After a brief pause I question him as quietly as I can. "Who gave the instructions?" Whoever it is has been watching me and following my every move, and then reversing my instructions and halting any activity.

"There was no name given. But it was definitely our office."

"Do you have any influence over the station master?"

"Yes. He has assured me the containers will be on their way today."

"How can you be sure?"

"I've just paid him the equivalent of a month's salary and I've promised him another month's salary when they arrive. I'll stay here until that happens. They should be here on Monday. In the meantime I will organise trucks to take the containers to the site. We can't rely on anyone else."

Bewildered and almost whispering I say, "OK, Vlad. Well done. Let's see what happens from here."

I stare numbly at the phone as my arms rest on the surface of my desk. My shoulders are slightly hunched. I feel impotent and insignificant. We're now 10 weeks behind schedule and the Siberian winter is closing in on us. The office is quiet despite four others sitting at their desks. Someone close to me is shafting me. But who could it be? There's one thing they all have in common: none of them has been in favour of the Altai projects. Leave it to the Altaians to sort themselves out, they say. There are easier places to do business here. Popov is so blatantly against me and the projects that he would be too obvious. The river runs deep for a few of the others. You'd never know what they were up to.

One thing's for sure, we have pissed someone off. Big time. Someone with the wherewithal to influence one of my colleagues in this office. This isn't someone who has been offended by a random derogatory comment or sleight. This is someone who is well and truly out of pocket or who has somehow been deprived of their usual control and influence.

The containers arrive the following week and are delivered to the two construction sites by a convoy of Kamaz trucks. Construction of the abattoirs accelerates, then falters. The electricity supply and installation of the power transformer just don't appear to be happening. The power is required to allow our guys to commission the machinery, and of course the locals need it to operate the facility. The power supply is the locals' responsibility, but we take control of the situation. I send one of our Moscow-based Russian engineers to the site with the sole responsibility of supervising the electrical installation. Construction is completed a month after the snow settles on the ground near the end of 1991. The delay-related costs have been significant. Our approach to construction management has changed: we will take control of every aspect of a project in the future.

I'm back in the "Smoke". When I'm back I enjoy regaling my mates with tales about what I've been up to and what I'm observing over there. My portrayals are skewed towards beautiful women, the lawlessness of the place, and how quickly a completely different world is evolving. I'm in full flight talking to Jonty and a couple of other characters at the Lock Tavern on Chalk Farm Road.

"At home we might see one beautiful woman out of a hundred, but in Russia I reckon there's one in 10. There are girls of German descent, Finnish, and Central Asian, beautiful dark-skinned girls from the Caucasus, and Russians, all mixed in the melting pot. And the thing about these women is that they're really into being feminine. They've got this innate ability to beautify themselves. Some of them take up to an hour to get ready before they leave home."

Looking incredulous Jonty says, "An hour! Bugger that."

"I asked one of the young women in our office how long it takes to get ready for work and she told me, 'Long enough to look beautiful.' When I shook my head she said, 'Grigori, you should know that for a Russian girl, leaving home without looking glamorous is just not an option.'"

"Huh," he responds.

I think, "Mate, if you could only see them you wouldn't mind if your wife or girlfriend took so long." I continue on: "The other thing is, as the seasons change the women wear clothes suited to every change in climate. There might only be two weeks of cool spring weather, and they'll have coats that suit just that short period. Light coats for the end of summer and the beginning of autumn, woollen fabrics for autumn, and if they can afford it they'll have a fur coat for winter. A lot of women make their own clothes, too. They'll see designs in magazines like *Vogue* and *Marie Clare* and copy them. Most of the time you can't tell the difference between an original and a copy."

"What are the typical occupations for women?" Jonty asks.

"Most women I've met have been side-tracked into relatively poorly paid occupations and professions – doctors, teachers and scientists. It's incredible, but doctors get paid a fraction of what our interpreters are paid. In fact, one of our part-time interpreters working on one of the construction sites is a neurosurgeon who earns 350 roubles a month in her profession. But on the black market the US$300 we pay her can be exchanged for 3000 roubles."

Jonty says, "I read an article in *The Independent* newspaper recently that stated that something like 60 per cent of Moscow secondary school girls taking part in a survey indicated they would exchange sex for hard currency. It went on to say that prostitution is eighth on a list of what women feel would be their top 20 most desirable jobs."

"It's understandable. Women working as prostitutes can earn between US$100 to US$200 per night," I say. "The Russians have a saying: 'When the women are strong, Russia is strong.' Clearly this isn't their current phase."

The following day Monica and I decide to spend the day relaxing together. We have lunch in Hampstead and a stroll through the Heath.

Not long after we return to the flat in the late afternoon Monica says, "Today was nice. It's not often we get a chance to spend some quiet time together. Do you realise that when we socialise with other people you tend to dominate the conversation with talk about Russia."

I feel embarrassed. "Oh, do I?"

"Yeah you do. There's not much room for me."

I continue to feel uncomfortable as I realise how it's all about me, even when I return for weekend visits to be with her. I don't mean to smother things. I know I couldn't do this without her. Not only has she fully supported this hare-brained idea of mine, but she's been living in London by herself and working full time to help pay her own way.

Then she looks at me with a matter-of-fact look, "And, you know, we are supposed to be trying to have children."

I nod, agreeing with her. Having a family is a big desire of Monica's, but my greatest desire seems to be increasingly about success. I also realise how difficult it is for me to talk about such things. Monica is so much more open than me. When she speaks openly it rattles me. I'd love to be able to communicate unimpeded, but I just don't seem to be able to. It's as if there is some internal resistance to it. It feels like such a risky thing to do.

"Well, maybe we can base ourselves back in New Zealand. I don't think I need to be living in Russia permanently."

Monica's face lights up. "Now you're talking."

"OK. Let's see if I can pull it off," I say, feeling that it's probably the only way we can achieve a mutually beneficial outcome from this Russian thing.

Within two months, and almost magically, the whole business dynamic changes to support both my ambition for success and Monica's desire to be living in New Zealand. The Soviet Union, formerly the world's best business partner, has just become the world's worst payer. So Ashfield wants out, and fair enough too, but Ashfield's withdrawal is an opportunity for Merv to step forward and establish a trading business and a project business. He offers me 50 per cent of the project outfit. Our new business may have more front than Harrods, but we're smaller than ever. I'm excited and charged full of confidence and wondrous expectations of success. Equally important, Monica and I get to return to New Zealand and have a shot at creating a family. It takes a bit of arranging, but eventually we get it sorted. Monica is happy and living in Christchurch. I should be happy, but once again the goal eludes me.

Soon it is the northern hemisphere spring of 1992. Spring is the least appealing time in Russia. The dust, oil and grit that have collected throughout the winter are exposed as the road-side snow begins melting. Murky water and mud lie in long strips beside the curbs. As we drive to see the general director of the steel mill in the Urals I look out at the pedestrians dodging the pooled water resting in the depressions in the pavement. All of them seem preoccupied with the daily grind. The colourless five-storey blocks of flats, identical to pretty much all the other buildings we've driven past in the last 10 minutes, are partially shielded by tree trunks and branches that are not yet budding.

The general director welcomes me into his office. Sitting around the meeting table are 12 deputies. They all stand to shake my hand. With an air of jubilation the general director announces that today is a very special day – the majority of the shares in the steel-making complex have been transferred to the workers and management. If his elation is anything to go by, he's got his trotters in a full trough. Individuals like this character have taken ownership of the state-owned industrial complex in the last few months. The transfer of wealth and influence from the state to private individuals is happening with such stealth that it's impossible to know if I'm dealing with a modestly paid functionary of six months ago or a multi-millionaire of today. Maybe this boy will become an oligarch?

EIGHT

It's October 1992 and I return to Sovetskaya in northern Kazakhstan to discuss the commissioning of the new meat-processing plant. Looking more manic than ever, Petr Brandt ushers me into his office. Walking in, I notice the portrait of Lenin has gone. So too have the red Soviet flag and the Communist-era photos that had previously been mounted on the wall. The turquoise Kazakh flag sits on his desk and photos of Petr shaking hands with various people have replaced the previous images.

"Petr, where's Lenin?" I ask.

"He's gone. Long gone," Petr says. "These are rapidly changing times in Kazakhstan. It's impossible to know what's happening from one day to the next." His face creases into a mixture of reflection and uncertainty. "Literally thousands of Germans are leaving every week for Germany."

"Thousands of Germans?" I ask, struggling to understand.

Almost impatiently he says, "Not long ago, there were nearly 1,000,000 Germans living in Kazakhstan."

Confused, all I do is repeat, "Germans?"

"That's right. Volga Germans were deported to Kazakhstan because Stalin feared we would join Hitler. During Khrushchev's virgin land programme in the 1950s, more Germans relocated here from Russia to convert the steppe to cropping farms. Once the farms had been developed, we were effectively prevented from leaving. Without us, the farms would have failed." Pointing out the window with his left hand Petr states, "Thirty-five years ago this land was virgin steppe." Then his expression changes suddenly as he swerves to a new topic. "Do you know the President of Kazakhstan is coming to the commissioning party?"

"Yes, I do," I respond as I struggle to keep up.

Before I came in here to see Petr I'd been mocking what's going on outside. The main street of the township, the area around the meat-processing plant and the road the President will drive along, are all undergoing a rapid clean-up by dozens of workers.

Petr puffs out his chest. "It's a great honour for us, and it will be a great advertisement for your company."

I've seen this carry-on a couple of times now. In the lead-up to the visit there's always a chaotic rush to paint every surface that might come into visual contact with the esteemed visitor. Grimy building walls, lamp posts and lichen-covered fences are all painted, road sides and rubbish-filled waterways are cleared, trees are planted, and generally any shit lying around is moved to a less obvious location. Yeltsin visited one of our milk-processing plants in the Far East before he ascended to the presidency.

Then Petr interrupts my train of thought. "Grigori, do you think I'm a fool?" he says unexpectedly. He paces the length of the office, unable to sit. "There's supposed to be a rendering plant included in this facility."

"That's not right, Petr," I say, reeling. "A rendering plant was never in the contract. Not once has it been mentioned in any discussion I've had with you."

"How can you build a meat-processing plant without the ability to process waste? What are we to do? We can't just dump the waste! Did you think we would bury it in the fields?"

He's got a valid point, but this twist of events is completely unexpected. "A decision must have been made during the development of the scope of supply not to include a rendering plant," I say.

I can never predict what angle Petr is going to come from, but this rendering plant idea is completely out of left field. And a whole new magnitude. Something is not right here. He's up to no good.

Petr runs his right hand through his hair and clasps the back of his neck. Tilting his forehead towards me, he looks up with a contrived scowl. "Grigori, you are very difficult man to deal with. I think you must be of Jewish descent."

I'm becoming even more wary of this mercurial bastard. "Thank you, but no, I'm not Jewish."

I notice that his collar-length hair looks like it has been dyed with a cheap Eastern European dye. The roots are white, but the remaining swathe suggests the mad bastard has used a two-pot mix of amber and black. His full-length coat and black-and-white-striped scarf add to his Dali-esque appearance. The bastard still owes us a million dollars, and this stunt, just weeks before our guys are about to complete the commissioning of the plant and return home, could leave us hugely out of pocket. I'm having difficulty thinking clearly here. Enveloped in dread, I notice the dull, heavy feeling centred in my stomach.

"The two meat plants located at Omsk and Petropavlovsk will be able to process the waste generated here," I say carefully. "Both plants are only three hours' drive away. Trucking offal to another facility is common in New Zealand. They'll be pleased with the additional intake, and it'll give you an income without having to invest more capital. Your abattoir manager has a good relationship with the management of the Petropavlovsk meat plant. I'm sure he can organise something."

Petr thrusts his extended right index finger at me. "Grigori, if there is one thing you need to understand it is that no one can be trusted."

"But things are changing."

"But some things never change. I will always need to be completely self-sufficient. I can't rely on anyone else."

Petr seems agitated beyond his normal level of erratic behaviour. "Merv assured me I would have a complete meat-processing facility. That is what I was promised and that is what must be delivered."

There's nothing more to say here. "Look, Petr. We have delivered all that we agreed to deliver. We always do." I point to the meat plant visible from the office windows. "What is constructed over there is the plant in its entirety. I can understand your concern, but this is what you contracted to buy."

I leave his office. My armpits are wet. It pisses me off. Personal hygiene is so important to me. I don't feel comfortable if I'm sweating. The gnawing in my stomach is still there. I need to walk, dissipate some tension. I might go back to my accommodation and have a coffee and some food.

No. I don't want to talk to anyone. I need time to myself. I've got to get clear on this. I'll go for a walk. I'll head over to the fields.

As I walk towards the fields I continue mulling things over. There's something not quite right here. The contract was finalised by . . . fucking Popov! Popov has got direct access to Petr. Is that prick meddling here? Fuck, I bet that's what's going on. My confusion subsides as I realise that maybe something bigger than me is at play in all of our dealings in Russia and Kazakhstan. I feel uneasy with the thought that Popov is lurking in the shadows just behind me all the time.

After dinner I decide to have a chat with the girls in an attempt to stop me thinking about the scale of interference that appears to be going on. The three of them are translating technical documents in preparation for the meat plant staff training. Within a state-owned organisation most of the translators probably couldn't be bothered doing much more than the bare minimum, but working with us they are all going for it. It's demanding work, but with the offer of hard currency these translators are as driven as anyone I know.

I wander over to their table and join them. After a few minutes of aimlessly chewing the fat I decide to share one of my observations, and it's relevant because all three are solo parents. "One of the surprising features of the female population here is the large number of single parents," I say.

Olga jiggles her right leg and says, "One of the problems we used to face was that effective contraception wasn't always readily available. When you are young and in love, it is easy to think that continuing with an unplanned pregnancy is the right thing to do. But once the baby arrives, the fathers often can't cope with the responsibility and they leave."

I say, "Someone was telling me recently that of all the abortions performed around the world, one in four are undertaken here."

"It's true," Sveta says ruefully. "Many women have multiple abortions."

Olga adds, "And the conditions in the clinics are simply terrible."

"That must be changing, though," I say. When I first arrived here Merv used to bring boxes of condoms with him to give away as gifts.

"No, there's less money available from the state than there was before."

The next morning Vlad and I are driven three hours to the airport. Despite Aeroflot being the largest airline in the world, there are many cancelled flights due to the scarcity of aviation fuel and the lack of people with money to spend on travel. So, as happens often, we have the opportunity to settle into a day of drinking and eating in the VIP lounge.

Vlad has been away for half an hour trying to organise our flights and I'm sitting here getting wound-up about Popov, despite a few vodkas. My forearms, biceps, shoulders and neck are tight. My solar plexus is tight too. I stretch my arms, then my hands, then I curl my spine slightly and screw up my face. With a guttural groan I release the tension in my body.

Realising I've missed most of the past 30 minutes, I decide I need a break. I gaze out the observation windows and suddenly wonder if I can get away with walking out onto the runway with a camera. Things have become so loose that I reckon I could. Purposefully stepping out onto what has been, until now, a high security area on the runway, I start snapping photos with my camera. I see a mobile radar mounted on a military truck on the side of the main runway. I walk towards it, clicking. Using the telescopic lens, I zoom in on other aspects of the airport.

After about 10 minutes Vlad rushes out. "Grigori, what do you think you are doing? The airport security are preparing to seize you. If you don't get back inside immediately, you'll be arrested."

"No, I won't. This sort of thing is going on all over the place."

"Grigori! They are serious. Stop it and come in."

I relent and return to the terminal building where I am apprehended by two police officers. Vlad's quick diplomacy gets me off with a reprimand and the removal of the film from my camera.

"You're getting too cocky," Vlad reproaches me. "What may be acceptable today may not be tomorrow. The pendulum may swing back. You have to be more careful."

The morning after my vodka-induced walk onto the tarmac I'm sitting on the bed in the VIP bedroom with a towel wrapped uncomfortably around my extended guts. I catch a glimpse of myself in the mirror. "You poor bastard," I say to my own reflection. "What a sight! How did you let yourself get this far out of shape?" I stare at myself in the mirror. The sight of my face shocks me even more. My skin is puffy and dry and the furrows on my forehead give a clear indication of the chaos within. I look so old.

I can't believe how unpredictable I'm becoming. Yesterday's episode was a reckless thing to do and completely unnecessary. So much for my search for a peaceful life. Peace and calm are becoming even more elusive. I attempt to regroup as Vlad organises our travel to visit the Altai.

The Mayor's independent streak has blossomed while I've been absent. It appears that Merv's mate, the Prime Minister, is in the decline and of course the Functionary is dead. This has left a power vacuum. The Mayor has moved from the shadows of the Gorny administrators and is now fully capable of funding projects himself. It's amazing, really, because the town has a population of only 4000, but it's clear his close relationship with the directors of the state farms around here has paid off.

Vlad has been doing a great job keeping in contact with the manager of the abattoir, so I've been aware the plant is all good on the operational front. What I wasn't aware of was that the Mayor had purchased a process-line capable of manufacturing sausages, salami and meat small goods from a German outfit. We've lost our monopoly. The Mayor told me that although something had been lost through my absence, there could still be opportunities to do business. He suggested we prepare a proposal to construct a building to house his new manufacturing equipment.

Over the past couple of months we have worked diligently to prepare a proposal for the construction of the building for the Mayor. I sent the Mayor the translated proposal a couple of weeks ago. Now I'm here to follow it up.

It's the 24th of December and the cold bites hard as Vlad and I leave the aircraft. The Mayor's new Toyota Land Cruiser is parked by the terminal building. Just two months ago the only foreign-made vehicles on the road were our two Nissan Patrols. We're no longer the only boys on the block. The Mayor has sent his driver to collect us. He's in a log hut in some remote valley with two of his mates. Apparently we will all be going hunting. As we drive along, the driver and Vlad are conversing, but Vlad's body language looks unnatural.

When the conversation stops I ask, "Vlad, what's up?"

He tells me, "The Prime Minister recently died."

"Really? What happened?"

Vlad shakes his head disparagingly, as if to say, "Not now."

What's going on here? I want to ask a dozen questions but I don't probe further.

We are driven along a valley and past several small settlements. The sky is dark and the muddy road is frozen. The sweet smell of silage hits me like a bad dose of halitosis. It's the lingering smell of decaying plant matter that permeates the countryside at this time of the year. I try to tell myself it smells like molasses.

It's a scene from another time. The housing consists of cabins constructed from logs bleached by the elements and sealed with white mortar. They are studded with small windows with white timber frames. Some houses have open gable ends, exposing the roof space to the weather. Yards, fenced with rough-sawn unpainted pickets, are stacked with hay nearly the height of houses and they're equipped with outbuildings of similar construction to the cabins. I guess that's where the farm animals live at this time of the year. Power lines draping from poles leaning at irregular angles add to the impression of decrepitude.

Two young women are walking beside the road, each immaculately dressed in a winter coat, a mink shapka and knee-high boots with elevated heels. They walk as if their role in life is to enliven this shambles. The grimness of this man-made environment accentuates their beauty and elegance. I've seen this concurrence many times. Not only do they preserve their dignity, but like cut diamonds, they radiate light.

Cautiously, the Mayor's driver steers the Land Cruiser over a ramshackle suspension bridge, past a horse-drawn sleigh, and then continues up into the head of the valley until the road comes to an end. A track formed through birch forest and snow-covered alpine meadows leads us towards the Mayor's hut. Within 20 minutes we come across two Altaians mounted on horseback and wearing traditional wool and fur winter clothing. Vlad asks them if we're walking in the right direction. We are. They tell us that the temperature dropped to minus 25 degrees last night and they'd slept in an open bivouac. Complaining that the hunting has been less than successful, they are on their way home for some comfort.

Twenty minutes further on the wood smoke wafting into the meadow leads us to the log cabin nestled on the edge of a birch forest. The whole area is blanketed in snow. The instant Vlad knocks, the door opens and the Mayor stands before us. His smile is contagious and has a calming effect on me. Following Russian protocol I step through the doorway before embracing him. We hug firmly and then kiss each other on the cheek. The lack of tension in his body indicates he is open and relaxed. In the past I've had a sense he was always controlled and guarded – as if he were scheming.

He introduces his two mates. Then he gives us a summary of what the general plan is, which involves staying here two nights. Oh dear. I'm not sure if I'm keen on two nights. Ah well, the things you do for business.

I respond, "Horoshyee." OK.

It's a small hut, but big enough to house a traditional wood-fired oven, a small table and five mismatched chairs. A cast-iron casserole dish is simmering on the oven top, and a large pot of water with snow floating on the surface sits alongside it. The sleeping place above the oven is packed with someone's rucksack. I also notice a large amount of food sitting on the window sill. Among other things there are a large glass jar of strawberry jam, probably homemade, a lump of butter wrapped loosely in greaseproof paper, a full length of salami, and half a dozen loaves of bread. Then I see my favourite. A small plate stacked with white portions, each the size of a box of matches. It's called salo. It's fat cut from the most prized part of the pig, the back, and seasoned with black pepper and salt. It's got to be the tastiest food in the world. Four bottles of vodka sit alongside the food.

"How is life for you, Grigori?" the Mayor asks.

"Monica and I are basing ourselves in New Zealand now, and that has made life busier for me," I reply. "Too busy. I figured out the other day that the longest I've slept in the same bed over the past 18 months is 10 days. And that wasn't my own bed. It was in a boy-catcher in northern Kazakhstan."

The Mayor frowns. "What's a boy-catcher?"

"A boy-catcher is a bed that sags in the middle. When a boy gets in such a bed with a girl, he can't easily get out and knows he's been caught."

The Mayor laughs and asks, "So you were sharing the boy-catcher with a girl?"

"No, no."

He smiles. "With all that pillow talk, you should be able to speak fluent Russian by now."

"Yeah, right," I respond.

"You need a Russian girlfriend to warm your bed," the Mayor says, matter-of-factly.

"Maybe. But maybe I'd never leave."

"Perfect. We would welcome you here. I'm sure your soul is Russian."

"Sometimes I think it is," I laugh.

The Mayor turns his attention to dishing up a venison stew and one of his mates cuts the bread. I notice the clove of garlic hanging around his neck and ask what it's for. Protection against colds and influenza, he tells me. The Mayor toasts to our arrival and to successful hunting. After two small shots of vodka I'm given a set of white hunting overalls, a pair of snow shoes and a rifle. I'm not into guns. They give me the shits, mainly because I'm such an unfocused bastard I could easily blow holes in things I shouldn't. Anyway, I'm here and I need to do the right thing.

Leading, and walking without talking, the Mayor carefully stalks up the valley. Wheezing like an asthmatic, I follow him. Suddenly he stops and raises his left hand to indicate to me to stop. Ahead and to the right is a mountain goat. The Mayor fires off two rounds. The animal bounds away into the cover of the forest. I use the rest to catch my laboured breath.

As we continue I find it difficult to remain focused on what I'm meant to be doing. Instead my mind wanders as I wonder what has happened to the Prime Minister. I'm aware that in the past the Mayor was often off side with the Prime Minister – always trying to avoid his control and go it alone. I decide to say nothing.

Back in the hut we commiserate over the unsuccessful afternoon. I don't mind: eviscerating some wild animal wouldn't have been high on the list of things I wanted to do on this trip.

"Grigori, do you know anything about the Chutotkas?" the Mayor asks.

"Nah, not really. I've heard of them, that's all."

"They are native people who live above the Arctic Circle, near the Bering Sea. Generally they're considered to be uneducated people, but in their naivety they say things that have relevance for all of us. So, I'll tell you a little joke. A Chutotka applies for membership to the Union of Russian Writers. He is asked what literature he is familiar with. 'Have you read Pushkin?' 'No.' 'Have you read Dostoevsky?' 'No.' 'How about Tolstoy?' 'No.' 'Can you read at all?' The Chutotka, offended, replies, 'Chutotka not reader. Chutotka writer!' "

I laugh.

He adds, "This phrase, 'Chutotka not reader, Chutotka writer' has become a popular saying in Russia. It's often said when someone uses ignorance to their benefit, and usually after the event."

Chuckling, I think to myself how my life started being more effective in the Soviet Union when I adopted the Chutotka writer approach to getting things done.

Then, growing more serious the Mayor asks, "You've stayed at Kiwi Lodge, haven't you, Grigori?"

"Yeah I have."

"Have you heard about what happened to the caretakers?" he asks.

Wondering whether Merv is still involved in the joint venture there I reply, "No I haven't."

"About a month ago they both went missing. Initially no one was concerned, but as the weeks went by neither of them had made contact with their families. About a week ago the police thoroughly searched the lodge and uncovered the woman's dismembered body in the chest freezer."

"Seriously?"

"Seriously," he responds.

"We supplied that freezer from New Zealand."

"Do not worry. You could not have foreseen that it would be used as a morgue."

"Neveroyatna," I say, thinking of my stay in the lodge.

Despite the significance of the Prime Minister in the Mayor's life, he doesn't mention him.

That night Vlad and I share a cramped bunk made from sacks nailed to timber framing. I can't sleep. The torment has kicked in again. My mind is hammering away. These situations with a group are fine for a few hours, but the idea of being here for two days is just too much. I feel imprisoned. I wish I wasn't like this, but I get anxious when I'm in close proximity to others for too long. I don't feel comfortable. All I want to do is go, be by myself somewhere else. I have difficulty making small talk. There's only so much you can talk about. I'm envious of those who find it easy. When I was a kid I used to be good at telling jokes, but these days I don't bother. It's such a contrived thing to do anyway. I much prefer spontaneity. Indiscriminate injection of comments into conversation is what I enjoy. The problem is, timing is important and the finer nuances are generally lost in translation. All I want is to get the deal done. Once the deal is done, I'll feel better.

Then I start thinking how the prevailing thread running through every aspect of this business grind is fear. Fear that I'm not capable of pulling it all off. Fear of failure. I wonder if he's going to sign the contract. You'd never know. He's a good party official – never gives much away, and when he does, he's pretty good at disinformation. After all, it was not long before my first visit here that the Mayor categorically stated that the release of toxic gas from that beryllium plant in Ust Kamenogorsk didn't happen. This region is located just over the mountains from where the explosion occurred. The foreign media covered it extensively, stating that the first thing the 300,000 people living in Ust Kamenogorsk were aware of was the random selection of people taken to hospital for tests for something unknown. They were unaware that the 'postal terminal' in the middle of the city was a secret beryllium plant.

Maybe he didn't know.

God, I wish I could sleep.

The next day is Christmas Day, but not here. Orthodox Christians celebrate Christmas on 7 January. In appreciation of his hospitality I decide to give the Mayor my new Swiss army knife. As I start explaining what I am about to do, Vlad stops interpreting and proceeds to rebuff me. Giving a knife is considered to be a bad omen. If I insist on giving it, then I need to receive a coin in return. Vlad explains to the Mayor what I am trying to do, and the Mayor responds that he would like to receive my gift, but he needs to buy it from me. He pulls out a kopek and gives it to me. I'm continually amazed at how superstitious the Russians are.

The Mayor seems to be picking up on my tension. "Grigori, you should relax and enjoy this time away from business."

"Yeah, I know I should, but I have a lot of work to do before going back to New Zealand."

"If you would prefer, we can spend the day shooting and then go to my banya tonight."

I'm instantly relieved. "That would be great. I'd appreciate that."

Before we go shooting I tell him, "I have a story to tell about my wife. Recently I was at a pub in my home town when I overheard a bloke telling his mates how his wife had gone to a male strip show. My home town isn't much bigger than Ust Koksa – you know what small towns are like – you can't get away with much. I'm the only person there who has anything to do with Russia. So this guy was explaining to his friends how most of the women at the strip show were whistling and calling out to the strippers, enticing them to come over by offering five dollar notes. Then he says some woman holds up a 50 dollar note, starts waving it madly and yells, 'Over here! Over here! My husband is in Russia! Over here!'"

The Mayor laughs.

After another unsuccessful day's shooting we leave the hut and drive back to his house. While we eat some entrées he lights the fire in his banya. After nearly an hour he invites us to have a sauna. Vlad, the Mayor and I sweat it out, taking turns to beat each other with the birch branch that has been soaking in water, after which the naked Mayor instructs me to join him outside for a snow scrub.

We go back inside the house and the Mayor says, "Steam treats not only your body but also your soul."

Feeling refreshed and cleansed, I agree fully. I feel relaxed and momentarily free of worry.

During the meal I decide it's time to break the news about the new business. I describe what has happened to Ashfield, that they want out of the project business.

"We're still the same guys with the same capabilities and we are here for the long haul."

I tell them that the company's name is now Arnicom, or АНИКОМ in Cyrillic, and that the majority of the shares will be owned by Merv and me.

"I'm the Managing Director of the business, but you'll still see plenty of me – my intention is to continue with a hands-on approach here in Russia."

I've had a series of brochures developed, illustrating some of the projects we've completed and showing off a few of the other technologies that we can deliver. The only marginal aspect is the photo of the building where our office is located: it would be easy to assume the whole building is ours, but it's not. We lease a corner space sufficient for four people. But that's OK. One of Merv's mates owns the building.

I pass a brochure to the Mayor. Predictably the photo that interests him most is the office building. I tell him the truth. I also tell him that my nickname is Arnie – a name I don't really like – but in a gesture of surrender I have named the new business Arnicom. He gets the joke and laughs.

At the end of the meal the Mayor suggests it's time to review the contract. Just before midnight on Christmas Day we sign the documents, shake hands, embrace and kiss each other and have a toast. A warm, robust sense of satisfaction permeates me. I've done it: the first contract signed by the new business! I've done the deal. I'm walking the walk. I experience a feeling of deep relief. My lower jaw and shoulders relax, and I stretch my fingers out, feeling the tension dissipating from my forearms and hands. Finally, I am a serious man.

The following day when we are at the airport I ask Vlad, "What happened to the Prime Minister?"

He raises his eyebrows as if to say it's an unlikely story, "He had a heart attack."

I nod. "OK."

NINE

It's October 1993 and I'm in Zhezkazgan to visit two meat plant sites. A sense of dismay and helplessness settles over me. I now know what a Central Kazakh steppe is. It's a vast, brown, treeless, dusty prairie exposed to 40 degrees in the summer and minus 50 degrees with the wind-chill factor in winter. The winds that are buffeting me now relentlessly hammer the place almost all year round. The conditions are so severe that the indigenous sheep only survive thanks to large fatty pads on their backs that protect their organs in winter.

I'd never heard of the place, but it turns out Zhezkazgan is a remote region the size of a European country located in the central Kazakh steppes. The capital is also known as Zhezkazgan. The Kazakhs in these parts live in state farms surveyed from land that is short on productivity and long on extreme conditions. The land supports horses and sheep and the odd human, but bugger all else. The only plus is that I'm close to the Baikonur Cosmodrome, where my hero Yuri Gagarin left the planet. In fact the two construction sites are located less than 100 kilometres from the launch site. This place is so different I've fired off a couple of rolls of film.

The hostel where I'm staying is a decrepit wooden cottage with no heating, and the bathroom is serviced by a pail of water collected from a tap down the road. The most distinctive feature is the lack of sunlight – the windows are all boarded over. There's a 40-watt incandescent bulb hanging from the ceiling in each room. For a moment I am drawn into melancholy, but then I refocus on what I have to do here. I've been invited to meet the State Farm Director.

Vlad is not with me on this trip, and later, entering the Director's home, I struggle to communicate to him that I'm here without an interpreter, who's away for a few hours. It's clear he's got about as much English as I have Russian. He indicates that everything is OK and gestures for me to come in and join him in his living room. My host is a refined character with the presence and charisma of a steady and reliable leader. His official role is State Farm Director, but he has a more important function: he's the tribal or community chief.

He sits me down at a dining table big enough to seat more than a dozen and proceeds to set up a backgammon board. Relative to the other dwellings in the village this is a big house. It appears it is home for his sons, their wives and their children. Producing two bottles of spirits, I'm given the choice of vodka or cognac. I go for the vodka with the unfamiliar label. He places it in front of me and puts the cognac on his side of the table. We've each got our own bottle to drain.

Aw, this vodka is shit! What is this? I look more closely at the label and see it's something I've never tried: Polish vodka. The Russians are always cursing and moaning about cheap Polish vodka. They claim the only thing the Poles are good at is trading products from the East to the West and never the other way around. I think there could be merit in their indignation.

There's a young woman sitting at the end of the table, adjacent to the Chief and me. She wears glasses with dark horn-rimmed frames that emphasise her intellect and her appeal. She's disgruntled. I attempt to communicate with her but she doesn't respond. The Chief's shoulders stiffen and he makes a facial expression that indicates it's inappropriate for me to do so.

Backgammon is proving to be a great way to communicate with the Chief. I get to see how reckless I am and how cautious he is. He's taking it seriously. He's a man who needs to win and he's dogged in his pursuit of a successful outcome. I'd like to win but I really don't care – I'm just enjoying engaging with this character. He is someone I could easily respect. Attempting the odd word of Russian and English, we toast each other. The young woman continues to sit attentively, topping up our cups of mare's milk before they're less than half empty.

My interpreter arrives. The Chief and I are on the upswing of two hours of drinking. Trust and rapport have been developed, but now she's here the Chief is eager to say something to me, "Grigori, maybe you work for the CIA?"

Tilting my head back in mock surprise, I'm not sure whether I should agree with him and tell him in fact I do work for the CIA. Instead I decide my humour would probably go the wrong way and I take a cautious line. "Why's that, Chief?"

"Do you think it is good manners to take photographs of people you don't know without their permission? How would you like it if someone walked around your home town taking photographs of the people who live there and their homes?"

Someone has obviously complained to him about my activities earlier in the day. I apologise for my indiscretion and assure him it won't happen again. I try to walk a mile in someone else's shoes to get an understanding of how their world looks before I do most things, but I guess I've been a bit insensitive.

The main course arrives.

Oh Jesus.

It's the dreaded baked goat's head, delivered on a dish of oversized lasagna, mutton fat and mutton. I've heard about this dish. It's considered to be the greatest delicacy by the locals but the most challenging for guests.

There are three of us eating here, but there's enough food for twelve. Holding the head in his hand, and with a twinkle of delight in his eyes, the Chief says, "Since you are a man of vision, a man with an eye to the future, it is appropriate that I offer you the most prized and tastiest part of the goat – the eye."

Good on ya, mate. First it was the Polish vodka, now it's the eye. It's a blue-grey gelatinous orb the size of a golf ball, and although I'm sure it's fresh it has the appearance of being 10 days old. I have to do the right thing and get on with it. Focusing on the vodka, I forcefully restrain myself from thinking about what I'm eating. The firmness requires several determined bites to break it up. Swallowing isn't straightforward. It's like dealing with oversized vitamin tablets.

I drain a glass of fire water and follow the Chief's lead, picking up a portion of fatty mutton and pasta with my left hand. No knives and forks here. I can't say I tasted the eye, but I'm pleased to have some mutton fat in my mouth to smother the taste of Polish vodka. The Chief lifts the head from the plate and slices portions of cheek, lip, tongue, ears and facial flesh. I choose a small portion of cheek meat. This is better. Nothing is said about my willing participation. There's only a sense that I did what was required.

In bed afterwards I reflect on how I seem to be able to blend in wherever I am. It isn't an effort for me to be one person in one environment and another in a home environment. I don't even think of it as compartmentalising. Maybe this is why I can function in this sort of environment and yet not bring this mentality back home with me.

The following day my next job is to attend the commissioning of the plant. It's 1.15pm and the dignitaries aren't here yet. We were ready with a pair of scissors to cut the ribbon at 1.00pm. The Zhezkazgan Regional Governor and his off-siders are coming from the capital, four hours away. It's an uncertain time for the old Governor. He's Ukrainian. During the last year most positions of power have been transferred to Kazakhs. The official language is no longer Russian; it's Kazakh. The political life expectancy of a non-Kazakh is very limited.

A dust storm is in full rage. Visibility is down to about half a football field and the landscape is being whipped into a frenzy by strong winds. We're all getting a bit twitchy. Much rides on an event like this. As much as anything, it's an opportunity to win favour with people in power.

It's 1.30pm and still there is no sign of the guests. Let's see if they front up. Keeping people waiting is common behaviour for political leaders around here. I never know if they do it to place others in an uncomfortable and subservient position or if they're just slack. Suddenly, out of the sandy blizzard comes a squadron of black Volgas, lights barely visible through the flurry of dust, engines racing, all driven as if there's a prize to be won for the first to cross the finish line. The driver of the second car slides his car to a halt outside the meat plant entrance. In total, nine cars emerge from the dust storm like an attack party led by Genghis Khan. In a frenzy the passengers and drivers leap out of their vehicles and wait for the Governor to arrive. It's so surreal – the collective energy of the group is almost manic. Maybe it's the dust storm or maybe these guys don't do public events well. If it was a different group you'd say they were cranked up on methamphetamine.

The Governor has arrived. All the bigwigs stand slightly removed from the locals and endeavour to look very important and accomplished. Wives, drivers, assistants, body guards and journalists are all here. The women look out of place in their elegant furs and high heels. I've never seen the wife of an apparatchik attend such an event, but their inclusion adds an uncertain tension to the event. It's an opportunity for the men to propel themselves higher in front of their spouses.

I engage in convivial chat with the Governor and have a chance to view his wife. She looks alright, but it's better to impress the man with our achievements rather than charm his wife. The locals are here in force and they're excited. The Governor, the Chief and I line up to cut the ribbon. Much applauding and celebration follows. The crowd of about a hundred Kazakhs, clothed in black and grey, some wearing shapkas, file into the meat plant. This is what we refer to as a mini meat plant. It is no bigger than a medium-sized house. We all go in. I'm on the leading edge of the group, attempting to show the Governor how the plant functions and what its features are.

Shit! I can barely move. I'm in a human crush. Leading the Governor I slowly manoeuvre my way towards the food display area. I want to show him the products the plant can produce. Our butcher has lovingly spent the last few days preparing a smorgasbord of sausages, salamis, cured and smoked cuts – you name it, he's made it – and not one morsel of pork amongst it. Delicacies never before seen in the central Kazakh steppe.

Bastards! The display has been decimated! The journalists and drivers have been tucking into the food presentation while I was leading the dignitaries around the plant. I don't know whether to laugh or bloody cry.

What to do? Nothing.

The Governor is pleased with himself for delivering a huge gift to the locals.

The Chief is chuffed that he is sufficiently respected to be granted the funding to construct the plant.

The locals who helped build the facility and have learnt to operate it are beaming with pride.

The residents are happy that their community has a brand spanking new toy that produces meat products in a hygienic environment and they have been propelled into the 21st century.

And of course our guys who built the plant are happy. Two months ago they had a set of plans and a bare piece of land. Despite the challenges along the way, they've created this.

I'm satisfied that we've done what we said we'd do. We are all feeling very pleased. It's an uplifting, festive day.

We relocate from the meat plant to the town hall. This hall was probably built when the steppe was conquered in the 1950s, but it isn't like any other small community hall built in that era. The walls are adorned with patterns moulded from plaster of Paris and painted shades of pastel green, turquoise and pink. Incandescent light bulbs hang from a patterned ceiling, all creating a wonderful ambience. The long, narrow room provides space for two parallel rows of tables running the length of the hall. Laden with food and beverages, the tables have been set with the names of the guests. The Governor and his key men are at the head table. There are no women up there. I'm seated with the Governor's wife and the wives of two other dignitaries. The only other women in the place are those serving.

Very quickly the speeches get underway. Looking decidedly insecure, the Governor leads with a few words about how, despite the challenges facing Kazakhstan at the moment, the Zhezkazgan region has developed rapidly under his leadership. The speech includes much praise for himself, particularly in relation to providing this very special meat plant.

An academic stands to share his vision. He sees a time soon when the level of education and health care will be higher here than anywhere else in the world. There will be direct flights connecting Zhezkazgan to New York. Zhezkazgan will be serviced by a Moscow-style underground commuter rail system and this village will, in time, be connected to the city of Zhezkazgan by train.

The academic's behaviour is becoming extremely erratic, his arms are flailing and his mouth is distorting. Frenzied, he continues. "Zhezkazgan will become a significant military power base in Central Asia and it will have a very influential role to play in world politics."

Far out, this is getting really loose. How did this dude get in here? What on earth does he do for a living?

Other speeches are delivered. Then it's my turn. I stand and share my pearls of wisdom. I want to tell them to forget about the direct flights to New York and world domination, but I figure it's way more fun to add to the mayhem. Absolutely this area has the ability to be influential, to be a broker between the states in the south and Russia in the north. With the great mineral wealth of the Zhezkazgan steppe plus the integrity and capability of the people, the future is boundless. In particular, we've enjoyed their hospitality and the support the locals have given us building the meat plant. I am especially grateful for the efforts and the offer of friendship from the Chief.

The speeches are finished and the Chief comes over. He's beaming. I embrace him as if he's the love of my life. He asks if I could take photos of the people here. The moratorium on photography seems to have been lifted. I recover the camera from a bag I brought along just in case there was a reversal in the earlier edict. The previously camera-shy locals line up to have their photos taken. Eagerly they await their turn to be targeted by the lens. It's as if they've never had their photos taken in their lives. I shoot three rolls, each 36 exposures, of Kazakh banjo players, catering ladies, people pulling faces, one character on his knee singing to his sweetheart, not to mention all the snaps of the Chief, his wife, son and grandson.

How do I get out of this? That's it! No more film. Sorry.

It's difficult to know what is going on anywhere here, but especially at the higher levels of state. But it appears there has been a breakdown in communication at the top. About a month ago Yeltsin issued a decree dissolving the Supreme Soviet of Russia and the Congress of People's Deputies of Russia – or Parliament. Just to juice things up, the next day the Supreme Soviet declared Yeltsin no longer the president and the vice president was sworn in as the new president. Since the Parliament was dissolved there have been a bunch of people holed up in the Parliament buildings.

I return to Moscow from Zhezkazgan just as things get out of hand. The Russian iron fist has come hammering down as it has so many times throughout history. Tanks surrounding the White House have started lobbing shells at the Parliament building under Yeltsin's orders. Merv is in the office when I arrive. We go into the board room to have a chat about what's happening down the road at the White House.

Merv says, "I've seen this carry on so many times. Someone will get pushed and shoved and shaken, but only up to a point, and then bang, like a shaken champagne bottle, the cork flies and all hell breaks loose. Can you imagine a dispute in the Parliament buildings in London being resolved by sending in a division of tanks with guns blazing?"

I respond, deadpan, "No, not really."

He laughs and says, "There's one thing I would never want to do – get caught in a tight spot where a Russian leader wants to make a point."

Raising my eyebrows I say, "The enemy must be destroyed at all costs." We finish chatting and I return to my desk. After I sit down I realise that maybe this Russian approach actually isn't too different to my own. My interactions with other people can become unclear, and that can lead me to become frustrated, and sometimes the frustration can overflow into an angry outburst.

TEN

It's 1994. I'm in the office in New Zealand and Merv wants to have a yarn. I hear from Merv these days only when he's got a serious business enquiry. His success rate in such situations is close to 100 per cent. So I'm very excited. Nonchalantly, he gives me a murky overview of the enquiry. Merv knows someone with direct access to people with money, money that has been made available for the development of small-scale businesses. We've got no idea where the money is from, nor are we interested. All that matters is that the guys on the sharp end have the ability to pull the deal off and we've got the ability to deliver the goods.

It's Monday morning. Merv received the call an hour ago. Innovation and urgency are the themes. The decision on who will be awarded the contract will be made by the end of the week.

There are no guidelines or terms of reference for this one. Brainstorming is all that's required, so we pull in the others. Ideas come quickly, many based on what we have prepared before and some on our understanding of the emerging consumer market. For me it's an opportunity to revisit some of the ideas I've had floating around from my time lurking around the streets of Moscow. We decide to develop a series of proposals based on 20- and 40-foot shipping containers, facilities capable of delivering consumer products and services anywhere in Moscow.

A range of small milk pasteurising and packaging plants are first off the rank. An ice-cream-making set-up, a cheese-making operation, a delicatessen, a pizza restaurant, an office bureau, a salami- and sausage-making facility, a range of refrigerated cold storage units. Shit, a coffee roaster and café based on an idea Merv set up in Riga. Bread bakeries of varying capacities. Someone even comes up with the suggestion of a small-scale oil refinery that some Aussie engineer has developed. I can't see that working too well on Leninsky Prospekt, but you never know. An open mind is a wonderful thing. A drycleaning outfit, and why not a laundromat? Hey, what about a dog-grooming salon? A sunglasses retail outlet.

And so it goes on. We are giving each random suggestion enough attention to string a few descriptive words together, prepare a CAD drawing and overlay each proposal with a scope of supply and a price. It's seat-of-the pants stuff. I've increased the profit margin to compensate for the inevitable errors. It'd be too easy to omit a bunch of expensive gear. We've got the international clock in our favour. The time differential between Christchurch and Moscow is 10 hours, so we work while our counterparts in the northern hemisphere sleep. I love this kind of activity: lots of creativity with bugger-all attention to detail, all fuelled by the prospect of selling a few units and making a few shekels. I'm keen for anyone's input, so I'm asking everyone I know for ideas. By Monday night we've faxed off eight proposals. I head home charged with excitement. The possibilities are endless.

As soon as I get in the door I greet Monica and briefly share the day's events with her. I roll a joint. Hungry for the hit, I greedily inhale every wisp of the blue smoke. I wait as long as I can. *Ahhhh.* Exhaling, my chest deflates. Yeah, it's a good brew. I love the comfort and familiarity of it. Just briefly it feels like home.

As I look around the room the initial sense of mellowness is superseded by my mind launching into overdrive. All those possibilities! I could make a fortune out of this deal. The intensity of projecting into the future overcomes me. I crank up the music, Joy Division, the edgy, almost metallic despair resonates with me. I gorge my dinner, completely unaware of anything other than the ideas and visions of what may happen.

I head out the door, uttering a few words to the effect that I'll do the dishes when I get back. I need to walk – I need space for my thoughts to clarify. I get so wired. It doesn't matter if I've been smoking, drinking or abstaining, my mind seldom settles. I walk purposefully uphill, trying to slow my head down. I do this every night. Lungs heaving, thigh muscles straining, my mind whirling in a tornado of thoughts. An hour of striding out is usually sufficient to defuse the intensity of the energy in my head and body and allow some clarity.

I return home and have a shower to relax myself further. It occurs to me that Monica spent an hour preparing another fine meal and all I've done is gulp it down and bugger off. But I can't stop myself. I spend the rest of the night thinking about the possibilities of the deal. The anticipation consumes me. I reach for a blue bomber. Halcyon days are back again. It's over and out.

It's Tuesday morning, and I feel the way I always do – like shit. I get in the shower. My diaphragm shudders as I hack away like a geriatric smoker. The bronchial tubes feel tight and inflamed from the smoke last night. I spit and direct the green mucus at the drain in the floor of the shower. I want another joint and a day off. But really, I want more than that. I want peace. Endless, unbroken peace.

Instead I instruct myself with my daily directive. 'Come on, pick yourself up, put your shoulder to the wheel. Keep going. There'll be an end to the grind soon.' I don't know when, but I hope it's soon. Every morning I instruct myself to keep going, to keep pushing my fair share of the load. Don't let yourself or anyone else down. Come on mate. Reward yourself with a smoke at the end of the day. Because of the massive flow of luxury cars into Moscow there's a lack of workshops equipped to service the newly purchased Mercedes, BMWs, Bentleys, Range Rovers, Jags, and Audis. We prepare a proposal for a transportable hi-tech workshop.

Tuesday night and another joint, more single malts than I can remember, rapid mind activity, again, and then bed. Oh, and a few words with Monica. I'm so caught up in the internal dialogue it's as if she isn't even there most of the time. If I go to bed unaided by pharmaceuticals, like tonight, I fall sleep for about an hour, then lie awake with my head racing like a mad bastard. Sleep deprivation pisses me off.

Here I am, awake again. Most nights I try counting down from a hundred to zero. It doesn't work that well. I usually peel off into diatribes, ranting about this or that. Or I try solving work-related problems. My body gets so wound up I can't lie still, tossing and turning. I don't know how Monica puts up with it. I wake her up most nights. The counting goes on for hours, but I rarely get to zero. I usually end up sliding out of bed, then I creep around the room like a cat burglar until I smack into a wall or the bedside table on my way to watch television.

Tonight, as usual, before getting to the living room I open the fridge door and stand and eat. Fat and sugar is what I target – it seems to momentarily appease the angst. Then I sit through hours of CNN recycling the same stories. Now that is inane shit.

In the end I have a beat. That calms me down. Masturbation has been a daily activity for me since I was thirteen. I must have had over 10,000 make-believe shags in my time. As Jonty says, the library of past encounters is a useful thing. I usually fall asleep after that, but if I'm having a real shocker of a night, or if I make the mistake of masturbating too early in the period of broken sleep, I end up beating myself off a couple of times. There's no pleasure in that: the few moments of respite from the torment are superseded by the discomfort of a sore cock.

It's 9.30 in the morning. Another shit night's sleep. The old gills feel like they've been etched with caustic. The head isn't too flash either. I struggle out of bed and manoeuvre to the bathroom to have a shower. I douse myself under the wonderfully large shower rose and the water cascading over my body recharges me. The time here gives me a chance to re-establish calmness and get my head around the frame of reference for the day.

These days I'm so jittery I can't seem to focus on too much. I'm not sure if it's the stress or the durry – but every day seems full of judders. About a dozen cups of coffee keep me sharp throughout the day. I don't want to disturb what little sleep I have, so I make sure the last one is at three in the afternoon.

Sensible, eh?

I choose a tie. I like my ties. I swing my arm into a jacket. Here we go.

Merv comes into my office just after I arrive. He wants to know how much margin we have in the workshops job. I've been in this situation with Merv before. He's driven by the rush of doing the deal rather than the profit in the deal. At this stage of the game I'm more interested in having some fat left over rather than just doing the bloody thing. It's time to make some money. Money will give me a chance to slow down and live life.

Any indication of margin I give him will be trimmed to the bone. Besides, this isn't a run-of-the-mill enquiry. For whatever reason, the purchaser wants this deal done quickly. It's not the uniqueness of our proposal but the pace of the enquiry that will protect our profit margin. "Look mate, there's bugger all in it," I say. I grit my teeth slightly. It's only a little white lie.

"Come on, we've got to give them something. That's how they work," Merv says.

"Yeah, I know," I say. "We can knock $20,000 off the price of each unit, but that's all we can afford."

There'll be good money if we sell five. I'll be punching the air if they buy ten. An hour later and Merv is back. Things are serious. Negotiations are going well, but they want a better price, especially given they could take up to 50 units. Yeah, right. How many times have I heard this sort of bullshit?

"OK, drop the price by a further $10,000, but that's it. It won't be worth doing the deal if we go lower."

An hour later and Merv is back beaming. "I've done the deal."

"Seriously?"

"Yep, it's done."

"How many workshops are they taking?"

"Fifty."

"Fifty!"

"How much did you sell them for?"

"The price we agreed."

"Far out!"

Actually, the margin is much better than Merv could ever have imagined. It's one of those pie-in-the-sky situations I've always dreamed about. Striding to my desk I tell him, "I'll get the costing spreadsheet for this proposal." I do some new calculations based on the price we just agreed and peruse the profit margin at the bottom of the right-hand column. I'm engulfed in supreme satisfaction and excitement. I call Merv over and show it to him.

He looks at the computer screen then at me. "Is this right?" If he's pissed off that I doubted his negotiation skills it doesn't show. Nor should it. We're about to make a shit-load. I feel so elated and full and expansive. My desire for money has finally been fulfilled and right now I don't have a care or concern in the world. There is nothing more I want. I can't wait to tell Monica.

It's the next morning and Merv tells me he has contracted to have the 50 units delivered to Moscow within four months. Merv has agreed to a timeframe that is really going to crank up the tension. "Four months! How the fuck am I going to do that?"

"You'll make it happen – you usually do."

I think how it sounds a lot like "I've done the deal, making it happen is your problem." Already the joy of yesterday is subsiding and the time restriction is beginning to induce concern. I prepare a Gantt chart that quickly gives me a visual overview of how we are going to use the three resources we have at our disposal – people, money and time.

Time is the trickiest. It always is. It's a funny thing, but if there is one thing that everyone on the planet seems to be poor in it's time. We never have enough of it. The lack of time creates so much stress for everyone, running around, pushing and shoving as we try to complete a job in a finite timeframe. It never ceases to amaze me how people universally underestimate how long it takes to complete a task. I learnt something a few years back from one of my mentors: there's no such thing as a five-minute job. A 'five-minute' job takes 30 minutes and a 30-minute task takes two hours. A job you think will take a couple of hours usually takes more than half a day. The stress caused by trying to complete a job

in five minutes is just plain daft. But this awareness still doesn't eliminate my stress and insomnia.

It's been two months since the workshops were delivered. Despite the
angst we do what we said we were going to do – we deliver the workshops
on time. The only glitch along the way was when some thugs attempted
to hold up the convoy of 50 trucks transporting the containers from Riga
to Moscow. I don't know what they thought was inside the containers
– maybe Polish vodka. Or maybe it was just the fuckability factor again.
In anticipation of such an event, we'd engaged some ex-military guys to
provide security for the convoy. One of them broke an arm in the melee,
and the hoods fled without inflicting too much grief.

But we've heard no more from the client. No request to commission
the facilities, no contact to initiate personnel training. Nee-chee-vore.
Nothing. They've just disappeared. But we got paid in full, so that was good.
And I have what I've dreamed about: filthy lucre in abundance. That was
satisfying – for a day or so.

If I said it aloud, my response would be a long, guttural growl, "A-h-h
f-u-c-k." I've just arrived in Moscow from New Zealand. I'll spend a few
days here before I head to St Petersburg to meet up with Merv and a bunch
of blokes he's been doing business with. I'm just passing through customs
inspection when I hear the dreaded words, "Come with me, please."

Recently there have been stories circulating of foreign business people
arriving in Moscow carrying more cash than the limit allows. They've been
apprehended by customs officials, like this bastard, questioned, released
with the money, followed to their accommodation, then mugged and
separated from their cash. It would appear to be a co-operative venture
between a mafia outfit and customs officers. And when you think about it,

I fit the profile perfectly: a regular visitor on a business visa, spending more time here than not, and young and cocky enough to give it a go.

The customs officer at Moscow's Sheremetyevo Airport instructs me to follow him. Taking my completed customs declaration form identifying that I have the maximum permissible amount of $5000 cash, he ushers me into a small room adjacent to the inspection area. What to do? Stay cool and calm. Deny it. I have $75,000 in $100 notes hidden in two money belts and the pockets of my overcoat and sports jacket. Fortunately it's winter. Just remain calm. Remember you've got $4500 in your right-hand coat pocket. Show him that, and if you have to, give it to him. Pointing to my handwriting he asks, "Is this correct?"

Frowning, I look close to see if I haven't been a silly prick and written down how much I've actually got on me. No. Thank fuck for that. I have written it correctly: $5000. My head is so cluttered I never know what I'm writing half the time. "Yes," I respond, wondering what this is all about. Maybe he's made a mistake. Or maybe he's been tipped off. The guys in the office know I'm bringing it in. But there's no way they'd dob me in.

"So, you have $50,000 with you?" He asks officiously.

"$50,000?" I reply with surprise, immediately thinking that maybe someone has set me up. A week before I departed from home I had discussed with the guys here in Moscow that I would be bringing $50,000 to keep the office functioning. They had informed me that the banking system was untrustworthy, and they needed money for salaries, travel, accommodation and cash to support the construction sites. Three days before my departure I decided to increase it to $75,000. They still think I'm bringing $50,000. I point at the amount I've written on the declaration. "No. I have $5000."

He holds the completed form up closer to his face and realises he has misread my scrawl. "Ah. Can you show me the money you have?"

The money belts are noticeable against my abdomen. I suppress a moment of dread. I need to remain calm. Preservation of life sharpens my wits. I focus. I calmly put my hand in my coat pocket, feel the pack of 45 $100 notes bound by a paper band, and remove them. I transfer the pack to my left hand as I proceed to remove the wallet from my right-hand trouser pocket, opening it to reveal a further $500. I'd prepared for this – where the money would be placed, how I'd respond to any questioning, and what I'd do if the money was uncovered. I hope I don't need to move to the next stage of the plan.

He asks, "This is all the money you have with you?"

"Dah. This is all I have."

The moment seems to extend forever as I remain focused as we look into each other's eyes. Then he hesitantly says, "Horoshyee. Spasibo."

A chink in his resolve – a doubt, maybe even compassion.

I respond identically, "Good. Thank you."

He moves to lead me out of the office. At the inspection station he stamps my documentation and waves me through. There was something dodgy about that encounter – the figure of $50,000 was a bit too sticky for my liking. I pass into the concourse to be met by Vlad. I embrace him firmly. I want to tell him what a close call I've just had but I restrain myself.

When I get to the flat I lie down on the sofa and start thinking about the sum of $50,000. Was it a coincidence? Am I paranoid? It's so marginal that it's difficult to differentiate between reality and fiction. Then I drift off thinking about how I always get out of tight spots like the customs incident. I know that in the end there is never anything to worry about, but I can't stop second guessing what may or may not happen. It's as if my mind has assigned a high level of risk to everything I do.

As Merv's flying mate said, "Doing business in Russia is like flying a helicopter. You're always on the edge of your seat waiting for something to go wrong."

This approach has served me well, but the preparedness for a cock-up has ousted innocence and engrained cynicism. I've adopted the attitude that at any given moment any number of events could occur to block my progress. Someone offering support today may change their position tomorrow, or one of Yeltsin's presidential decrees could shut down a whole aspect of the economy. Or Popov could be pulling strings again. I'm perpetually prepared for failure, and this is making me increasingly stressed.

The Russians are so used to the insurmountable inertia of the place. If the going gets tough they shrug their shoulders and say, "Chto delat?" What to do? And the response is always "Nee-chee-vore." Nothing. They surrender to the knowledge that they are impotent to do anything.

I remember Vlad telling me early on, "If we have to bribe someone, what is there to do? Nothing. Just pay. Resistance won't work."

Inevitably "Nee-chee-vore" prevails. If only I could master surrender.

The following day is International Women's Day. As far as holidays go, nothing matches this day – it's such a reversal of status. On this one day of the year the men celebrate women. The daily lunch prepared by the office cook is expanded to a banquet of caviar with blinis, raw salmon, borsch, salads, favourite dishes, dessert, chocolates and champagne.

Before lunch I follow the aroma into the kitchen. I ask the cook how she prepares a dish called pelmeni – soft, doughy meat dumplings shaped like Chinese wantons.

She tells me, "I hand knead dough and wrap a mixture of lean beef, pork fat, butter, oil, onions and salt and pepper, and then boil it in water. Each family has its own slight variation of the recipe. My mother taught me. So, I expect you to eat as many dumplings as a Russian man does."

About half an hour later all 11 of the office staff sit at the table and the celebration begins. The men fuss over the women, giving each of them a bunch of flowers and kissing them on the cheeks. Superstition prevails. Each bunch is arranged with an odd number of stems. God help anyone if they receive an even number of flowers. Very soon the toasts commence. The men praise the wisdom of our female colleagues. They appreciate them for their capabilities, their beauty and their patience.

I'm surprised by how elated the women are as they receive so much attention and praise. It's as if all is forgiven for the chauvinistic behaviour they have to deal with the rest of the year. As the women are showered with appreciation and flattery, their delight intoxicates all of us.

After I leave the dining room I reflect on the ways in which the whole structure of government organisations and society is skewed in favour of men.

The next morning I'm off to discuss a proposed joint venture south of Moscow. To be honest, the last thing I want is to invest our hard-earned cash with a bunch of novice entrepreneurs. There's just too much opportunity for grief. This trip really is a waste of time. Sometimes I make decisions when my gut instinct tells me otherwise. Basically, I'm down here to please Vlad. It's his idea and his contact. He doesn't often get much of a say, and he's been as irritable as buggery lately, so I'm trying to humour him.

This isn't the first joint venture we've investigated, but the conclusion I draw is always the same. Trust is a fundamental element of life, but it just isn't in abundance here. It's understandable. The old Russians have been physically and psychologically hammered since the beginning of time, not only by others but by their own. They don't trust each other, so how the hell are they going to trust me?

So now here I am talking to them. The main man disparagingly claims the enterprise has gone broke because of the ineptitude of the previous management.

"The fish rots from the head down. If the chief isn't doing his or her job of leading and communicating, or if their ethics aren't right, the fish begins to rot, starting at the head. That's what happened here."

Shit, there's no truer statement than that. What a pearler.

As the meeting fizzles out I make a few meaningless and non-committal comments that effectively give little hope. Despite my obvious apathy, we're invited to visit a military firing range for a few rounds of pistol target shooting. The firing range is dual-purpose: it trials Russian missile and armaments technology, and it's used to test captured weaponry from Afghanistan, such as US-made Stinger missiles. It's also close enough to

Moscow to allow the upper echelons to view the incendiary displays.

Dressed in his summer uniform, the army colonel who runs the firing range greets us with great bonhomie. His primary role is to supervise the facility. As usual, it's a boys only affair, with Vlad translating. A building used as a viewing platform for the hierarchy sits on the north side of the sealed quadrangle. A small man-made hillock providing the backdrop to a series of targets is located on the opposite side. The observation area of the range is ringed with floodlights mounted on poles. The colonel presents a collection of pistols and rifles.

We each choose one and begin firing. The tempo of the event escalates as every bloke shows off his prowess with a gun in hand. Make my day, you sucker! *Bang, bang, bang, bang.* You beauty! A bull's eye. Every bull's eye hit is celebrated with a slug of fire water. Things get loose. There are near misses, and then shots that completely miss the hillock are celebrated. The banter becomes increasingly raucous.

The colonel, who has joined in the party, suddenly targets a floodlight, fires a round, and glass sprays onto the car park. What a spectacle. Encouraged by our applause and guffawing, he fires in quick succession until every floodlight surrounding the quadrangle has been vandalised. As he chortles his eyes reveal the glee of anarchy. It's a snapshot of indifference, and how wanton it can get when we just don't care anymore.

It's exactly how I feel, mate. I don't give a fuck anymore either. I don't give a fuck about doing business here, or making money, or any other fucking thing. I don't actually know what I want any more.

Back at our accommodation the vodka is amplifying the chaos within me. I'm in a state of mind I refer to as "fucked in the head". It's a state in which my thoughts are erratic and very, very loud. I feel like every aspect of my world is rapidly shrinking and I feel more isolated than ever. I tip another oversized vodka back without toasting.

"Grigori, have you considered going to see a psychiatrist?" Vlad asks.

I'm appalled. Anger surges through my body. I try to hold it back but I can't.

"Fuck you, ya arrogant prick. You're the one who should see a shrink."

Looking affronted he says, "Grigori! Your behaviour is becoming very intense and unpredictable."

The intensity of the anger increases. My eyes feel like they're going to explode and my voice shouts out: "That's great coming from a fucking Russian."

I struggle to contain myself as I stand up. I want to smack the self-righteous bastard in the head. He stands in response. My aggression is displaced by fear as we glare at each other. A moment of apprehension suspends each of us and then we lunge at each other. His strength surprises me as we grapple each other. I thought I'd be much stronger, but I'm not. We are equally matched. Very quickly I stop when I glimpse the madness. Vlad stops also.

"Fuck you," is all I can say.

I turn away and make my way to bed. There's no way I'm going to see a fucking shrink.

It's the next morning and I feel terrible about what I said and did the night before. The guilt hits me like a freight train full of despair. I was the perpetrator of the antagonism. Normally I don't get pissed off in a nasty, aggressive way. It's more like gnarly belligerence. I get so cranked up I want to take on the world and that scares people sometimes. Shit, sometimes I even scare myself. But this violence has broken new ground. I've never been physically violent before. I realise that the analogy of "The fish rots from the head down" applies to me. I don't enjoy being fucked in the head like this. I've had enough of living like this. I don't like what I've become.

I cover my mouth with the palm of my left hand. I feel depressed. What can I do? I realise that I'm becoming harder by the day. The gentleness within seems to have dwindled. Maybe it's gone forever. I've fortified myself so much that access to the real me is impossible. They say you have to be a hard man to do business in Russia. The reality is you have to be harder than the Russians because you're on their turf, a sitting duck. A few of my mates have been telling me I've become a hard man. There's not much I can do. It goes with the territory. I have to protect myself.

The problem is, toughening is not what I seek. This approach to life has become devoid of enthusiasm and freshness and love. I seldom derive any pleasure from any outcome. I'm moving further and further away from what I crave. I apologise to Vlad, but it's clear some connection has been lost.

When I arrive back in Moscow I call Monica. I tell her what happened with Vlad.

She says, "You poor thing. Why don't you take a week off when you get home. We can go over to the lake."

It strikes me how she supports me through all of it. She could just as easily have accosted me about my propensity to create these situations.

"That would be good. I need a break."

She continues, "You have to be the most courageous man I know."

Again I'm taken aback by her love for me. "You know, I've made more money in the last year than I could have ever imagined and I'm probably the unhappiest I've ever been."

"Maybe it's time to take a break and do what you really want. You've been working too hard for so long now."

I get off the phone and think about how I've been working pretty much every waking moment for all this time in Russia. The only privacy and solitude I've experienced is when I've been in the flat in Moscow by myself for maybe three nights a month. It would be nearly impossible for any Westerner to travel around the Soviet Union more than me. I've probably been more exposed at the coalface of these changes than any other English-speaking businessman. And through it all, Vlad has been there with me, through thick and thin, in every moment.

The only respite we've had from each other is when I listen to music while we fly. I've thrashed the same albums for more than two years – Madonna, Billy Idol and Texas. Punk hammers me too much these days. Although the boys at home would mock me for listening to Madonna, she gives me hope. It's bizarre, but she inspires me.

I sit at the table and think about the intensity of my abnormal life. Grimacing, I nod my head from side to side and say aloud, "Jesus. No wonder I'm fucked in the head."

ELEVEN

I'm back home in Christchurch, but I don't quit. I don't know how to change direction. To be honest, the only thing I enjoy about Russia these days is collecting art. They say fine art offers us something every time we look at it. That resonates with me. A lot of the art I've collected sings to my soul. I love the depth of it, the way it draws me in and the way I engage with it. It calms me down and I appreciate that.

A few weeks ago Merv hauled me up to his Wellington office and explained how he had the opportunity to sell three interesting technologies developed by the Soviet military. Aware that my passion for Russia has waned, he piqued my interest with the offer of 10 per cent of any profit derived from any successful outcome. It was a good strategy. I'm more enthusiastic now than I've been for a long time.

This is how it goes. Merv has been selling bulk food products into St Petersburg. Such business activity requires the protection from a "roof", or a mafia group. From all accounts, the Mafia Dude, as I'll call him, is a good partner. As well as ensuring there is security in any dealings Merv has, the Mafia Dude is also open to involving Merv in some new business opportunities, such as this. It doesn't stop Merv sleeping with a shotgun on his bed when he's in St Petersburg though.

In addition to protection, the Mafia Dude derives income from casinos, but he's decided it's time to move into a more socially acceptable segment of the economy, one that won't give him the grief of competing for territory with other mafia dudes. Commercialising emerging technologies is his new focus. The Mafia Dude has secured an interest in some out-there technologies, but he needs a trustworthy foreign partner in order to sell the intellectual property to a suitable Western buyer. Who knows, the buyer might be a multinational specialising in the development and distribution of technology.

The Mafia Dude has teamed up with a creative genius who developed many technologies within the military complex during the Cold War. The inventions have diverse applications beyond the military arena in the wider manufacturing and consumer sectors. The know-how and the Genius have been closely guarded by the state, but as the structures have collapsed the technologies have become accessible. The potential is vast.

So here I am in St Petersburg again. We've just been collected from our hotel by three top-end Mercs. The driver of my car looks like a useful sort of a character to get you out of a tight spot. Merv and the Mafia Dude are in the middle car, and I'm in the rear car with a scientist we've brought with us, and Vlad. We are on our way to meet the Genius.

We make our way to a mansion located on a small island in the Niva River. Brezhnev used it as his Leningrad dacha. The location is perfect. It's close to the centre of St Petersburg and yet isolated by the river. It's a bizarre scene: Brezhnev's dacha, forbidden technology, a mafia outfit, a genius and a couple of shufflers from New Zealand.

The Genius has a PhD in chemistry and another in philosophy. He tells us that to allow the development of these creations he meditates, progressively focusing on the stillness within, and that allows the knowledge to flow to him. This weird shit is all well and good, but all I want to do is to find out how the technology works – get a look at something tangible, something that actually works from a practical perspective – and get out of here.

Technology number one: the Genius has devised a simple, low-temperature chemical reaction that alters the structure of graphite, enhancing its natural ability to absorb all sorts of compounds such as oil and industrial pollutants. It has the potential to purify water from oil and contaminants, to purify air from pollutants, and, who knows, it could even be a highly effective medium for cigarette filters.

We are led outside onto the lawn, where three bodyguards lift an old cast-iron bath into position. In true form the bath is missing one foot. The hoods prop it up with some wood and proceed to fill it with water. It reminds me of a recent quote by the notoriously tongue-tied Prime Minister, Viktor Chernomyrdin: "We wanted it to be better, but it turned out as usual." To initiate the process, graphite powder is placed in a galvanised pail, then the Genius adds a liquid of secret composition (we are informed it's very cheap to prepare). The mixture spontaneously combusts, popping and banging as black smoke wafts from the receptacle. The reaction dies out after about 10 minutes, and the expanded graphite is ready for application.

In the interim, one of the likely lads has emptied a jerry can of oil onto the surface of the water in the bath. The Genius sprinkles the modified graphite into the bath. Instantly the graphite and oil coagulate to form oily clumps on the surface. Scooping the black material from the surface of the bath with a very fine fish net, similar to those sold in pet stores, one of the hoods ladles it into a large bucket. Crystal clear, completely uncontaminated water is all that remains in the bath.

"Not only that," preens the Genius, "but the oil can be extracted from this matter in its purity." Wearing protective gloves, he squeezes a clump, and clean oil drains from the mass.

This has to be a winner. The potential applications are vast. It's so simple and effective. This could minimise the impact of potential environmental disasters anywhere in the world. How cool is that? Let's sell it to 3M or a similar business. I could make some serious dosh from this. Despite knowing he's onto a winner, the Mafia Dude looks even more angst ridden than me.

Technology number two in the trilogy, and this is very intriguing. "Nothing complex about it," the Genius says, puffing his chest out. "I have the process running at home in my study."

The Genius has downloaded from the stillness within (yeah, good one) a chemical process for producing 30 grams of a very rare isotope every 24 hours. The isotope functions as if it has access to a perpetual supply of energy. When a beam of energy, such as light, is directed onto a very small quantity, it responds by radiating a unique energy, a quantum more powerful than it receives. The isotope was initially developed to allow for the identification of military hardware and personnel when a beam of light is directed at it from a long distance, such as from a helicopter or plane.

"The isotope has many possible uses," the Genius explains. "We have recently commenced discussions with the reserve bank of a European country to investigate the viability of implanting unique identification marking on credit cards to prevent credit card fraud. An application such as this requires a minuscule quantity of the isotope."

Before I left home I undertook some cursory research and uncovered an offer on the internet by the US Navy to buy the isotope for $30,000 a gram. If the story has any validity, this means the Genius's home-based chemical process is producing about $900,000 per day, and it implies that the Americans don't have the technology to produce it. He is, therefore, a very wealthy man indeed. So why is he selling this technology? And, who really owns it? The Genius? Or the state? What expectations does the Mafia Dude have?

Soon the meeting is over and we leave the island and make our way in the cars to a manufacturing facility belonging to the military complex located in a suburb of St Petersburg.

Technology number three: single-crystal sapphires are produced here, in any shape or form. The primary application is in missile manufacture.

"Now remember, you're not to talk, only look," I am instructed for the third time in less than 10 minutes. It's been decided I'll be the only foreigner to go inside. The decision has been based on two attributes. The most important is that I look like a Russian, and the lesser is that I'm an engineer. Merv wouldn't know the difference between a car and a tractor, and he looks more like a bloody Irishman than a Russian.

So, it's agreed. Any questions directed at me, or any invitation to talk, will be deflected by the Genius. I love it. Led by someone who works at the joint, the Genius, two bodyguards and I are shown around the facility. Security is lax.

I follow the host into a small workshop dominated by a cylindrical furnace. Electrical cables the size of my forearms are connected to the furnace. Large hydraulic rams mounted at each end of the cylinder, like the ones on a large bulldozer, control the pressure inside. Interesting manufacturing process, but what are we going do with sapphires twice the size of my fist?

We exit from the factory and I indicate to Merv that the cursory inspection was interesting, but it's probably best to have a chat later. We leave in the cars and make our way to a restaurant located in one of the casinos owned by the Mafia Dude. "Nice one," I think as we sit down. I've drawn the short straw. The Mafia Dude has positioned himself with his back to the wall, flanked by two bodyguards. My back is facing the entrance door. Let's hope he hasn't pissed anyone off lately, like the rightful owner of the technology.

The conversation trundles along between Merv and the Mafia Dude, and I drift off, conjuring up visions of us selling the technology for $50 million. I imagine the Mafia Dude's troubled face and his ensuing shouts after we report the price.

"Fifty million dollars! But where's the money? The technology is worth at least $300 million. You should have got $300 million! What have you done with my money? Neveroyatno. I don't believe you. Fifty million – this is nothing. I trusted you. *You bastards!*"

Then I project another scenario in which we have sold the intellectual property satisfactorily, the Genius and the Mafia Dude all live happily ever after, but the KGB are on our tails to inflict retribution for selling highly secret state technologies. I spend the rest of my life looking over my shoulder, like I am now in this bloody casino in St Petersburg, and employing a bunch of hoods to look after my safety.

It's impossible to visualise a happy outcome. Either way, we're on a hiding to nothing. For sure, I'm intrigued by the science and the potential widespread beneficial applications, but to be frank it just doesn't feel right.

I'm just too tired to get genuinely excited. I'm tired of the pace of life and weary from doing business here. If I keep going I'll end up operating on the margins, just like these mafia boys. I crave a normal life again. But most of all I want a respite from the torment in my head.

I've had enough.

I want out.

You have to move quickly here. Running on gut instinct and turning on the balls of your feet is essential. I used to be able to do it. I knew when something was right and when it was not right. But I've lost touch with my intuition. I spend too much time intellectualising and trying to second-guess outcomes, worrying and grappling as I try to decide what to do. Trying to work things out has become incessant – it consumes me. But this time I'm going act on my gut instinct. It's time to get out of Russia. It's over and out for me.

I get Merv alone later and start to roll it out. "Merv, look mate, I don't feel too comfortable about this technology deal. It doesn't feel right," I say.

Looking agitated, Merv says, "What do you mean, it doesn't feel right?"

"I think the technology is too closely linked to the state. The true ownership is murky."

"I don't know, Arnie. Sometimes you're a complicated one."

"You know Russia far better than I do, but have you ever read Churchill's view on Russia in full? I think it's appropriate."

"What, the riddle in an enigma one?"

"Yeah, but there's more to it than what is normally quoted."

Merv shrugs, suggesting he doesn't know. I have the quote written in my notebook and I read it aloud. "I cannot forecast to you the action of Russia. It is a riddle, wrapped in a mystery, inside an enigma, but perhaps there is a key. That key is Russian national interest."

We look at each other and he shrugs again, one of those Russian "What to do?"-type shrugs. Well, I want to do something – I want out. If there is one thing I have no interest in, it's getting between the upper echelons of the state and intellectual property like this.

"Look mate, I've been giving it some serious consideration and I've run out of juice for this game. I've had enough."

"You can't just bail from the business like that."

"Well, I've always said I'd give it a go for five years, and that's long gone." I'm surprised Merv looks so aggrieved. I thought he'd be pleased to see the end of me. But before I go, I want to find out about something that has always troubled me.

"Merv, you know when you usurped the Moscow bloke who was the head of the Soviet Ministry selling deer velvet. Did he ever indicate any displeasure?" I ask.

"You mean Andropov?"

"Yeah, him," I say.

"Of course," Merv replies. "Andropov invited me to an up-market restaurant for lunch. When we arrived there were six other diners there and a classical quartet playing background music. He wasn't happy. He paid the quartet and the other diners to leave, and he paid the restaurant owner to close the restaurant. He launched into a tirade telling me how if I didn't stop meddling in the velvet business immediately he would well and truly fuck me over. He was ranting and shouting like a crazed man."

"What did you do?"

"What could I do? I tried to appease him, but it was too late. The gates were wide open for anyone to get into the velvet business."

"Did he actually do anything?"

"Well, our relationships in the Altai died and we lost a lot in the joint venture farm and the hotel operations."

"Did Popov have any connection with Andropov?"

"Yeah, he did. Popov and Andropov were good mates. Popov was on his payroll."

Incredulous, I say, "While he was working for us?"

"Yeah. In the beginning we were doing hundreds of millions of dollars worth of trade through Andropov's outfit. We needed someone who had direct access to Andropov. He ran the state organisation as if it was his own."

"Did I ever tell you what happened with the delayed containers in the

Altai and the instructions that came from our office?"

"I was aware of the events, but not in any real detail."

I tell him, and as I sit there talking I finally have no doubt about what had been going on. I tell Merv how I have suspected Popov was trying to derail us the whole time. We both pause, and in that instant there is the recognition that much happened around us as we scrambled trying to keep up with the massive scale of the change over the past few years.

"What is Popov up to these days?" I say.

"Didn't you hear? He's dead."

"Dead?" I start getting the feeling that this happens to everyone we do business with. "How?"

"The details are a bit hazy, but it seems he was found dead in an apartment by his wife. Apparently he'd been in a drunken stupor. There's also some suggestion he had been dead for a few days."

The drunken stupor bit sounds familiar. "What about Andropov?"

Merv says, "You'll like this one. It has to be the most implausible story I've ever heard, but apparently he was struck by lightning on a beach in Cuba."

I nod my head almost nonchalantly. It's definitely time to be getting out of this game. Not only because it's getting hairy, but also because I realise how unaffected I am by all this news of death and retribution.

"The cover-ups get more outrageous by the day," I say. Apparently a hit costs US$5000 these days. I suppose if you're going to go, the more unlikely the story the more difficult it is for your family to come to terms with it. "The Prime Minister, the Functionary and the Functionary's son – they all died in mysterious circumstances too."

Looking slightly numb, Merv replies, "Look, their deaths weren't overly mysterious, but they were unlikely." He pauses, "But then we can't forget the caretaker's wife at Kiwi Lodge."

The one who ended up in the New Zealand freezer.

No, it's hard to forget that.

I recollect another half dozen people we've had dealings with who are no longer with us.

"It's amazing we came through it all unscathed. If you think about it, we could easily have been identified as the common link with all of them."

Nodding his head, Merv responds quietly, "Yeah, I know."

"It's something else, isn't it?"

Merv looks at me grimly. "The death that shocked me the most was the shooting of my friend in the mink trade. Shot in the head in a lift."

Not much mystery there.

TWELVE

Monica and I arrived at the Hayman Island Resort in Queensland yesterday. It's rated in the top five resorts internationally and we've both been looking forward to this treat for a long time. Mostly we've been looking forward to the calmness and relaxation that's so conspicuously missing from our daily lives. If I thought just getting away from Russia would do the trick, so far I've been wrong.

A couple of days earlier I was standing in a spray booth getting a suntan for our holiday. A young woman was staring hesitantly at my Y-fronts. She'd never sprayed a bloke before, so instead of giving me a G-string she told me to leave my Y-fronts on. All was well and good until I got home and realised what she'd done. The top of my Y-fronts came up as far as my belly-button and they weren't on straight. So only half of my stomach got tanned, and the lower white part was demarcated by a sloping line. I told myself it wasn't going to ruin the holiday.

And so far it hasn't. We got off to a magical start when our accommodation was upgraded to a contemporary apartment completely decorated in white. It's got white walls, white leather furniture, white curtains, white carpet, white linen, even the artwork is white. Not long after walking into the apartment Monica declared that we should go for anything and everything on offer. I enthusiastically agreed.

Today we took a float plane to a lagoon in the Great Barrier Reef so we could go snorkelling. When I sink beneath the surface the iridescent orange and green and yellow of the fish mesmerise me. Suspended, all I can do is be here and observe. I'm in awe. There's nothing for me to do but be drawn into their colours and shapes. The fish and the exquisite vegetation move and wave with the flow of the water. Everything is perfect, absolutely perfect. Gently rising to the surface I feel completely at ease. As I break the surface my awareness is drawn to the azure sky above, then it gently moves to the light blues on the horizon. It's as if I'm at one with everything.

The next evening we go to one of the restaurants. It has gold-plated cutlery that apparently cost a million bucks. We eat Monica's game fish – earlier in the day she'd landed the biggest Spanish mackerel anyone had caught all season. The sommelier befriends us and plies us with 30-year-old wine and 70-year-old port – at no extra cost. The following day, equipped with champagne and a picnic hamper, we are dropped off by launch on a sandbar elevated a metre above the high-tide mark. There's no one there but us. The day after that we have dinner prepared on our balcony and we top it off with a sail on a yacht at sunset. It's obvious that Monica is enjoying all of it. Life should be just great.

And yet, in spite of my glimpses of deep peace while snorkelling, I keep transporting myself into the future and worrying about starting a new business. If it's not the business, it's some other thing that pulls me away from where I am and what I'm doing. It's like a sick joke: I'm here on the dream holiday but I'm trapped in a continuous dialogue in my head. Monica can't quite understand why I want to start another business when I've achieved everything I set out to do.

"Well, what am I going to do if I haven't got a business?" I ask.

"I don't know. Go fishing? Have a go at relaxing or try to find that peace you're forever looking for."

"I'm not sure peace is possible. We've been here a week and I can't seem to relax. Anyway, I have no interests other than business." What would I be without business? A fringe dweller? I'd be nothing. I'd feel completely inadequate. I'd have nothing to think about.

To add to my state of tension we've been trying for a child and it hasn't been working out. In fact, it's just about time to move to the next step, which is for me to go to Sydney for micro-surgery on my vas. Before the operation the surgeon will try to extract some sperm in case the surgery is unsuccessful. There's no point shagging around. I should get the operation done as soon I can.

⁓

Three weeks later the surgeon has had a poke around but the results aren't looking great. I have a few beers with Cliffy and decide to tell him what's going on. I like being able to share what's going on in my life with a mate. I've missed him.

"If you want some sperm, I can give you some," Cliffy says immediately. "I wouldn't offer it to just anyone, but I'm offering it to you."

Wow, this comes from left field! I can't believe it. What a generous thing to offer. I don't know what to say. After a moment of confusion I say, "Man, that's something else. I really appreciate it. Let's see how things go."

Any doubt I had about the closeness of our friendship has just evaporated.

The conversation moves on to business prospects. I tell him I'm starting another business. I want to create something that Monica and I can be involved in together. "I've realised that if you want to make serious money you need to be close to it, and there's nothing closer than getting your sticky fingers on the lucre in the financial game. But I haven't got the right make up. From what I can tell, the next best thing is to develop a brand. We've researched some ideas and have decided to develop a chain of pet stores. Not your ordinary pet stores, though. We want full-service vet clinics, dog grooming, dog training – every possible pet and pet product you could ever imagine all under one roof."

"A pet shop! You don't even like animals."

"It wasn't my idea. Jonty came up with it. He's on board, both as a shareholder and an active participant. And having Monica involved will add to the business, too. You know how she loves pets. Plus she's a born shopper. She knows what shoppers want."

"First it was gold mining, then Russia, now it's building a chain of pet shops. I don't know, Arnie. Sometimes you're truly random."

"Yeah, I know, mate. But the vision isn't just a pet shop or two. It's to develop a brand throughout New Zealand and Australia. Ultimately we want to list it on the share market. We've spent a year researching the concept. We've looked at what is happening overseas in the same market segment. There's a pet store operator in the US that is one of the fastest growing businesses listed on the NASDAQ. They've gone from seven stores five years ago to 500 today. We want to refine their model by being more focused on technical advice – we want to encourage responsible pet ownership. Plus we want to provide an interactive experience for shoppers, with lots of pets in store."

"Well, frankly," Cliffy says, "I don't know how your pride could let you own a pet shop."

I carry on. "Sixty per cent of households in the English-speaking world have a pet, and most of them love their pets more than any other member of their family." As I say this I think how daft it is that we love pets more than we love each other.

―

A month after we open for business in Christchurch I walk into the store and I'm overcome with dread. The place feels like failure. It feels lifeless, despite having enthusiastic and technically capable staff. I walk to the middle of the retail space and stop in front of a huge aviary fitted around a three-metre landscaped waterfall. Trevor, an Australian sulphur-crested cockatoo, sits on the branch of a tree that has nearly been annihilated by his jaw-like beak. I look directly into Trevor's eyes.

"Fuck off," he squawks.

Despite appreciating Trevor's humour, I go home feeling discouraged. I've got a tiger by the tail, and if I don't do something soon we'll be haemorrhaging financially. I thought I'd front up at the end of each week, fill a canvas bag with Johnny Cash and head home with a smile on my face. It was supposed to provide an income so Monica and I could have some fun in early retirement and live the dream.

I start asking anyone I meet if they've heard of the business. Most have, and thank God for that, because we've been spending a king's ransom on radio and newspaper advertising. When I ask these same people if they know where the store is located, most don't have any idea, even though many of them drive past the high-profile site on a regular basis.

We decide to change our image. Research suggests that the most effective colour combinations are black lettering on a yellow background or white lettering on a red background. We decide to run with the black and yellow and terminate our advertising campaign.

Soon we are attracting a huge number of people to the store. But we can't seem to sell to them. I soon realise that our staff don't know how to sell. I arrogantly thought that most retailers were uninterested in customer service and I didn't want to employ staff who'd worked in that environment. Accentuating our inexperience is the fact that our sales training is effectively non-existent.

I've figured out there are three M's of business growth – money, management and mentoring. I decide to forge ahead into raising funds. My clumsy tongue seems to transform into a silvery one. All the people I contact are keen. The big plus for me is that their life doesn't depend on it. This is a secondary investment for them.

I meet Frank for only the second time. We had our first encounter a month earlier when he called into the office and offered me space in a new retail centre he's developing. During our 30-minute conversation he accosted me with the same questions, but I wasn't in a position to respond. His bald countenance shining, he leans forward with his palms on the table and asks in a gravelly voice, "Now listen, how much dough do ya need?"

You gotta love this guy. I tell him how much we need and add, "But I've already raised half of that."

Frank flicks the tip of his tongue between his lips. "What shareholding does $650,000 give me?"

I quickly do the numbers and tell him.

"How did ya determine that?" he enquires.

"You might recall I was having Deloittes prepare a valuation. We've just received it."

"OK, count me in for $650,000."

After successfully securing investment funds I start making inquiries about management coaching. I've had enough of doing it all alone. I need help to get clarity and direction, to see where I'm losing objectivity. I need guidance from someone who has done what I'm trying to do. All roads lead to a character called Bob. Until recently he was the managing director and a substantial shareholder of one of New Zealand's most successful publicly listed companies. He sounds promising, but getting hold of him proves easier said than done. I finally get his telephone number, but he doesn't answer my multiple phone messages. Nor does he respond to the two letters I send him.

I learnt long ago that tenacity is one of the primary keys to success. I decide to speak to a couple of blokes who know him and ask them to have a word with the elusive Bob. I finally get a call from him a week later.

"Look mate, I've got no interest in pet stores," he growls at me down the phone line.

"Nor do I," I say smoothly. "But I'm onto a winner, and I need guidance and systems to get it to where I want it to go."

He pauses and says, "This is what I'll do. I'll meet you at your store and we can spend the day together. Then I'll give you my view of things. I charge two and a half grand a day." I'm buzzing with excitement when I get off the phone.

Later that week, as promised, I'm waiting at the airport to pick him up. As the passengers walk into the arrivals area, a character dressed in black catches sight of me and starts guffawing. "I was told you look like a Russian!" he says, striding towards me. "It would've been impossible to miss you." I laugh at his cockiness.

An hour later, the cockiness is all mine.

"This is the best retail concept I've seen outside of the one I've just left," Bob enthuses as we review the business. "You've done well. But frankly, you're all over the place."

"Thanks, but I'm not paying you to tell me what I already know. What I want to know is whether you're available to be a director of the company?"

"No," Bob responds immediately. "I'm only prepared to commit myself to giving you guidance one day a month for six months. If everything is going alright at the end of that time we can agree to extend it. Or not."

I hold out my hand and we shake. "Fantastic."

Things are looking up.

⁓

Monica has done what many of our customers have done – fallen in love with a puppy. The current love of Monica's life is a cross between a Chihuahua and a Papillon. This morning she's been walking around with the little thing in her dressing gown – its head and huge ears (with 10-centimetre tassels) hang over the top of the dressing gown pocket. Monica has started calling him Little Arnie. She brought him home wearing a Driza-Bone cowboy jacket, ostensibly to keep him warm, but in reality it was to take the piss out of me – I have an identical human version. Some people say your world is a reflection of yourself. If Little Arnie is anything to go by, I'm in decidedly bad shape.

Never mind. The brand is quickly building recognition that our stores are fun places to shop. We encourage customers to bring their pets shopping and allow staff to bring their fur buddies to work. On any given day there are numerous dogs, colourful parrots on shoulders, and even pet rats. But equally importantly, our stores are becoming places to get sound advice. We win a Retailer of the Year award, and Bob soon tells me he's sufficiently confident in the success of the business that he's keen to invest $250,000. He's also got his old cadre of management from his last business who are looking for a new home.

But everything isn't as rosy as it seems on the outside. I meet Cliffy for a few beers one Friday night and confide, "If the retail judges had access to our financial statements the place wouldn't look anything like Retailer of the Year. To be honest, I feel like an outsider in the retail game. I miss the creativity and comradeship of engineering. In retail you're dominated by the daily budget. Everything is geared to achieve that budget. Every morning we start with a zero balance and we all grind and chisel our way to the budget by 6pm. Then the next day the same thing happens. Day in and day out."

"Then why don't you get out of it?"

"I can't, mate. The shareholders have invested in a growth business, and, as egotistical as this sounds, they've also invested in me. I was the one who painted the big picture, so I can't let them down."

"Well then, you created a rod for your own back."

"Yeah, I know. But this growth model requires us to continually push at every facet of the business. We're forever trying new ideas and stretching the envelope. It all needs money and quite a lot of risk taking."

These confidences I've just shared with Cliffy aren't the only problems. There's worse.

THIRTEEN

Monica is sobbing uncontrollably. It's so sad. We've just been told we can never have children.

I want to cry too, but I can't. My eyes are watering and I feel like I've got a book stuck in my throat. I wipe the tears from my eyes with my fingers and I open my mouth, but I can't say anything. I can't cry. The discomfort is unbearable. I try to comfort her with a hug, but I feel isolated. It wasn't meant to be like this. All she wanted was a big family, in a lovely country home, with a garden and a simple life. I've fucked it up. I'm sorry, but I don't know how to say I'm sorry. We stand in silence in the street outside the fertility clinic.

A few months later Monica and I are lying wide awake in bed. It's 2am on a Saturday morning. My 44th birthday. She asks me how I think our relationship is going. For the first time in a long time I admit that I think we're in bad shape. She agrees. We spend the next three hours discussing separation. We fall asleep together and wake up at nine. By midday we've agreed on the division of our assets and belongings. It's clear each of us has known the end was imminent and we've both thought about the material things we'd like to keep. There's little overlap. We each have our favourite paintings and pieces of furniture.

The next day I talk to a friend about our decision and she suggests we talk to a psychologist. My friend thinks there's hope of saving the relationship. Monica can't understand quite why we should reconsider the decision, but she agrees to come along. I think we're both hoping the psychologist will validate our decision.

She does. After talking to us for a long time she agrees that it's best for us to separate. She says we could spend the time, probably months or even longer, revisiting and working through the things that have happened, but really there has been just too much water under the bridge.

"My only advice is that when you leave here, immediately start putting the practical steps in place to separate." Monica and I look at each other, instantly relieved. Then, turning to look directly at me, the psychologist says, "And I need to see you again as soon as possible. Your stress levels are so elevated that I feel I should award you an honorary doctorate in anxiety. I have an appointment available next Friday at two. Does that suit you?"

"Ah, yes." I knew I was stressed, but a doctorate?

Monica and I leave the psychologist's rooms and walk to a nearby café. We sit down, feeling like we've just completed a marathon without training. After an extended period of numbness Monica says, "That was the best piece of advice anyone could have given us."

I nod. "Better to have the truth than sympathy. Let's take our time getting organised. There's no need to hurry. We can still live together for a while and support each other through the transition."

Staring out the window of the café at nothing in particular Monica says, "That would be good."

I, too, gaze at the nothingness of the grey day outside. I then remember my first encounter with Monica. Her beauty and presence were something I'd never encountered before. It was obvious she had an impact on everyone in the room. I feel more love for her now than I have for a long time, but there's no doubt I know this is the right thing for us to do. Still, I can't bring myself to apologise. I feel so shut down. I haven't got the courage to look sideways, let alone face my demons.

At my first session with the psychologist she says, "I would rate your ambient level of anxiety at eight out of ten." Then she smiles in a comforting way. I feel safe, and also glad that I can share my torment with a professional. God knows, I've shared it enough with Cliffy. He hasn't been able to do much except reinforce my despair with similar stories of helplessness.

"Well," I respond, "if you rate my anxiety at eight, then I can tell you it peaks at 10 many times every day."

Soon enough, and inevitably, we end up on the topic of Monica. I say, "A day didn't go by without Monica making me laugh. Even now she cracks me up. A couple of days ago we were driving past a wedding. She pretended to wind the window down and then she yelled out, 'Don't do it! Don't do it! Don't marry the bastard!'"

I sigh. "To be fair, I wanted to be there for her, but in reality I wasn't. I just didn't show up. Whenever I was with her I was incessantly thinking about work, and near the end I was fantasising about other women. I couldn't help it. It was maniacal. This is how stupid it got: a mate was describing a woman he'd met and I immediately haired off into a make-believe relationship with her." Shaking my head I look at the psychologist and ask, "Can you believe I was infatuated with a woman I'd never even met?"

She raises her eyebrows but doesn't respond. What could she say?

"In the short time since we've split I've been amazed at how all the women I've been infatuated with hold absolutely no appeal for me. It's completely unviable for me to date or have a relationship with any one of them."

Back in the psychologist's office for the second visit the following week I notice I feel lighter than the last time. Maybe I'm down to seven out of ten? I tap the top of my stomach with my left hand. "I often have this dull discomfort right here. It seems to be there when I'm feeling geared up. The only way I can calm down is to have a joint. That settles me down – for a while anyway."

"How often do you smoke?"

"Most days."

"Why do you think you smoke so much?"

I'm enjoying this little exploration with the psychologist. She's nice. I like her. "Well, I suppose I look forward to being wasted. I love it. Well, maybe not everything about it. I don't enjoy the hammering my respiratory system receives, or the intensity of the chatter in my head sometimes, or the murkiness the morning after, but the anticipation of moving into an altered state is what inspires me to smoke as much as I do. It's a state where I have a chance to escape the anxiety, where I can appreciate the things around me more, things that I don't normally notice, and I especially enjoy the creative space I get into. You know? The ideas that come from nowhere."

"It won't be doing you any good. I'm dumbfounded that most people who smoke marijuana think it's a relaxant. Its effect is quite the opposite. The active ingredient of marijuana actually stimulates the flow of adrenaline in the body."

"Funny you should say that. I began noticing a few months ago that it did actually wind me up rather than relax me." I chuckle at myself. "It only took me 25 years to notice it."

"Do you smoke with others?"

"Yeah, I do. I dunno how I could interact with most people without it. I struggle to string more than a few words together when I'm straight. When I smoke I feel like I can communicate naturally, unencumbered by self-doubt." I pause. "Yeah. It allows me to express myself, to be who I really am."

"Are you aware that you have no difficulty expressing yourself right now?"

"Yeah, but this is different."

"How?'

"Well, it's a non-threatening environment. You're here to help me and I want to change, and I think being open and interactive will allow me to change quickly." I continue to reflect on my social behaviour. "When I socialise under the influence with people I don't know that well, or people I don't feel that comfortable with, I can take on a superior, combative approach. I think some people think I'm a bit arrogant."

"Why don't you try reducing the amount you smoke? You may find that you don't need to smoke to socialise."

"Yeah, I want to. I can do without it." I pause for a long moment and then say, "I want to give up drinking as well."

When the hour appointment draws to a close the psychologist says, "I have a colleague that I refer some clients to. She's a physiotherapist who specialises in stress management. Here's her business card. I suggest you arrange an appointment with her."

A short visit to the stress management therapist reveals I've spent my whole life hyperventilating. My short, shallow, wheezy breaths through my mouth deliver insufficient oxygen to my respiratory system and inhibit the proper expulsion of carbon dioxide from my lungs. This apparently alters the pH in my body, and this chemical imbalance has been disturbing my ability to be calm and to focus.

"Extend your diaphragm slowly, pushing it out, and allow your breath to be drawn in through your nose, but not forcibly," the therapist instructs.

I never thought I'd get lessons in how to breathe.

"Keep the rise and fall motion of your diaphragm steady so the contraction and expansion of your lungs remains constant throughout each cycle. Breathe slowly. That's it. Raise the diaphragm gently and the lungs will exhale then continue to smoothly lower the diaphragm and notice the lungs filling. That's it. You've got it."

Until now, I've found it impossible to breathe through my nose, but hopefully this will change.

"Some yogis taught that the best way to regulate the nervous system, and in turn the mind and the body, was through proper breathing," the therapist says. "They said that the breath was the most important thing for survival, and consequently they considered the diaphragm the most important muscle in the body."

I've always known that I breathe like a steam locomotive pulling a load of coal up an incline. But now I get it: the lungs sit on top of the diaphragm, they don't have muscles of their own. The lungs need the diaphragm to do the work rather than ancillary muscles around the lungs, like the chest muscles.

"The internal motion of the diaphragm also stimulates the blood circulation to the organs so they function better," she tells me. "Your shoulders and neck have been so stiff because when we get stressed our tongue becomes elevated, causing our neck and shoulders to tighten. Clenched fists are also a common tell-tale sign of stress, and this action also applies tension to our forearms, biceps and shoulders."

She explains to me how to notice what is happening with my tongue when I get stressed. If it's raised, then I should release it and focus on my breathing. I leave her office feeling calm and full of optimism. I feel for the first time that a stress-free life is within my reach.

But a few weeks later my illusion is shattered. I'm sitting outside the clinic waiting for my fourth appointment. The breathing therapist hasn't arrived yet and I decide to use the time to concentrate on breathing with my diaphragm. In the beginning my nasal passages felt tender, but they've settled down now. I close my eyes and focus on the movement of my diaphragm.

Suddenly the therapist arrives, breaking me out of my reverie. She's here and she's in a frenzy. She'd misplaced the keys to the office. She's absolutely stressed to the max. Bemused, I ask myself, how can this be? Isn't a stress management therapist supposed to be stress free?

Later that week I talk to the psychologist about it. "This breathing technique is a great thing," I say. "I feel much better. But when I saw her stressed I knew what she had to offer wasn't enough. Her guidance has been beneficial, but I want more peace than this technique can provide." I want more than just the odd respite from stress. I want to be completely stress-free.

A week later Monica is about to walk out the door of our house for the last time. Using her index finger like a weapon she jabs me in the chest. "Get your hearing tested."

Either I've been the archetypal husband and haven't been listening or my hearing really is severely impaired. Maybe it's time to do something, because Monica isn't going to do it for me. It's over and out and I'm home alone. I've agreed to stay here until the house sells so she has a clear run at starting a new life. It's the least I can do.

I follow Monica's instructions and have my hearing checked by my GP. He places a tuning fork on each side of my head and determines that my hearing on the left side isn't what it should be. Always one to present the worst possible outcome first, he tells me it's possible I have a brain tumour. He refers me to an audiologist, who confirms the results from the tuning fork test. Yes, my hearing is impaired on the left side.

I'm sent for an MRI. The magnets clatter and bang away, then the noise stops and the platform I'm lying on ejects me from the tunnel of the scanner. The radiographer talks to me through the headphones I have on, "We need to inject some dye into your arm. You may notice a metallic taste in your mouth, but there's nothing to be concerned about. If you feel nauseous, just press this button."

Oh shit.

My radiology mate claimed there was less than a one per cent chance they'd need to inject some contrast into my blood stream. Now it's happening. The dye is injected and I return to the tunnel for a full scan of my head. The following week I receive a phone call from the ear, nose and throat specialist. "Now, before I start, you haven't got cancer. But you do have a benign tumour growing on the nerves running from the brain to your left ear. It's called an acoustic neuroma. It's treatable."

Rather alarmed I ask, "How is it treated?"

"We access the tumour by cutting a hole in your skull and, effectively, we scrape the tumour from the nerves. It will take up to 12 months to fully recover from the surgery. I've made an appointment for you to visit me tomorrow. Are you available at 11am?"

I get off the phone and I'm overcome with emotion. Monica and I still work in the same building. I open the door of my office and wave her in. Distraught, I tell her the news. After less than a minute of talking I stop. The dark clouds separate, revealing bright blue skies. I get it. This is my way out! This is my legitimate exit from this business and every other possible idea of a business. The responsibility I have felt towards my shareholders has trapped me. But this is the opportunity to change my life, to live in peace. I definitely don't want to cock it up.

I leave the office, literally punching the air with my fist as I walk down the stairway to the car park. I drive home full of bliss and joy. My desire has been delivered. And we've been prudent, too. We've had good succession planning in place for the past 12 months. The guy we ultimately want to run the outfit can step up straight away.

That night a group of us get together for a jog and then a yarn over a beer. Jonty looks troubled as I ecstatically inform him about my discovery.

"Arnie, are you sure you're not in some form of denial?"

"You've got no idea how life-changing this is for me. I don't know where it's all leading, but I have an overwhelming sense of freedom."

Since Jonty is a shareholder in the business I try to couch my explanation in such a way that he doesn't become uneasy about the safety of his investment. But he continues to look concerned about my behaviour.

The next day I meet with a professor of interventional radiology and the ear, nose and throat specialist. The specialist tells me that four nerves run from the brain to an area near the ear. Two are for balance, one for hearing and the other for facial control. A tumour has grown on this cluster of nerves and has started pressing against my brain stem. Because the membrane around the brain will be ruptured during surgery, there's a chance of meningitis, not to mention the dreaded facial palsy. Most definitely my hearing will be damaged further and my balance will be even wonkier than it is now. A month in bed after the surgery will be followed by about 12 months of rehabilitation. There's a one per cent chance of death. The neurosurgeon is available to perform the procedure in a month's time.

I'm given the names and phone numbers of a couple of people who've had the operation. I call one of them. He's in his mid-thirties and the father of a young family. He had the surgery two years ago. He tells me he can't run, nor can he chew or smile on the left hand side. His left eyelid doesn't function, so he places drops in his eye, which is all well and good until the spring and summer winds blow. He experiences intense headaches often, but especially when he laughs or coughs. For a moment this worries me, but as far as I'm concerned the tumour is in there and it has to come out.

Monica offers to move back into the house with me for the first few weeks to nurse me through the worst of it. Can you believe that?

I decide to give my radiology mate a call. He lives in Melbourne and he's an expert in all things relating to the brain. But most importantly he has an extremely pragmatic approach to medicine.

"Do you want a caved-in face for the rest of your life?" he asks frankly. "Listen, you're 44 and single. If you have this operation there's a 70 per cent chance of sporting a facial palsy. Arnie, you have enough trouble lunging on women as it is. Imagine what it'll be like when you've got a distorted face! You'll never get another woman."

Shit. He's right.

"Don't do it. Come over here and have your head torched with the rays. If it doesn't work, there's a chance you'll be able to follow up with surgery in a few years' time. By then you'll have a new woman."

"But I've got the neurosurgeon and the ENT boy lined up to do the job next month," I protest.

"Don't let them anywhere near you. Whatever surgeons operate on never fully heals. Last year I had surgery on my finger and it still isn't right, and it probably never will be. Remember what the commando did to your nose when he removed those polyps?"

"Ah yeah." I think back to how my nose was accidentally broken during a straightforward procedure a few years back.

"There's no conclusive evidence that surgery is more effective than radiotherapy."

"Can you organise it over there for me?"

"Yeah, course I can. No problem."

I decide to take the Melbourne option and cancel the surgery.

Meanwhile I'm still seeing the psychologist. We have been discussing my neuroma, and my intense feelings of liberation. We come back to discussing my relationships with women.

"I used to maintain a bloke should never get into a relationship," I say at the next appointment.

"When did you first adopt this position?" she asks.

"Maybe when I was six or seven. I can recall being adamant at a very early age that I never wanted to have a girlfriend. I definitely didn't want to get married. I took this approach because I thought my parents' marriage and my two brothers' relationships were severely flawed."

Thinking back, I begin chuckling. "This approach did, however, present a challenging dilemma when I reached adolescence. It became very apparent that I was attracted to lots of girls, so my dogma evolved: it was possible to have a liaison with a girl, preferably succeeding in having sex with her, but I was prohibited from revisiting her. The mantra 'Never go back' was firmly established by the time I was 15. I was disturbed whenever any of my friends started a relationship, or even if they had a friendship with a girl. I'd say, 'What on earth are you doing? Most certainly shag her, but don't have a relationship. You won't be happy. It'll only lead to misery, mate.' The problem was that as I grew older my desire for love grew. I was often besotted by a girl, but I was tortured by my inability to start a relationship."

"Given your propensity to think that a relationship wasn't for you, how did you manage to commit yourself to Monica?"

"I loved her. She was a good woman, and I knew I wanted to share my life with a good woman. We were well suited. It was easy to have fun together and we enjoyed each other's sense of humour. We wanted the same things. We were both ambitious. We wanted to be successful and to live well. I pause. "Actually, I still love her."

"And how do you feel about relationships now?"

"I'm probably less open than I was. I'm practically incapable of letting anyone get close enough for me to really experience love. It's funny. As well as peace, it's love I want. I want to be in love again. I enjoy the intimacy and happiness and contentment when I'm in love. I'd love to be able to do it again. But I'm too wary of relationships."

"The only way you're going to learn how to have a relationship is to practise," she tells me.

"I suppose that's true," I admit. I go home and feel sad about Monica not being in my life. I miss her.

The next week I'm off to Melbourne for six weeks of daily nuking. I set myself up in a serviced apartment in South Yarra after deciding that this thing inside my skull shouldn't interfere with my desire to party. Monica comes to settle me in for the first four days. I appreciate the support, doubly so given that she has a new man in her life.

I'm lying with my head secured to the cast-steel bed of some computer-controlled apparatus that looks like a huge robot for creating precision machinery. A mouth mould made specifically for my teeth and jaws is fastened to a metal frame that's positioned around my head. The frame is bolted to the bed. The head of the robot swings through arcs programmed to ensure the tumour is accurately struck with the rays.

"Now, you need to remain as still as possible for the next 20 minutes," the radiographer instructs me.

I hope my wee chest doesn't do what it has a propensity to do: break into a coughing spasm. We don't want to torch my brain and brain stem, now, do we? If the rays hit the stem it's all over red rover. Here's the thing: the rays are accurate to within 1 mm and I've just been told to move my head up relative to the mouth guard. But it's impossible to know how far I've moved. It feels like the gap between my teeth and the guard has allowed me to move way more than one millimetre. Oh well, nothing to do but lie back and think of England.

I get into the swing of having my treatment at 1pm every week day, returning home for a two-hour nap, and then meeting up with friends and having a night out. My three-month resting period actually gives me a chance to unwind, de-stress and start thinking about how I can live life with more harmony – and not just by breathing through my nose. I start being more careful about my decision making. I continue to feel light and even content because I'm doing things that I love doing instead of doing things that I don't really want to do. These choices make me feel lighter and uplifted rather than heavy and uncomfortable. I've realised that my ambitions of owning a mansion, several holiday homes and having 10 mill in the bank is just nonsense. I haven't got the ability to accumulate that sort of filth and it isn't going to make me happy anyway.

Day after day my resolve to take a different approach to life strengthens. My expectations lower to the basics: once the house is sold, I'm going to rent for a few years. I have no need of a luxury car nor do I need flash holidays. I focus more on what I want, rather than what I don't want. I ceremoniously turn the television off for the last time and within days I notice how much more time I've got to do the things I'm passionate about. And that feels so energising.

I return to work refreshed and relaxed and with a desire to maintain this relative peace. The new general manager has stepped up to the position and is doing well. In my new role as managing director I will focus on strategy, a far less stressful role than being responsible for staff and operations. However, this newfound me gets a shaking when our human resources manager gives me a written summary of my 15-page personality profile. It reads:

> This is an extremely competitive and goal-orientated individual who can be aggressive in resolving uncertainties. Winning is very important to him and he will seek to lead the way when facing new challenges. He will not hesitate to take chances, assume risks and is comfortable being accountable for getting things done. He faces troublesome issues, resistance, and obstacles willingly and despite them, or maybe because of them, he will be determined to attain his goals. He is ambitious, needs to succeed, and not only welcomes but often expects authority over others as well as responsibility for them. He is exceptionally assertive and success-orientated. He will be very dissatisfied unless he can achieve his goals and he is so aggressive that it is unlikely he will let anyone stop him.

And so it goes on . . . I'm flabbergasted. I can't believe I'm that aggressive and that hard. I reread it several times and finally decide to track down

Monica and get her to read it.

"Is this really what I'm like?" I ask.

She looks up at me from the report with a slightly mystified look on her face.

"Yeah. You are aware of what you're like, aren't you?"

"Well, no, I don't think I am." I take the document back from her. "This is awful."

"It's not awful, it's just how you are," she responds.

I'm dumbfounded. "It must have been difficult living with someone like this."

She raises her eyebrows and nods her head. "It certainly had its moments."

I leave the office for the rest of the day. I know I'm driven and that I can get a bit carried away, but this is terrible. We do this same personality profiling for all our staff, but I bet our human resources manager hasn't seen anything like this before.

That same week I have to go in for a six-monthly check-up at the doctor. It's part of my new strategy to monitor my progress. The personality profile is still running through my mind.

"What was that reading again?" the GP asks the undergraduate medical student who has just taken my blood pressure. She takes it again.

"Wow. That's high," he says, looking over her shoulder.

"I know what the problem will be," I say. I tell him I was out last night with three mates. We all had an E and things got cranking. I bought a round of eight straight tequilas, with the usual condiments. Each had one shot and then abstained from the remainder of my hospitality. Oh well, waste not, want not, I'd thought and knocked back the remaining four shots. I must have had a momentary black-out because the next thing I knew I was dancing on a bar top with a young blonde.

The GP looks at me as if to say, what the hell is an E? And what's a middle-aged bloke doing hammering himself with chemicals? "Your blood pressure is too high," he says finally, "and the results from the blood test show that your cholesterol is too high too."

I've been resisting taking the cholesterol-lowering pharmaceuticals. I want to try a natural approach. On the way home I reflect that my public behaviour might soon start to have an impact on our business. This is a small city, and the brand has high recognition as a professionally run ethical business. My continued wayward behaviour could become common knowledge. I never thought I'd develop a brand that was more respectable than I am. Maybe there was something to that personality profile.

Within a month the new-found peace and harmony from my three months of rest has nearly disappeared. I still have moments of sadness when I wish I hadn't cocked things up with Monica. I'm back to suffering from insomnia, getting wound up about this and that, worrying how the hell we're going to make a decent return on our investment in the business. And so on. I don't completely regress. I guess the difference is I notice my own behaviour now. In the past I was so wound up in it all I had no idea what was going on.

I decide to move to Wellington. If three months off work can't deliver permanent calmness, then maybe relocating to another city will help. If I'm out of sight of the Christchurch head office, hopefully the head office will be out of *my* head. Plus I like the social life in Wellington. There are plenty of single women up there and no one knows me, so I should have a better chance of finding the love of my life. I'm excited about the opportunity to reinvent myself. It will be so liberating to leave my demons behind in Christchurch.

That weekend I catch a flight to Wellington to check things out. I'm not willing to commit myself to a permanent move without testing the waters first. I meet up with a couple of friends who offer me a chance to go on a blind date. Apparently their friend is the same age as me, she's divorced without children, and she's currently designing her own home. She's also a successful entrepreneur, apparently managing three businesses simultaneously. Maybe she'll be too much for me?

Oh Jesus! I'm shuddering on the inside as a woman joins our group for the evening. She's apparently the one I've been waiting for, although she's completely unaware that this is a set-up by our mutual friend. She has short blonde hair cut in an unusual way and I notice she has a great figure. She's wearing high-heeled boots and a red leather jacket. But, although she's attractive and wearing high-quality clothing, from my perspective she seems way too intense – and too straight. She immediately walks to the bar and buys herself a drink, thus depriving me of the opportunity to buy one for her. How could anyone think I'd be keen on this woman? I'm keen, or some would say driven, to meet a woman I can spend the rest of my life with, but this one looks like a dud.

Oh well, I'm here and so is she.

I begin sharing with her my view that Wellington is populated with the most empowered women on the planet. Most women I know here are successful entrepreneurs or are at the peak of their careers, while many blokes are languishing. At this point in time the Prime Minister, the CEO of the largest publicly listed company, the Mayor, the Attorney General and the Governor General are all women. "I think it's great," I venture. "Let's face it, men have been at the helm for centuries and all we seem to do is continually lurch from one war to another, or alienate some group of the population in one way or another."

"Women are more empowered now," Esther the set-up agrees, "but many men appear to struggle with successful women. It's difficult to find a man who isn't intimidated."

Around midnight three of the women leave the bar rather abruptly. It has come down to Esther and me. I could be in.

"I've got this theory about kissing," I say to her. "You can determine the compatibility of a couple if they kiss well together. I think the kiss is truly the most telling interaction that two people can have."

She responds immediately. "Well, let's try it then."

Reaching across we kiss each other tenderly on the lips.

"Stop it! Stop it! It's time to go."

Lobbing ice cubes at us, the bar staff look less than impressed. It's been close to quarter of an hour since we started kissing and the bar is now empty. On the flight back to Christchurch I reflect that the idea of moving to Wellington has become significantly more appealing.

FOURTEEN

Tapping my right temple the GP says, "The problem is in your head, it's not your pecker."

In anguish for the past 36 hours, I've finally made it to his clinic. I'm feeling awful. Two weeks after I met Esther I got her into bed. We'd had an afternoon and evening of discovery, all the time liking one another more and more. It was wonderful. We'd barbequed lobster on the fire outside and we'd drunk a lot of good wine. I knew it was good wine because I'd paid a fortune for it. And then it happened. We were all ready to go and my pecker wouldn't function. The bloody thing just hung there, flaccid. I was gutted. I thought I had more testosterone than you could poke a stick at and now the bloody thing wouldn't even work.

Reluctantly the GP prescribes Viagra.

"How can this happen to me?" I demand later that week from the psychologist. "I'm only 45. I've fantasised about women forever, and I'm lucky I've still got my eyesight after all the years of masturbation. Now I meet someone I like and my penis won't do the job." I pause for a moment and then admit, "Actually, I was with a woman a month ago and I had no problem. In fact, we had a great time. Come to think of it, I've successfully had sex with a few women over the last six months."

"What was different about those women compared to Esther?" the psychologist asks.

After pondering the question for a moment, I start talking. "They weren't women I wanted to see again. I had no expectations of them or myself. These encounters were never going to lead to any relationships. I guess I wasn't feeling self-conscious, and maybe I wasn't judging them."

"So maybe your judgements or expectations inhibited your performance with Esther? How did she deal with your erectile dysfunction?"

"She was fine. She didn't see it as her problem. She saw it as my problem. And she didn't necessarily see it as a physical dysfunction. She thought it was a head issue. So that made it easier for me."

"Well, that's good, isn't it?" the psychologist asks, trying to shore me up.

"So much for me not having any baggage," I comment wryly.

"Well, why don't you use this as an opportunity to learn how to be in a relationship? Why don't you give her a call and see if she wants to give it another try? I suggest you try doing nothing other than kissing this time. Don't attempt anything else. OK?"

"OK. I'll give her a call and see if she's up for it."

I call Esther and lucky for me she's keen for a rematch. We follow the psychologist's instructions and our physical interaction is kept above the neckline for about 20 minutes, but my cock is rearing to go. So I suggest we break the rules and play further. It all works. Yay! I'm back on track.

Lying alongside me afterwards, Esther asks, "What do you think that was all about?"

"I dunno. Maybe when I get close to someone I like, I get scared."

"Scared of what?"

"I don't know. Maybe scared of being vulnerable. Scared of opening the fortress doors. Who knows?"

At this time I still haven't made a permanent move to the capital. The periods of separation from Esther allow fantasy to flourish wildly and the first evening of a weekend together we always engage in wanton sex. But the next day, sex is interspersed with strained, inarticulate conversation and, for me, prolonged periods of judgement and discomfort. By Sunday afternoon the discomfort is displaced by angst and a sense of isolation, intensified by being in someone else's home and socialising with people

I don't know. By Sunday evening all I want to do is get the hell out of there and never return.

For all that, I am continually drawn back to Esther and don't want what we have together to end. I decide a move to Wellington might allow the relationship to grow into something more loving. And at first the move does wonders. But a few weeks later my feelings of intimacy have largely dissipated. The openness Esther and I initially enjoyed has vanished and we've regressed into a pattern where we are preventing each other from getting close. We seem to be continually trying to control each other and we seldom communicate any appreciation.

A few months on and the relationship has become a cocktail of passion, intense judgement and angst. I've never felt so isolated or doubted myself so much. In the end it seems there's nothing endearing about the relationship or the woman. She lacks any ability to nurture, although others think she's a warm, caring person. How that works I don't know. She's definitely incapable of sustaining a relationship.

"This new woman I'm going out with at the moment is a horror show, mate," I tell Jonty on the phone. "She rejects and resists pretty much everything I say and suggest. She comes at me from every angle like a bloody fox terrier. It's like I'm playing squash with myself and she's the walls. Every time I hit the ball, it comes back and hits me in the side of the head."

I don't know why I'm confiding in the poor bastard about this. His wife has just left him for another guy, and Mitsubishi has launched a new range of vehicles with a television advertising campaign using one of his songs. Jonty hasn't been able to watch the box for nearly three weeks.

Against my better judgement I persist. "At some stage in my relationships the old judgements always come back, and it just becomes a matter-of-fact march through life again. If only that initial joy and passion would continue rather than turning into such terrible angst."

"Why don't you just bail out?" he asks, sounding even more depressed than me.

"I should, but I just can't seem to do it. There's something there that keeps reeling me in."

"Well, it's up to you how much horror you want, but I've always been a proponent of Newton's law. For every action there's an equal and opposite reaction. Maybe if you stop pushing and shoving she might have nothing to react to."

Fine words of wisdom, and that's all well and good. But what am I supposed to do: just sit there like the Buddha? Anyway, look at what's just happened to Jonty. I sigh and decide to change the subject. He's just developed a new cream for healing skin cracking and abrasions. The advertisement reads, "Jonty's crack cream. Guaranteed to close any crack."

"Hey," I say, "I pissed myself when I saw your advertisement in a lifestyle magazine the other day. The one for your new cream. Have you had any response?"

"Shit yeah. I'm selling it by the litre."

～

Now that I'm down to 10 hours' work a week I've decided to use the time to get my body fit and my head straight. I buy myself a kayak and decide to paddle out to Somes Island. It's a stunning Wednesday morning and, despite not receiving any tuition at all, including how to keep upright, I'm now trying to circumnavigate the island. Unfortunately I wasn't so successful at finding anyone to join in on the fun. I called five friends in a row and couldn't reach any of them. I left a message for Jonty: "Hey, mate, you're probably being run ragged trying to keep up with the crack cream sales, but I thought I'd just let you know I'm enjoying a perfect, windless day on Wellington harbour. I'll talk to you soon."

A blue penguin surfaces about three metres away and then effortlessly dives under again. As I look down into the sea past the reflection of the sky on the water's surface I see a forest of bull kelp below me. A feeling of peace falls upon me as I observe the penguin darting about. The peace expands to a sense of completeness and absolute contentment. I realise I always love spending time in nature.

Then I look around and I realise there's no one else on this part of the harbour. Almost at the same moment I notice the wind changing.

Oh Jeesuz.

A southerly is coming. Now I have to knuckle down and grind my way back home.

It took a mere 40 minutes to get to the island and already I've been paddling back for two hours. The phone has rung at least four times but I've been unable to answer it. I can't take my eye off the ball here or I'll be in the drink. The wave caps are white and they've got to be over a metre high, but the decidedly scary thing is that the interisland ferry, a ship that must be all of 20,000 tonnes and two football fields long, is now bearing down on me. My vague memory from Sea Scouts is that all motorised craft should give way to non-motorised craft. Either the helmsman can't see me or I don't know the rules within the harbour.

Paddling like a madder bastard than I normally am, I manage to back-pedal out of her path. Oh Christ, she's following me. Maybe this boy has had enough of kayakers. My body is nearly broken but I've got to pull on these paddles.

Jeesuz!

I look up at the blue wall of steel as it slides past only 20 metres away. I negotiate the wake, then turn around into the southerly again and beg my body to get on and get me home.

At last I feel the golden sand rub against the bottom of the kayak. Nearly crippled I struggle out of the cockpit and look around. People walking past barely notice me. Or if they do they couldn't give a shit. I struggle across the road to my apartment with the kayak and head upstairs. An hour later I get a call from Jonty on my mobile. He's answering my pompous message.

"Arnie, what are you doing to yourself now?"

I tell him about my run-in with the ferry. He laughs and informs me that all water craft in the harbour must give way to the interisland ferries. Oh shit.

A few days later Esther tells me she wants out of the relationship. Frankly, I'm relieved. I wanted to pull the pin but didn't have the guts. Actually, I'm elated. I'll have a clean slate again. I'll be free to create a new and better relationship with someone else.

The following day I go to the airport to collect Little Arnie. Monica is away for a few weeks and it's my turn to look after him. I arrive just as Little Arnie's cage comes along the baggage carousel. I let him out of his cage in front of about 150 travellers and he excitedly dances on two legs. He's dressed in his cowboy coat. Over the next week I walk him in his coat along Oriental Parade twice a day. I make sure I don't wear my own cowboy jacket. Immediately it's apparent he's very effective at attracting women. They stop to pet him and chat away, although the blokes look at me as if I'm half gay. I don't care. It does, however, strike me that I don't give a stuff what anyone thinks. It's a new experience for me. I reflect how empowering it is not to care what other people think. And it's relaxing, too. I feel more relaxed than I've felt for ages.

About a month later Esther and I get together for a drink and decide that we get on alright together after all. We agree to meet up on a weekly basis for a bit of fun and, quite unexpectedly, I experience moments of affection and love. I've started liking her. I love chatting with her and being around her. The calm and peace she radiates draw me in like a magnet. She's such a powerful anchor for me. It's surprising because I didn't see it before.

She's been playing with being aware of all the things around her, as well as being aware of what is happening in her mind and body, and this allows her to maintain a peaceful presence. She has been trying to focus on one thing at a time. If she gets stressed or upset she spends time looking at things such as a bunch of flowers, inhaling their fragrance and appreciating their beauty. Or she'll do things like focus on a cluster of stars at night. She suggests I have a go at it.

"Just gently place your attention on something on the wall, like the corner of that painting, and be alert to it. Continue to observe it and then at the same time let your awareness move wide."

I follow her instructions and notice how easy it is to remain focused and how calming it is.

A couple of months later I meet up with Esther to have lunch. We've just sat down at the table when she looks at me with a serious expression.

"I have something to tell you," she says. "I've started dating a guy and I'm very fond of him. I first met him five years ago and I liked him then. We're very attracted to each other, so I don't think it's appropriate for you and me to keep on seeing each other."

"That's fine. Good on you."

We continue chit-chatting over lunch and I pretend to be relaxed about her new romance. That was always the deal. But when I get home I'm overwhelmed with grief. How could she? This isn't right. Her behaviour was never normal and nor is this.

I feel a great weight pressing down on me as I wander distractedly around the flat. It's like I'm grieving for her. I feel so alone and rejected. She's rejected me for some other boy. Can you believe that? She's never had a boy like me. The new boy is bound to be a spoon, because that's what she is – a fucking spoon. Fuck her!

I sit down at the kitchen table until the anger dissipates. I suddenly realise that she's the perfect woman for me. How could this happen? I'll never find anyone like her again. I had my chance and I've blown it. If only I hadn't taken her for granted. I got cocky. I could have been more open about showing my love, but I held back. Shit, it was only two weeks ago she told me she loved me. I've been gypped.

Mate, you're going mad! Stop talking to yourself!

Later I receive a text from Esther asking if I'm OK.

No. I'm not, but there's no way I'm going to let her know that.

I reply, "Yes, I'm fine."

~

It's been several weeks and there has been no respite from the heaviness of loss and the feeling of frustration. I feel entombed in despair. I'm a broken man. Fuck, I admonish myself, she's not that great, you're carrying on like a teenager. You couldn't have cared less a month ago when you had full access to her. Now she's with someone else and you're putting on a performance?

Bugger this. I'm supposed to be seeking peace but it seems to be more elusive than ever. I need to get her back. I stand at the window of my flat and look out over the water. My attention is drawn by the lights of the city on the other side of Oriental Bay. I remain focused on the shapes and colours of one of the high-rise buildings. A blanket of peace envelops me and I start taking stock. I have an abundant life, I have a bunch of good mates, and I'm involved in a successful business. I'm fitter and healthier than I've ever been. I get to kayak around the bays to have breakfast a couple of times a week. I'm only working part-time. And yet here I am as tormented as a madman.

I decide I've had enough. I've got the time and the resources to pursue this peace of mind thing. I have to do it. I'm going to pursue it until I achieve it. I'll show Esther how it's done. I decide to make an appointment with a new counsellor in Wellington.

"It often takes an intense, sharp shock to initiate the journey of self-discovery," she tells me at our first session. "At some point we need to take responsibility for changing our own lives. It's up to us to be happy, no one else. So, well done."

"Thank you," I say. Then it all rushes out. "I've been in a frenzy for weeks. I haven't been able to stop thinking about her. It's been very loud and painful. I've taken up running, bush walking and kayaking to try to crank up the endorphins to keep me high. It's gotten really silly. But the suffering won't go away. It's so intense."

"It's amazing how much the mind perseverates, isn't it?"

"That sounds like a fascinating word. What does it mean?"

"Perseveration is the tendency for a pattern of thinking or emotional reaction to recur over and over again in other situations. Eventually these patterns become mental grooves. Many of those grooves involve judgements about ourselves and others, or about things that have happened to us."

"I like that word. Perseverate."

"I like it too," she replies.

I give the counsellor the background to what's happened and how I got to be in the position I'm in. I tell her about my habitual drinking and marijuana smoking, and my occasional joy ride with pharmaceuticals. She says I've done well in spite of myself. I probably have. She tells me she wants to go back to the beginning of my life. Of course. That's what shrinks do. "What was it like growing up at home?" she asks.

"It was chaotic at times. My father would have periods of uncontrollable anger or deep depression. In my teenage years nearly every day he would have outbursts of Herculean proportions. He was bipolar. He drank every day and that seemed to react with his nervous system, or maybe with the medication he was on. I don't think he was well managed by his doctor."

"Did the anger ever manifest itself as physical violence?"

"No. Not once. He knew his boundaries, even in the midst of his ferocious anger. Thank God for that, because he was built like a brick shit house."

"How was your mother during all of this?"

"She tried her best to cope, but as you can imagine it was a wild ride. It was hard to maintain a sense of stability. In retrospect I guess she was symbiotically depressed."

That bit of jargon will impress her. I read about it somewhere and it seemed to sum up Mum and Dad perfectly: mutually dependent, locked together in the hell of depression. But the counsellor doesn't blink.

"That's generally the case when one partner is deeply depressed," she comments.

"Still, even though she lived in all the turbulence, she had the strength and determination to hold the show together. She was the foundation and the structure of our family."

The counsellor nods. "Do you have any siblings?"

"Yeah, two brothers, but they're quite a bit older than me. My oldest brother was 12 when I was born and my other brother was nine."

"Were they there at the time your father was unwell?"

"By the time the old man was experiencing the worst of his illness I was home by myself. The other two were at university. In spite of what I've just told you, I was mollycoddled by both my parents. They doted on me. I didn't go without, that's for sure."

"Tell me more about your father's illness."

I think about this for a moment. I haven't done this amount of digging around for a long time. "His intense anxiety and depression led him to be hospitalised eight times, and from what I gather, during most of those visits he received shock treatment. He had nightmares till the day he died, yelling and shrieking in the middle of the night. He said it was the reliving of one of the shock treatments when he came out of the sedative. Mental health has got a lot to answer for, eh?"

"That particular form of treatment was certainly barbaric," she responds evenly. She writes something down then lifts her head to focus on me again. "So, you were the only child living at home when your parents were both struggling with varying degrees of depression, and your father was often in a rage. How did you deal with it?"

"Well, I loved school – everything about it. As a kid I'd literally run to school in anticipation. I had an above average intellect, so academically school was relatively easy and I didn't take it too seriously. I had lots of mates I loved hanging out with. We'd get up to all sorts of mischief."

Laughing, I tell her some of the things we did. "I learnt how to activate the railway signals by placing the back axle of my bike on one rail and then placing the front axle on the other. As long as the bike was within 100 metres of the level crossing, the lights would start flashing and the bell ringing. It was a laugh stopping motorists, but I got a bit carried away. One day I set the alarm going when the old man was about to cross the railway line. He looked down the line and saw me, and started waving his fist in the air and yelling at me. I high-tailed it out of there, but when he got home he didn't mention it. He must have thought it was someone else."

"How was it when you were at home with your parents?" she enquires.

"I kept clear of the old man as much as possible. But I wasn't scared of him. Actually I developed a sense that I was afraid of no man."

"Why do you think you weren't afraid of anyone?"

"Because Dad was so fearsome that I didn't think anyone else could be more frightening."

"What did you feel when your father was angry?"

"I just stood up to him. I never backed away."

"Can you remember how that felt?"

I stop and think about one of the times when the old man was ranting and raving about something he thought my mother had done, but I'd done it and I didn't have the courage to own up. The intensity of the event washes over me as I describe it to the counsellor.

"I was ashamed that I was letting my mother down. And then there was a deep sense of isolation. It felt like fear and loneliness."

"How did you deal with that fear and loneliness?"

"I sheepishly went to my bedroom, trying not to disturb the peace and feeling decidedly uncomfortable for what I'd done."

"That must have been frightening for you?"

"Yeah, it was. I felt more alone than normal, and I didn't know if my relationship with my mother would recover."

"How old were you?"

"Maybe 11."

"Well, it would have been tough for an 11-year-old to stand up to a grown man. You can forgive yourself for not standing up for your mother, and you can forgive your father as well. The first step in changing the way we behave is to forgive those in our lives who we think have hurt us. I'd like you to have a go at forgiving your father."

"Ah, look, I really have nothing to forgive him for. Both my parents tried their best. I knew the old man had a shattered nervous system – his behaviour was so extreme and abnormal that I knew it wasn't about me. It was his mental health. I know I've painted a picture of an unloving environment, but I knew he loved me very much. He was trying his best. He was the most generous character I knew – not only with money, but with his time and concern and effort. He really looked out for people. He'd do things like deliver a load of wood to someone out of the blue to help them out. It was just that the poor bastard was hammered by his make-up."

"Have a go at forgiving him over the next week anyway. On some level you may not have really forgiven him."

Over the next week I notice how much I think about the past and I toy with forgiving the old man. I have moments of crying – crying the way I've been taught not to. It's uncomfortable and it feels like there's a lifetime of trapped anguish and emotion being released. I even cry on the way home from the pub on Friday night. It's cleansing. I decide that I'm going to make weekly appointments. I'm determined to heal myself.

Back at the shrink's she asks how my homework topic of forgiveness went. I tell her about all my blubbing and how much lighter I feel. She says, "Well done. It takes a lot of courage to do what you're doing. In many ways forgiveness is letting go – letting go of the past memories that on some level have dogged us and influence the way we currently live. Now you have the opportunity to make a new start."

PART TWO

Revealing Happiness

You might have gained the impression that my life was still a bit of a mess at this stage. I'd solved some problems, but I hadn't solved the problem of the chattering in my head driving me crazy. There are only so many runs you can go on and only so many chemicals you can take on board to drown out the racket. I needed something else – something stable and permanent, something that could provide me with the enduring happiness I was seeking rather than just brief bursts.

In this second part of the book I describe my search for lasting happiness and inner peace.

So the story takes a bit of a different turn now. It's a different exploration from here. If you've ever been unsatisfied with how your life's going, if you've ever been bugged by those perseverating thoughts going round and round your head on a continuous groove, and if you've ever wanted to do something about it, then read on.

You'll have gathered I was no saint, no stare-at-your navel, bean-eating hippy in ragged clothes. I was a man of the world, grabbing the bull by the horns, living it to the max, draining the glass to the bottom, and a few other metaphors you can think of. But in the end it all just made me miserable and destroyed any meaningful relationships I attempted to have.

So here it is – my accelerated search for happiness and love.

And by the way, I found it.

FIFTEEN

My friend Denise has just loaned me a book her brother suggested I read. It's called *The Power of Now* by Eckhart Tolle. Apparently her brother is a monk. I don't know what a monk is, or what he does, but it seems pretty strange that a boy from Dunedin is one. I consult the dictionary.

"Monk: a male member of a religious community bound by vows of poverty, chastity and obedience."

That doesn't sound like her brother from what I've heard. But he says it's a good book. She seems to listen to what he says and I rate her opinion, so I decide to give it a go.

Some things in the book really strike a chord. Like the idea that your mind is continually thinking about either the past or the future. It's seldom still, resting, here in the present moment. The *Now*, as Eckhart Tolle calls it. When the mind thinks about the past it usually evokes sadness or anger or guilt about what's happened. Thinking about the future induces fear and anxiety and worry about what may or may not happen.

Yeah, that sounds about right.

Sitting alone in my lounge one evening after work, away from the hustle and bustle, I close my eyes and I quietly observe and wait for a thought to start moving. As the thought appears I watch it. It's as if I have a torch shining on it and the thought fades away. And I feel calm. This observing works! I just watched a thought about Esther and it retreated and left me in a momentary state of peace. It was the first glimpse of peace I've had for a long, long time. What a discovery! I can't wait to tell the counsellor about it, along with a few other insights.

"Tell me how you got on with your homework – noticing what was happening when you were feeling anxious or stressed," she says.

"I noticed that whenever I'm anxious, I'm usually judging someone as being inadequate or arrogant, or they haven't done something as well as I wanted them to, and it winds me up. It's unbelievable how much monologue and even dialogue is going on in my head, and how much of that is me judging others. Every time I see someone – anyone, people I know or even people I don't know – the judgements kick in automatically. And then I get wound up."

"Good job. Noticing our thoughts is a big shift in awareness."

I continue on, excited about my discoveries.

"For example, one of my life-long obsessions has been well-made shoes. As far back as I can remember shoes have been a bellwether for me to determine if someone is a person I want to interact with. I'm always looking to see what shoes someone is wearing. If the shoes aren't stylish, or high-quality, I launch into a tirade in my head. Look at those shoes! What kind of spoon would wear shoes like that? And look at the shirt he's wearing. What a lemon. I quickly decide whether I'm interested in conversing with someone or not, all based on my judgement of the shoes he's wearing. Man, it's amazing how these judgements drive my behaviour."

"Have you noticed how you behave when you are judging others?"

"Yeah," I quickly answer, well prepared with another gem I've discovered. "On a couple of occasions I've noticed how twitchy and even manic I become."

"Good," she replies. "You're my star pupil. That's great you've noticed the judgements and how they induce anxiety. Typically judgements about others are based on a habit of rejecting others before they reject us. The mind uses a collection of judgements, beliefs and positions to protect itself."

I think about that. I get it. My incessant judgements, as uncontrollable as they are, could well be a flawed device to protect myself, but what I'm also realising is that rather than protecting me, they're limiting me. My judgements are actually isolating me from other people and the many good aspects of my life. I think how much Esther and I rejected and resisted each other. It was probably almost impossible for either of us to have a relationship.

"I see so many people who struggle in relationships because of two things: they are either judgemental of each other or they are judgemental of themselves," the counsellor says.

"But how do you stop the judgements?"

"Well, noticing them is necessary to start changing the way we react to them."

I'm already halfway there, then.

I start doing a series of stretching exercises called Tibetan Rites. My body has been as stiff as a strip of biltong from years of sitting around like a lounge lizard. I love the release of endorphins – it makes me feel good. Apparently they're the body's natural morphine to neutralise the pain associated with the muscular tearing that occurs when we exercise. Increasingly I'm noticing how calm and grounded I feel after doing the exercises.

One evening I'm on one of my endorphin jogs, there's still that chatter in my head. I struggle to the top of Mount Vic and decide to do an exercise I read in a self-help book. I stand with my eyes closed and consciously feel the wind interact with my body. I'm aware of my body moving with each small gust. The wind depresses my cheek and the movement against my face makes my skin feel alive. The attentiveness makes me feel relaxed and enlivened. As I start running back down the hill I give myself a goal: one day I'll run up Mount Vic completely free of the chatter. That will truly be a great day.

I'm following Eckhart Tolle's writings as diligently as I can, and am trying to remain focused in the Now. I try hard not to get caught up in the chatter that pulls me into the past or the future. I only remember to focus half a dozen times a day, but most times I'm instantly rewarded with freedom from the chatter. I had a powerful experience the other day. I got caught at the airport. It was a busy time of the day and I was running late, and I thought I might miss my plane, so I got a bit geed up. I paused and consciously listened to the Silence. Eckhart Tolle says that by paying more attention to the Silence than to sounds, the mind becomes still. And it worked. It calmed me down.

Despite experiencing extended moments like this, the chatter in my head doesn't stop for long and I'm only having moments of peace. I've started closing my eyes to focus, even at work, and I'm attempting to meditate. I haven't received any direct guidance, but I've read a couple of books. It's a bit hit and miss, though. I'm not sure it's working. I think I need to attend a course. I've never been into courses. I usually do a runner halfway through a weekend. But I'm hungry to have more of this peace.

It has been fascinating observing the new things appearing in my life. They appeared from the moment I first committed to seeking inner peace – not the half-arsed sort of commitment to which I've paid lip service all my life, but a *total* commitment to finding peace.

It's May 2005 and I've just finished breakfast in a Wellington beachside café on Oriental Parade, a place where I've eaten twice a week for the past year. I get up from the table and go to the cash register. I consciously decide to thank the boy behind the counter for his service. He looks pleased. As I'm walking out a yellow flyer catches my attention. I stop and read it. It's promoting a weekend course for a meditation technique called the Brightpath Ishayas' Ascension. The brochure describes Ascension as a meditation technique that reveals peace and joy on a perpetual basis. It's a strange name, though. I bet these guys are woo-woo types. But, hey, if the technique can deliver what I want, who cares?

Three days later and I'm at an introductory talk about this Ascension thing. There are six of us here. The talk is being convened by a young bloke and a young woman. They're both dressed in white and they look to be about 30. They introduce themselves as monks.

I thought monks were supposed to be men.

His name is Arjuna and her name is Karuna. Strange names. I can hardly pronounce them in my head. But she's deliciously joyful. Arjuna starts with, "What is the single thing you want more in life than anything else? What is your heart's greatest desire?"

That's a no-brainer. I want peace and I want love.

He responds, "Chances are you desire peace of mind. Not just short glimpses of peace, but peace that permeates every moment of the day, undisturbed by the people and events unfolding in your life." He looks at me directly. "You may also want to experience unconditional, rock solid love. Love that's there regardless of what you do, or don't do. A grounded, unmoving love that doesn't depend on having someone in your life to provide that love."

Absolutely. I want all of that. Yeah, I do.

"And most of us want continuous contentment and happiness in our lives. This is indeed possible, but to be in this state in an ongoing way we need to disengage the internal voices. We need a tool that allows us to cease identifying with the endless stream of thoughts and emotions passing through our existence."

It sounds great, but I wonder if it's really possible.

Arjuna looks around the group and asks, "Can you remember a moment when you were stopped in your tracks by awe, or when you fell into a state of profound peace or joy?"

Actually I remember moments like that. The time at the Bolshoi Ballet in Moscow, and even intimate moments during sex. After a moment's hesitation a boyish-looking bloke with a grey beard speaks.

"Sometimes I fall into a state of awe simply going for a walk. There's a track along the south coast I walk twice a week. I often feel very tranquil when I'm there."

An immaculately dressed middle-aged woman tells us, "For me one of the most wonderful moments in my life was the overwhelming sense of love I felt when our first baby was born. I actually fell in love as soon as I first saw her."

Someone else says, "One of the loveliest moments of my life was my wedding day. There was an uplifting sense of love and support for my husband and me. It was such a joyful day. I'd go so far as to say it was blissful."

Ah well, I suppose I may as well join in. "Years ago I lived near a lake at a time when there was a lot of stress in my life. I loved looking at the reflections of the mountains on the lake. It was so soothing. I would sit there for what seemed like hours, fully engaged with the lake and the bush . . ." I tail off, remembering the feeling. Then I look around the room. Everyone looks peaceful and happy.

Now Karuna, the joyful monk babe I'd like to fall in love with, says, "These experiences are the result of our full engagement with the present moment. In this state we're in total harmony with all that exists. And here's the thing: that moment of peace and bliss happened without you doing a thing. All that happened was that you stopped thinking. And when we stop thinking, everything is perfect and peaceful."

She pauses, then continues. "Can you imagine living in that state all the time?"

No, I can't. But I want it.

She says that deep inside each one of us there's an ocean of peace and love. And, amazingly, that's the peace and love each and every one of us is looking for. But we don't find what we're seeking because the voices in our head distract us. The internal voices continually direct our awareness outwards, to the world around us. And those voices tell us, directly and indirectly, that there's something wrong with our lives, that happiness will only be bestowed upon us at some time other than now, or even that we are unworthy of any happiness.

"But," she says with a smile, "the good news is that it is possible to experience peace, love and happiness on a continual basis. This state, which is a state free of internal voices, is our natural state of being. But we need a solid meditation technique that allows us to disengage from thinking. We need a meditation technique that allows us to do this not only with our eyes closed, but also with our eyes open as we go about our ordinary day."

Ten days later I'm sitting in front of the same two monks on the Friday night of the weekend meditation course. There are four of us left: the boy-man with the beard, the immaculately dressed middle-aged woman, plus one other. I guess two dropped out. Not me. I'm going to give this all I've got.

I like the room. It's got big comfortable chairs covered in a red-and-green floral fabric. They look almost Japanese. The oil painting on the wall is a slightly abstract scene of a wave breaking onto a gravel beach with an upturned tree stump on the foreshore. The warmth of the room is accentuated by the knowledge that outside it's actually a bleak winter evening. About 20 minutes into the course, Arjuna says, "The reality is, we're not actively engaged in life here and now because our minds distract us from it."

This is exactly what Eckhart Tolle says.

"It's amazing we can even do the things we do. Just think. How many times do we drive a car and arrive at our destination then wonder what happened to the last 10 minutes? We're often barely aware of the environment we drive through because we're preoccupied with the internal dialogue in our heads. Often, when we're talking with someone, we're not actually listening to them. Instead, we're thinking of something else, or we can't wait to say what we want to say, or we are judging that person."

I chuckle to myself as I have a glimpse of myself in meetings at work. Most of the time I'm not listening at all. Before I know it, I've missed what Arjuna is talking about. I consciously try to focus on what he's saying.

"Seven billion of us are walking around on this planet in our bodies while our heads are thinking about something that's happening at some other time. Our bodies are here, but we are not. Most of the distractions are irrelevant to what we are physically doing right now. We miss out on life because we are in a dream, a dream about the past, or a fantasy or projection about the future.

But the past has gone. And the reality is, our memory of past events is distorted by our opinions and judgements rather than being accurate and purely objective. As for the future, it nearly always unfolds completely differently from what we can ever imagine. In reality we can never predict what is going to happen in the next month, or even in the next minute."

Ain't that the truth.

Karuna takes over and explains that over the weekend we will learn the first four meditation techniques or Attitudes. These Attitudes are based on praise, gratitude, love and compassion. The Attitudes function on many levels. They release the attachment to thoughts and feelings, instantly revealing the underlying peace and stillness. They also act like keys, unlocking stress that has accumulated in your nervous system.

She writes on the white board: *Appreciation*. She says that when we praise someone, the first response from the recipient of praise is gratitude. In the exchange of praise and gratitude we experience a connection with each other.

"Praise is an active aspect of appreciation," she continues. "The act of giving or receiving authentic praise has become increasingly unfamiliar for many of us. Many of us effectively live in a praise-free zone, going months without receiving recognition, or – the other side of the coin – without appreciating others. Sometimes it appears like we do a hundred things well but when we make one error the whole world comes crashing down around us.

It can feel difficult to praise the attributes or actions of another person. But it's actually very easy. It's not necessary to experience the emotion of appreciation before we communicate it. All that's required is to choose to do it. Initially it can take courage to overcome any sense of vulnerability, but by actively appreciating someone we can change their day, and ours. For example, recognition from a work colleague or a manager can bolster our confidence. It can even quash any doubt we have about ourselves."

I think about some of the work meetings I've had recently and imagine praising some of the people I got stuck into. It sounds like a tough ask.

Then Karuna leads us into our first meditation, or Ascension. I close my eyes. I gently think the technique and the commentary in my head quickly ceases. It's still and peaceful.

I wonder if Karuna and Arjuna are in a relationship together.

Ah – that's a really distracting thought! I gently introduce the technique again. Peace and stillness are again revealed.

In an incredibly soothing voice Karuna says, "Now, gently open your eyes." Looking at the group she asks, "Was that relaxing and peaceful?"

"Yeah, it was very peaceful," I reply. In fact the moments of being free of chatter reminded me of the experiences of love and happiness I've had at different times in my life. It felt like coming home.

"Did you notice your thoughts drift away when you introduced the praise Attitude?"

"Yeah, I did. I caught myself thinking a couple of times, but even though it was appealing to keep thinking I was able to introduce the technique and let it go. Then there was peace again."

She responds, "Excellent. Now you can continue experiencing that peace using the Attitude with your eyes open."

Imagine if the boys saw me tonight, I think as I walk out of the course venue. They'd have a bloody field day if they knew what Arnie was up to. But I don't care. I've just experienced the peace I've been looking for. As I drive into town for a beer I actively use the technique and I notice the internal chatter is interrupted every time I use it. What remains is attentiveness. As I drive along this familiar road I'm noticing buildings and structures and colours more than I ever have.

Very cool.

I stand in the bar calmly observing people dance. Normally I'd feel awkward standing here by myself, but I keep playing gently with the technique. I feel very grounded and connected. I notice that I'm staying calm for longer periods. I'm also noticing that when the internal chatter starts, the calmness is replaced with unease.

It's Saturday morning and I'm back in the comfy room with the big arm-chairs. We're asked to share how our attempts at meditation went overnight.

I start. "Man, when I closed my eyes this morning to Ascend there were just so many thoughts. But when I became aware that I was caught up in them, I gently introduced the technique and it was like I dissolved into a vast tranquil space. I felt so relaxed."

Karuna responds: "Perfect. That's all you have to do. Keep gently doing that and you will naturally reveal that peaceful space more and more easily. The gentler we are in our approach, the more powerfully we reveal the peace."

Arjuna writes on the whiteboard: *Gratitude*. "The second Attitude is based on gratitude. The emotion of gratitude is more powerful than praise, but in our society we seem to take most of our lives for granted – we effectively ignore our world. It's just a habit to ignore what we have, or to be negative, but this has a profound effect on our energy, our bodies and the world around us.

Yet there is so much to be grateful for in our lives. We are often only grateful for something when it appears to be threatened or it is no longer there. How many times do we hear of people becoming grateful for their health only after they've survived a severe illness? Many of us feel grateful for our partner, or family, only when we are apart, or when they are no longer with us."

A feeling of regret and melancholy over my failed relationship with Esther envelopes me like a duvet. If only I hadn't taken her for granted. Maybe we could've still been together.

"Gratitude is the opposite of taking things for granted. Just think about the times you have helped someone out. When that person was truly grateful for what you had done for them I bet you felt uplifted and would've been prepared to do more for them. But those times when the recipient of your generosity took what you had done for granted you probably didn't feel inclined to help them out again. In exactly the same way, life is a giver of endless gifts, and as we engage in gratitude for those things in our life we receive more. It never stops growing; the more grateful we are, the more we receive. By being thankful for what we do have, exactly as it is, everything has the opportunity to change and grow and we naturally begin to experience more happiness and contentment."

Maybe I need to be more grateful for what I have. I've got a shit load more than most.

Arjuna writes the full technique on the board and then leads us into another period of meditating with our eyes closed. There's tension in my arms and hands and stomach. I realise I'm thinking about Esther again. I gently introduce the technique. Instantly it's peaceful and my body relaxes. Magic.

Over lunch I say to Karuna, "I thought monks were all men? Why are you called a monk?"

"In its purest form *monk* means someone, male or a female, who commits their life to remaining perpetually present. This state is achieved by surrendering, or letting go of every thought, feeling and action to the will of the universe. Such a commitment can be made by anyone, not just men."

I want to ask if she is allowed to have sex, but I resort to, "So have you renounced any aspects of your ordinary life?"

"No. Full engagement in life is a natural outcome of remaining present. We are here to live fully and to have fun. Renunciation is unnecessary."

Seizing the opportunity I ask, "Do you have a partner?"

"Yes, I do. Arjuna."

Oh well. That's the end of that then.

One of the course participants, Martin, is a humorous character who has Parkinson's disease. He asks, "Where's your garbage can? I want to smell it."

Looking pretty surprised Karuna says, "Under the sink, Martin."

As he reaches for the bucket positioned in the cupboard, he explains, "I think I've got my sense of smell back." He inhales through his nose and starts beaming. "I lost my sense of smell and taste three years ago. I haven't been able to smell anything since."

Far out. He's got two of his five senses back. I wait for an opportunity to talk to him privately and ask him how he copes with having Parkinson's.

"I learnt long ago that it's pointless getting stressed about the things you can't change in your life. I accept it, and that makes it easier." Then he points to the T-shirt he is wearing. Printed above and below the image of an alien is the statement *Resistance is futile.* We both laugh.

After lunch Karuna writes the word *Love* on the whiteboard. "Most of you have probably had experience with babies."

Ah, no. I haven't.

"One minute they're giggling with delight, then a few minutes later they're crying. Babies aren't distracted by what happened five minutes ago, nor are they interested in what could happen in the next five minutes. They are continually engaged in the present moment. It's a wondrous, carefree state infused with joy and love."

She says babies love life unconditionally. Then at some point in their early development they receive discouragement or a reprimand from someone close to them, usually from a parent. Whatever the nature of the feedback, the young mind begins developing a belief there's something wrong. The child's awareness has started moving away from the state of unconditional love, to a state of thinking. For example, they may start thinking a sibling is more favoured than they are, or they develop a belief they are not good enough. These beliefs create a sense of victimhood and distrust in love.

Karuna continues, saying that as we grew up many of us have troubling experiences along the way. Someone close to us, like a parent or a sibling, may die prematurely, or we may be physically or emotionally abused. Whatever the event, our reaction is often a feeling that we have been abandoned by the love that we were once bathed in. We start to develop and refine certain behaviours we think will support and protect us. But instead these behaviours isolate us, leading to a repression of our true personality and our innocence. This thinking causes us to react in fear, to see things as imperfect, to worry, or long for something other than what we have right now. We become experts at limiting the boundless love we truly are. And we become afraid to expose to other people who we truly are."

I'm definitely an expert at that.

All I know is I want love and the sooner the better.

I can't contain myself. "Why can't we experience love all the time?"

She responds, "Love is always there. It can never be destroyed. It just appears to be elusive because it is hidden by our continual thinking. If we can let go of our thinking, then we experience unconditional love. Really, it is very simple: experiencing love or experiencing fear is just a matter of choosing where we place our attention. As we begin using the Attitudes, we become less interested in fear-based thinking, and we become more attentive to the Stillness and love that is always there."

We close our eyes to meditate. I'm becoming more aware of the thoughts and commentary in my mind. I'm noticing how identification with these thoughts causes me to react. But I'm also discovering that Ascension is a purely mechanical approach. It's a tool to allow you to let go of your thoughts and reveal the peace that you're seeking. And the very cool thing is that it works every time.

The next morning Arjuna starts talking about compassion. "There's a saying: don't judge someone till you've walked a mile in their shoes. In other words, imagine what it's like to be that person in that same situation. We may not agree with the way they go about things, but we can accept them anyway. Compassion is about accepting people as they are. See them in their perfection: there is nothing wrong with them."

I ask what the difference is between sympathy and compassion.

Karuna says, "In our society compassion has become confused with sympathy. Sympathy or feeling sorry for someone is actually based on a judgement that something is wrong with that person. Such a judgement is based on the assumption that we are superior, and that they need fixing."

"Compassion is allowing people to be just as they are, without judging them. It is about treating others how we all want to be treated – we all want to be recognised for our full potential."

It's now Sunday afternoon and I notice how calm and relaxed I am. It's like I'm finally comfortable in my own skin.

Arjuna is wrapping up the course and adds, "Also, have a play with appreciating the people and things in your life and see what happens. Our teacher always says if you are having a rough day, get active praising others and see what happens to your own day."

Someone asks, "You always use the term 'play' when you teach. What do you mean by 'play'?"

"Play means to approach life like a child – taking nothing seriously or personally, having the courage to let go of any resistance or judgement. Watch and notice what happens. The trick is to play with letting go of all the positions of wanting to be right, or the desire to control certain aspects of your life, and letting go of the judgements you may have about yourself, or others. Then life becomes fresh and alive."

Karuna also mentions that for those seeking perpetual peace and contentment, a six-month course called The Mastery of the Self is convened in Canada. I start thinking I might go to Canada.

In the meantime life and work go on. Three weeks later I'm at Christchurch airport waiting for a boarding announcement. The terminal is under reconstruction. Beyond a temporary wall a vibrating hammer is rattling and punching through concrete. I'm a bit agitated because I wanted to use the opportunity to meditate. I give it a go anyway. I sit down and close my eyes. After a minute or so the noise has no impact on me. Soon the drilling stops. A few seconds later the boarding announcement is made. As I open my eyes and stand up I see Jonty walking towards the gate. I smile. I'd just thought how I'd like to catch up with him soon.

"Jonty, how are you doing?" I ask, falling into step with him.

He turns, surprised. "Arnie! Good. How've you been?"

"Great. You won't believe what I've been doing."

He looks at me with guarded interest. "What have you been up to now?"

"I've learnt to meditate."

"Oh yeah," he says chuckling.

"It's true. I've been meditating for about three weeks."

"Well, make sure you don't drift off on some magic carpet."

Knowing Jonty is a fellow insomniac I say, "You'd love it. I'm noticing a lot of changes already. I'm sleeping much better and I'm feeling so much more relaxed and energised."

We're standing in line at the check-in and Jonty is looking in his pockets for his ticket. "I haven't got the time. My life is too busy with work."

"One of the interesting things is that it seems to create time. I'm finding I do the things I really need to do rather than running around doing everything my mind tells me to. Now that I look back I'm amazed at how much time I used to waste doing things that didn't need doing."

"Ha," he says, pulling out his ticket. Then he looks me in the eye. "Let's wait and see."

For a break, I go with a friend to a remote part of the West Coast. As we walk along the beach, the shades of grey unfolding in the sky are reflected on the sea.

"Have you got the insect repellant?" my friend asks. We've been walking for about half an hour. The sun has been out and the beach has been clear of insects. But then the sky clouds over and instantly the conditions are perfect for sandflies to appear. She'd asked me earlier if I could bring the repellant, but I'd forgotten.

"Ah, no."

She shakes her head in mock displeasure.

I walk another two steps and there lying on the sand in front of me is a tube of insect repellant. I pick up the unused tube and toss it to her. I've been saved. The only people walking this far up the beach would be fishermen, and the season finished two months ago. I've been using the techniques for three months and magic like this is becoming common. If I trust it – it works.

The day after I return home the iridologist tells me, "This is fascinating. I don't think I've ever seen anyone's eyes change so much in such a short time." About two weeks before I learned to meditate I'd had my eyes analysed and he'd told me what I already knew: I have a strong predisposition to stress and anxiety. "This is miraculous. Look at this new image compared to the first one. This indicates that your whole nervous system has calmed down."

I peer at the images. It's easy to see the difference. One eye is clear, the other inflamed and ragged.

I'm noticing how much easier it is to make life changing decisions and not to procrastinate. I'm functioning with great clarity. I immediately know if I should do something or not, and I find it so easy to fully commit to that decision. I've pretty much given up smoking marijuana and I'm drinking alcohol and coffee in moderation. My stress levels have plummeted and what I'm noticing is that I'm making better choices about what I eat – far less fat and less sugar. After a lifetime of nose blowing, my previously unstoppable sinuses have almost ceased running. Even my propensity to sweat appears to have diminished. I no longer need a swig of Phenergan every night to ease me into a slumber, and that in itself is helping me to be more alert and effective during the day.

I go back to my GP for a full check-up, including blood tests. I'm keen to get objective feedback. My blood pressure is now in the normal range without the aid of pharmaceuticals. And the bad cholesterol has dropped to an acceptable level, probably due to me not reaching for junk food whenever I'm stressed. My exhaling air flow rate has increased by 20 per cent, no doubt because my bronchial tubes are loving the respite from smoke. I leave feeling very pleased with myself.

As a managing director my communications with people used to be laced with anxiety and impatience. A typical meeting would start with me arriving first and waiting for the others to turn up. I'd become increasingly edgy when people didn't arrive on time: "What a waste of bloody time and money," "How inconsiderate," and so the internal commentary would go. By the time the meeting started I was cranked with anxiety, off in a little world of my own, completely unfocused.

These days, when I arrive early for a meeting I use the time to sit and close my eyes until the other people arrive. I actually look forward to it because it refines my focus and I feel so refreshed. Meetings have become fluid and creative. People who didn't have the confidence to step forward in the past are going for it. When someone suggests an idea, I used to have a tendency to reject their suggestions, but now instead of discouraging them I remain attentive and open. And I'm finding that what they have to say is often a very useful suggestion or signpost to help me make decisions effortlessly. And there's a lot more laughter. But the really exciting thing from a business perspective is that every key performance indicator in the business continues to move in the right direction. Staff retention is tracking up, sales are up, the gross margin is up, staff costs are down, and the bottom line is angling up. What a beautiful thing.

As disturbing as my first personality profile was a year or so ago, I've decided to have another one done to see if any changes in my behaviour can be detected. It's now four months since I learned to meditate and the summary reads:

> This is an extremely considerate and accepting individual who goes out of his way to get along with others. He sees himself as part of a team and will be supportive of its efforts. Harmony is important to him, both in his job and in his relations with people. He can be quite selfless, occasionally going above and beyond for the good of the team and the company. He will carefully avoid conflicts with others. He approaches work in a very unhurried manner and has a calming influence on others. He takes things as they come and does not have to make continual changes. He is patient with people and does not push them around to get results quickly. He is very calm, cool and composed. People are important to him and he is comfortable working with them. He is congenial, optimistic and more

likely to focus on what is right in others. He is understanding, empathetic, caring, and he relates very well to people. He believes in others, likes and mixes well with them.

This is as surprising as the first profile, but this one feels much better.

SIXTEEN

It's 10 o'clock at night and I'm sitting around outside on a warm night in the bush with a group of mates. I decide to actively use the Attitudes while I sit here with my eyes open. Suddenly showers of iridescent blue stars sweep over the horizon, raining down onto me. It's magic. Every time I introduce an Attitude, another shower of digital symbols arcs over the skyline and connects with me.

Now I'm viewing my body and the bush from an indefinable place of knowing. My body is continuous with the surrounding bush and the diverging rush of electronic shapes and symbols. The light moves in diverging paths, flowing from the surroundings and then through me. Suddenly it seems as if it's not *my* body I am looking at, but rather *a* body. A body for me to use in the world I live in. I am much, much greater than the body standing there. It's just one infinitesimal aspect of what I am. We are all connected. There is no separation, only an appearance that we are separate. No one or one thing is separate. We are one.

I share my experience with people I think may be intrigued but no one is interested. After a month of talking about it, one of my acquaintances finally says, "Look, lots of people have these experiences. I know it was special for you, but give it a break. I don't want to hear about it anymore. It's tedious. You've had an out-of-body experience. So what? Big deal."

Finally, I call one of the Ishaya monks to share my experience and she tells me, "What you have described is an exalted experience. It's a bit like the thoughts, emotions and energy that pass through our nervous system. It's just movement, it isn't a stable state of consciousness. It sounds like it was a cool experience, but it's gone. Let it go. You never know, you may have more exalted experiences or you may not. Many people think exalted experiences are an important aspect of being enlightened. They aren't. They are just movement."

That puts an end to my self-importance.

"Nonetheless, you have had a clear experience of knowing that you are infinitely more than just your body."

It's now five months since I learnt to meditate and I'm on a three-day retreat with Arjuna and Karuna and three other people. In my daily life I'm experiencing an increasingly stable experience of calmness and peace.

Arjuna starts talking: "The mind and the body are fully integrated. They are not two separate entities. The active mind drives and controls the body. As soon as the mind engages in thinking, the body instantaneously responds. For example, if we have nervous thoughts, butterflies flutter in our stomach; or we might have an embarrassing thought and our face looks like a stop light."

I sit there nodding to myself as I remember the breathing coach who told me that an elevated tongue and clenched fists were a by-product of stressful thinking. I decide it's not appropriate for me to share my experience of the GP tapping me on the side of the head when I was distraught about my dysfunctional penis. Nonetheless, I am aware now of the power of the mind to cause bodily malfunctions.

Karuna says, "We've got a little exercise for you. It'll only take a few minutes yet it can irreversibly change your approach to life. It's an exercise in noticing the power of appreciation. Praise moves in quite the opposite direction to condemnation. While judgement contracts and limits, praise is the initiator of connection and joy. So, I just want you to have a look around the room and find two things to criticise. Find fault in two things that just aren't your cup of tea. As you're doing this, be aware of how your body feels. Do this for a minute or so."

As I judge the chair I'm sitting on for being uncomfortable, I notice a dull sensation in my body that almost feels like a contraction. Then I look at a vase on a side table and notice that I don't particularly like the pattern on it. I think it lacks taste. As I think how much I don't like it, I notice the same heaviness I felt when I was criticising the chair.

Karuna asks, "What was your experience when you criticised the things in the room? What did you notice?"

Someone responds, "It felt heavy and draining." Someone else says, "It was constricting, and I even felt tired."

Nodding her head Karuna says, "You've just experienced the down-ward-spiralling effect of judgement and condemnation. When we judge something, our body experiences a contraction. Now we'll play with appreciation. Have a look around the room and find two things to appreciate. Again, as you are identifying the things you like, be aware of what is going on in your body."

Instantly I feel energised as I appreciate the painting on the wall. As I enjoy its proportion and style I feel uplifted and almost joyous. After a minute or so she asks, "Did it feel lighter, expansive and energising? Were you happier and uplifted?" We all agree. "The mind and the body are fully integrated. They are not two separate entities. If the mind is enjoying an uplifting experience, it causes the body to feel lighter and more expanded. Conversely, if the mind is moving in a downward direction, the body feels heavy and constricted.

But the really powerful aspect of appreciation is that every time we praise someone it has the dual effect of uplifting both us and them. Conversely, when we are judging and condemning someone, verbally or just thinking it, this has a profoundly negative impact on that person, as well as on ourselves.

For the third part of this exercise I want you to revisit the things we condemned a moment ago. This time, make the choice to appreciate at least some aspect of those items."

I look more closely at the chair I am sitting on and decide to appreciate the fabric. The chair may be boney and uncomfortable, but I quite like the pattern. I feel a lightness and almost calmness as I observe it. I look at the vase and decide to appreciate it for its shape.

"Did you experience a sense of wellbeing and expansion?"

"Yeah, I did," I reply.

"Interesting, isn't it, Greg?"

She looks at me curiously for a moment and then carries on. "We have the ability to see fault in something one minute, and then in the next moment we can easily choose to appreciate that same thing. The impact of each position has a noticeable impact on our bodies and our experience of the moment. As long as we are authentic, we can choose to praise any aspect of our life. Equally as easily we can choose to ridicule, condemn and find fault in the same thing. But as we praise more actively, we notice more to appreciate, and increasingly we become the recipients of more appreciation."

We have a brief break, then we close our eyes. Occasional thoughts and faint commentaries float by. The thoughts are random and they don't last. They have a beginning and an end. They are unable to distract my attention. An ocean of bliss draws me in ever deeper.

"Now, slowly open your eyes," Arjuna instructs quietly. Reluctantly I open my eyes. The deep peace prevails as I continue to gently think a technique with my eyes open. I notice the clock on the wall. I've been having this experience for two hours and yet it feels like it was no more than 10 minutes. I need look no further. This tool allows me access to everything I seek.

I share with the teachers what I have just experienced and how it was similar to the experience in the avalanche. Arjuna says, "What you have described is an unbroken awareness of the Stillness, Greg."

"What exactly is the Stillness?"

"The Stillness is the source of everything. It is the essence of life and it permeates all that exists."

"So that's who I really am?" Greg grounded in Stillness and not Arnie in chaos, I add in my head.

Karuna replies, "That's right. We appear to be individuals functioning in a material universe. Our bodies and minds, and the world around us, appear to make up the totality of who we are. But we are much more than this. We are unaware that we're the ocean because we're so distracted by the waves on the surface. The reality is, every single one of us and everything around us is a manifestation of the vast ocean of Stillness."

I'm mesmerised as Karuna speaks. I have no doubt that what I am experiencing now is the essence of life. I tell the monks I'm going to the six-month Mastery of the Self course in Canada.

One of the cool things is how empowering it is to observe an obsessive train of thinking being ended by making a choice. Any story can be terminated at any moment by introducing a technique. I'm no longer a slave to the chatter and the suffering it induces. And that is so empowering. But the really wonderful thing is, the Stillness is becoming more familiar – it is becoming easier and easier to rest peacefully, and I am spending more time in the present moment.

I've turned into a bit of a zealot. I want everyone to experience this peace and magic. I've been surprised by the number of friends who are keen to learn. "Mate, I've found the greatest drug on earth," I tell Jonty.

"Arnie, this isn't the first time you've told me you've discovered the greatest thing."

"Seriously mate," I insist. "I'm finally in control of my peace. I have a choice to be peaceful or to be stressed. The stress and frustration I used to experience have almost completely fallen away. I'm feeling so relaxed and grounded."

"Well, that is a biggie for you."

"Yeah, it's huge. The odd day when I don't close my eyes to meditate I'm very aware of the difference in my day. Things speed up and I start getting wound up again. But on the days when I do meditate, I'm much more focused and engaged and this allows me to do things to a much higher quality."

"Like what?"

"Well, like revising a business plan, for example. Instead of worrying about possible outcomes I'm able to let go of worrying and remain attentive to whatever I'm doing. From there I can calmly assess different aspects of the business and, with clarity, prepare for the future. What I'm finding is that when I am undertaking a task I'm no longer distracted by thinking about other things. And the increased focus is allowing me to complete activities in much less time, and that's providing me with more opportunity to do things that I really want to do."

"You know what I've been like – always stressed. The reality is that everything always works out. Worrying is futile."

Surprisingly Jonty calls me later and says he wants to learn.

Cliffy takes umbrage when I tell him he needs meditation as much as I did. He says, "Get your retinas off that navel of yours Arnie or they'll burn a hole in it." Although a shrink told Cliffy that his life is joyless, it appears he's addicted to the angst and isolation.

I also get excited about having a workplace free of stress and conflict, where people genuinely appreciate each other and creativity flows without ridicule. Ten out of about 130 employees are interested, so I pay for them to attend the meditation course.

SEVENTEEN

A year after I first learn to meditate I arrive at the Kamloops Airport in British Columbia. As I walk into the airport building I look for the person who is here to meet me. It appears the middle-aged hippy woman standing over the back may be my host. I introduce myself and she confirms that she is indeed the one I'm looking for.

Jeesuz.

What have I got myself into?

My view of hippies hammers away at me: fringe-dwelling free-loaders, the whole lot of them. They've never done a day's work in their lives and they expect the rest of us to support them. I bet the place is packed to the rafters with bloody hippies. I soon realise my judgements about hippies are causing me a lot of discomfort. This is old Arnie suddenly spewing forth. I introduce an Attitude and the judgements cease.

As we drive to our destination the woman explains there are about 60 people at the retreat centre in total: 12 on my intake, about 20 in the group that started their six-month course three months ago, and about 30 teachers. She explains the daily routine: yoga at 7am, breakfast at 8, the group meditates together from 9 till 10, dinner is at 6pm in the dining room, and the evening meeting is convened at 7.30pm. Wednesday is a day of silence.

I ask a number of questions as I try to find out more about the place and the people. Thankfully I'm not required to get up at four in the morning to scrub the floor, nor do I have to sit all day in the lotus position. She tells me the people at the centre are from all walks of life. There's a part-time model from Mexico City, a former presenter from MTV Mexico, plus a bunch of young women from Oslo. That sounds exciting.

The trees cast long shadows in the late May afternoon as we drive along the back road leading to the rural retreat. I feel the way I did when my mother dropped me off at the university halls of residence for the first time, or the time I was taken to hospital to have an operation when I was five. I remember saying to my parents, "You're not leaving me here are you?"

I feel unsure and alone.

But I know I have to do it. I want a different experience of life and I hope that when I leave here in six months I'll be a different person. I want to be perpetually happy. The thought of that state reduces my apprehension, but it doesn't eliminate it completely.

I'm greeted by a young Canadian woman. Not only is she attractive, she's a lovely person, and she tells me to take my time settling in. I feel better already.

The accommodation is a three-storeyed wooden building with a commercial kitchen and dining room on the ground floor, and an office and large yoga room on the second floor. She takes me to my bedroom on the top floor. I'm sharing with five others.

Then she walks with me up a sealed driveway. She stops to introduce me to Betty, a stunning Latin American woman.

"This is Greg. He's here for the six-month course."

She greets me with a heavy Spanish accent, "Hi Greg. I'm pleased to meet you. Well done making it here."

She seems so joyful and her eyes are so clear and powerful that I'm stunned. I want what she's got.

Feeling intimidated, all I can say is, "Pleased to meet you too."

My guide leads me up to the entrance of a yurt. Just before entering she says in a hushed tone, "During the day most people meditate together in this room, and in the evening we use it as the meeting room. Now, if you need anything don't hesitate to ask anyone for help."

I thank her and she opens the door. The yurt is completely silent. I walk tentatively through the doorway towards a spare chair. I hesitantly cast my attention around the room. It is populated with adults of all ages. Most are wearing white clothes. I lower myself into the chair and attempt to settle into meditating. After five minutes I open my right eye and surreptitiously look around the room. I can't believe it: they are *all* women. And some of them look very appealing. If I can't find the love of my life here, I'll never find it.

At 7pm that night I close my eyes to meditate before the evening meeting starts. After half an hour I open my eyes and look around. The full group, consisting of about 60 people, also has a high proportion of women. Far out! Then I catch myself. In an instant I recommit to a single strategy: to use every moment to develop an intimate relationship with what is inside me and avoid trying to develop a relationship with any of these beautiful women. I don't want the distraction, nor do I want the complication.

The teacher, Maharishi, enters the room and sits at the front. Surprisingly, he looks like a normal bloke. He wears a black, long-sleeved top and black trousers. His graying temple and the crow's feet around his eyes suggest that he's in his 50s. He welcomes the new arrivals and asks us to introduce ourselves. His accent is American. After the introductions are out of the way he says, "Over the next few days you'll be releasing a lot of stress and you may sleep a lot. Just be gentle. All you need to do is relax."

Then he changes direction and starts talking about the mind. He refers to the mind or the ego as a kind of "mini-me". The internal voice that sounds like "me" and behaves like "me" is actually a kind of "mini-me". "Mini-me's" continuous self-dialogue is like a panel of commentators that appear to be housed inside our heads. The voices are so constant that we think it is ourselves talking and commenting.

"Mini-me" has a propensity to judge aspects of our world as imperfect, and this creates a nagging sense that something is wrong. It appears we live in an unsatisfactory world. Why is there always something wrong in my life? "Mini-me" can be particularly scathing about who and what we are. It tells us we are incapable of doing certain things, constantly doubting what we do and how we do it.

"I am unable to sustain a loving relationship."

"I feel incomplete, there's something missing."

"Ah well, I guess life is a compromise."

I chuckle as I recognise the familiar torture my mind has flogged me with for most of my life. And I realise that "Mini-me" is Arnie. He is the one I needed to let go of. He is the one who made all the critical judgements of everyone and everything. Arnie is the Perseverator, I think to myself, and smile at my own joke.

The following day when I close my eyes I notice that Arnie is back and in full swing. Sometimes he's talking to Esther and she is talking back, or he's moaning about Esther, or he's trying to work things out because that's what he's good at. There's Arnie instructing me what to do, or mocking these "bloody hippies" that are here. Then there's the really appealing scenario of Arnie and the model from Mexico City in a love affair. Or he is rebuking me for something I could have done better. And so on.

These internal discussions get me so wound up. One minute Arnie is dealing with Popov, who I've just remembered is dead. The next minute he's remorseful for some of the things he did when he and Monica were married. It's stupid because most of the people he's talking to exist in another time and place. I gently introduce an Attitude and the peace is revealed again. The tension in my body subsides.

For the next few days I keep an eye out for Arnie. He's tenacious. He doesn't like being here on this retreat, and he's got a lot of judgement going on about the people around me. But I do have a choice – I let Arnie's raving go. And the reassuring thing is, whenever I do this, the underlying peace is always revealed.

As the first week of the retreat progresses I'm coming up with – or, more accurately, Arnie is coming up with – every reason why I should leave. I've started dividing the total six-month course fee by the number of days I've been here. I figure that once I get to the end of the first month I can financially justify my time here as being equivalent to a resort holiday.

The second week kicks off with a new format. Morning meetings are being convened for an hour for newbies. *Newbies* sounds like such a silly description, but I go along with it anyway. What else can I do? Manyu, the dude convening the meetings, looks and sounds as though he's had an interesting life.

He starts off by asking, "Are you prepared to walk through pain to experience freedom and endless joy?"

Nearly everyone emphatically responds, "*Yes.*"

"Yes," I say, feeling slightly uneasy.

"Great. Now are you prepared to walk through joy to be free from suffering?"

What is this? A trick question? It's such a wet thing to ask that I don't respond. One person half-heartedly raises his hand to indicate reluctant assent. Manyu starts laughing and says, "You have chosen well. This path is the path of joy. You don't have to walk through pain and suffering anymore." Yeah right, I think. But then I feel hopeful, even relieved, at his enthusiastic and encouraging response.

"It's interesting how we are conditioned to think that there's an element of 'no pain, no gain' in any undertaking in life, especially when we're on a path towards happiness. Fortunately this isn't the reality."

Someone asks him, "How has it been for you?"

"I grew up in Vegas, and I did pretty much everything that Vegas had on offer. But I was continually tortured by guilt about my behaviour. The saying 'Whatever happens in Vegas stays in Vegas' just didn't cut the mustard for me. Everywhere I went in my travels the things I'd done in Vegas were there with me. They hadn't stayed in Vegas like I'd told them to!"

I laugh. This dude is a character.

He adds, "That was hell. But once I mastered letting go I've lived in peace ever since. And what happened in Vegas has truly stayed in Vegas. Thank God for that."

As my laughter subsides I realise that so many things I've done in my life were motivated by wanting to leave the past behind. I got into the pet business so I could leave my demons behind in Russia, but they followed me. And then those demons recreated the same dynamics in my new life.

Maharishi conducts the meeting in the evening. That evening a young English lad stands and confesses, "I've felt out of place throughout my entire life. I can't seem to fit in anywhere."

Maharishi responds, "You are exactly where you need to be. Just be gentle with yourself." Looking at the group he says, "In fact you are all exactly where you need to be, not one second behind."

Being exactly where I need to be is definitely my experience, but I don't think that this English boy is exactly where he needs to be. He's always getting caught in some drama or other.

It's four in the afternoon the next day and I've spent about half an hour getting wound up about the English boy. Every time I see him he's doing something other than meditating – reading a book, walking, or talking with someone. Yet he continues to have these dramas about being unworthy.

Mate, just meditate. Just do it. It's simple – let go of the drama.

I decide enough is enough. I need to have a chat with one of the monks. She says, "Just be aware that you are getting caught up in your judgements about him and that it is causing you discomfort."

I chuckle, then say, "The funny thing is that I'm judgemental about him thinking he is a misfit, but I feel like a misfit as well."

She says, "Ultimately all judgement falls away as we become continually attentive to the Stillness, but until you've developed that level of surrender, try to have the intention of accepting people as they are. Remember what Maharishi said – 'Everyone is exactly where they need to be.'" I decide to accept the English boy exactly where he's at. I start meditating again and the peace is blissful.

Two days later in a meeting I share what I've discovered.

"I've noticed that just by intending to accept people as they are I have no desire to identify with my judgements about those people. And the peculiar thing is, this approach not only eliminates discomfort for me, it also appears to induce happiness and joy in the people I've been judging. I'm also discovering that if I accept anything in life, it eliminates drama for me. So, I've got a new statement of truth: acceptance equals no drama."

Maharishi says, "Good job, Greg. That's a great thing to see."

It's 8pm later in the week and I sit looking around the room. Everyone has their eyes closed, meditating. Maharishi walks in and takes his seat at the front. I'm aware of energy in my solar plexus. Maybe it's there because I want to be first in with a question. I ask, "Maharishi, why are we here? What is our purpose in life?"

We make intense eye contact as he begins answering my question. "We are here to live fully in this present moment, to be alive in every moment and to have fun. Or in other words we are here to be actively attentive to the Stillness within. In this state we are able to fully engage with the world around us, free from the limitations of Mini-me. As we flow in this eternal moment, following our intuition and passion, we function harmoniously and our lives naturally become ones of service and of helping humanity to heal. We don't have to work out what we are here to do, all we need to do is let go of the internal chatter and remain attentive to this present moment."

He pauses to have a drink, and then with a mischievous smile says, "There are three ways we can become free of Mini-me. We can be born enlightened, or we can be struck by lightning and wake up free, or we can be guided to freedom by a teacher. Given that the first two events haven't occurred for you yet, option three is your last hope."

I laugh then I realise I've never hesitated to take a mentor in business, but I've been resisting asking Maharishi to be my teacher. I've run out of reasons why I shouldn't ask him. I know I'm here to get free, and I need him to lead me to that level of consciousness.

"Maharishi, will you be my teacher?" I ask.

"Are you willing to do whatever it takes to be free?"

"Absolutely."

"Then it would be my honour to be your teacher."

"Thank you."

Finally, I'm not alone. That night I meditate for hours. It appears my experience has shifted. There is less trying and forcing involved. It's as if my nervous system has finally relaxed.

The next step is to take novitiate vows. There's to be a ceremony in four nights' time. They are the first vows and involve a commitment for one year. Seven of us are here receiving an explanation of the vows and the practicalities of the period leading up to the ceremony.

Jaya, one of the five leading teachers at the retreat, says, "Starting tonight after dinner you will all go into a three-day period of fasting and silence. The purpose of this is to purify the body and still the mind. It's a wonderful opportunity to observe the addiction the mind has to thinking. We get to see how much energy we put into outward attention. But we also notice that the peace we seek is always there. Most importantly, we get an uninterrupted opportunity to commit our life to freedom, and the first words we say after coming out of the period of silence will be our vows."

She pauses, then continues. "You will all be taking white vows. White is the path of joy and purity. This means you will need to wear white clothes for the vows ceremony and quite possibly for the remainder of your time here, unless Maharishi thinks that another path serves you better. You also need a ring to place on your wedding finger, and you won't be able to cut your hair. Greg, you won't be able to shave."

Shit!

"The purpose of not shaving or cutting your hair is to master contentment," she explains. "Oh, and I nearly forgot. You are also prohibited from having sex for the rest of the time you're here."

I knew about the sex thing, but as I read the words of the vows printed on the sheet of paper the word *obedience* stands out.

Huh. Not sure if I'm keen on that.

"What does obedience mean in the context of this teaching?" I ask hesitantly.

She responds, "In my life I always wanted to do things my way. It was always my way or the highway. In the context of the vows, obedience means to allow the greater will to flow rather than resisting it."

I nod and Jaya begins explaining the five vows that are printed on the sheet of paper I'm holding.

The first is *Ahimsa*, or non-violence. She says we all come to Ascension with violent or harsh tendencies. Harshness stems from judgement. This vow is the commitment not to identify with our judgements.

The second is *Satya*, or truthfulness. Only truth exists when we rest in the Stillness.

The third is *Asteya*, or non-stealing. The mind has a tendency to take ownership of every emotion and thought and make it all about us. The reality is that every movement of thought and feeling comes from the Stillness. When we master non-stealing, we don't hold on to anything, and allow all thoughts and feelings to return to the Stillness.

The next vow is *Brahmacharya*, or self-restraint. Jaya explains that throughout our daily lives it's important to create boundaries that will establish and maintain our peace, to make decisions that will serve our growth in consciousness. For example, we might commit ourselves to meditating for two to three hours every day in order to maintain and refine our attentiveness to the Stillness.

The final vow is *Aparigraha*, or non-grasping. Too often we want to take full control of everything in our lives. This vow reminds us to cease trying to control events and to allow the flow of the Infinite to make its own way.

On the evening I'm taking my vows I sit on the floor looking directly at Maharishi. He is sitting just over a metre away from me. The Stillness is palpable as I begin speaking for the first time in three days.

"I dedicate my life, my heart, my body, my soul to the White Ishaya path . . ." At the end of my recital he tells me that my Ishaya name, a Sanskrit name, is Mahakala. I feel so happy and content. It feels as if I love myself way more than I could ever have imagined.

Maharishi says to the seven of us sitting around him, "I'm very pleased for you. I'm so happy it has worked out for you and I honour your commitment. It's such an important commitment. I encourage you to read your vows at the start of each day – it will give a different quality to your experience of the day."

I'm meditating for hours on end in a reclining chair and it's bliss. I'm loving it. I'm feeling so much more relaxed and alert at the same time. As the days turn into weeks I feel more comfortable and less judgemental. I'm conversing more freely. My daily calculations of how much it would cost per day if I left have ceased. I'm laughing spontaneously and I'm remaining in a state of not thinking for longer periods.

I'm aware my old beliefs and positions are dissolving. I'm making a lot of new friends, and interestingly most of them are women. I've never had female friends in my whole life.

Having said that, I've always thought, "I'll only be happy when I find the right woman". Miraculously, my obsession with finding that woman is diminishing. I know I don't need a woman to be happy.

For me there's no doubt that this teaching is not just a concept. It works. The instant I apply the guidance from Maharishi and the other monks is the instant an expansion of my awareness occurs. I decide on the spur of the moment to give Esther a call. I share my experience and suggest this path could be hers too. She tells me that she's on her own path, that she's learning a lot from her new partner and that at the moment he is her teacher. I get off the phone and instantly a pang of loss hits me. Then I become aware of what's happening and disengage the story. The dull feelings dissolve. I realise how fortunate I am to have a teacher who can lead me to freedom. No more cocoons of melancholy for me.

EIGHTEEN

I've been here four months eating vegetarian food and drinking water. Apart from yoga once a day and a 30-minute walk, I'm meditating up to eight hours a day and most of the remaining time I'm sitting in evening meetings. Even with this reduction in exercise I've lost about 10 kilos and I feel so much more energetic.

I've been exploring the impact different foods and beverages have on my pure body. The first time I went to town I ate a steak and that slowed me down big time. I fell asleep an hour after eating it. The second time I drank two cups of coffee. The caffeine cranked me up for a couple of hours.

Last night I went for sugar. When I returned from town after stuffing myself with ice cream and chocolate I was manic. It was difficult to calm either my mind or my body. If I had to label the energy passing through my nervous system and body after my big sugar hit I would say it was depression. It was hard to swallow, my throat was dry, and there was a dull tingling sensation in my stomach. Around 1am I managed to rest and focus, and I spent the remainder of the night meditating. The experience gave new meaning to a sign I saw in a gift shop: "Unattended children will be given two cans of soda pop and an ice-cream".

Now it's 7am the following morning and I'm lying in bed, bearded cheek on the pillow. My skin feels abraded from the coarse facial hair. I decide not to rub or aggravate my face so I get out of bed, wrap a towel around my waist and make my way to the bathroom, eager to wash my beard and face. I can't wait to feel clean again. I look in the mirror and see the patches of grey melded with brown. I look 10 years older.

A few weeks later I go off to the evening meeting. My group has formed a tight-knit team that works effortlessly together. We each look after each other without being prompted. Being the only man with 11 women means it's important that I avoid developing a relationship with any one of them. The dynamics could get a bit twitchy if I did. So I'm blown away when near the end of the meeting one of my buddies, Juliet, suddenly says, "Mahakala, why do you have such resistance to having a relationship with me? You know we are both fond of each other. When we kissed it was so tender and loving."

Jesus! What's this all about? I look around the room. No one has a clue what's going on, but most are looking sideways at me. This woman must be mad. Fortunately Maharishi isn't here. I don't respond. How can I? These meetings aren't designed for people to harpoon each other in front of 60 others. I've just been hit from left field by an accusation of non-compliance and I've got no idea what it's all about. After about half a minute Jaya, who is leading the meeting, says, "OK, this is probably a good time to wrap up."

Thanks sister. You've just saved my day. I seek out a different woman from our little social outing last night. "What was that all about?" I ask.

"Don't you remember? When we arrived back from the nightclub you went off with Juliet for about 10 minutes. I saw you kissing her in the car park, then you came back and insisted I lie on the drive with you so we could look up at the night sky."

"You're joking!"

"No. I'm not."

Walking away I shake my head as I slowly begin to recall last night's activities. I'd decided that after abstaining from alcohol for four months it was time to have a taste. I'd organised to go into town to participate in the prohibited activity with two of my female buddies. I didn't give too much away other than suggesting we'd have a light meal. We kicked off at one of the local bars and the first beer in what seemed like a lifetime went down a treat. After we'd consumed three rounds we headed across the road to a nightclub. I forged ahead with a martini. I can't remember if the other two had one or not. I don't know how we got home.

Clearly I was up to my old tricks.

Maybe my experimentation with evenings away from the retreat centre should be moderated. I'd better talk with my accuser and tell her I'm sorry. I'm fond of her, but I have no interest in a relationship.

A week later I ask Maharishi if I can take the next vows. He agrees and tells me to take Black Novice Vows – the path of ruthless compassion. These vows don't require a period of silence and fasting, but the commitment is greater on many levels. These vows are for a lifetime, and as significant as my first vows were, they involved a different level of consciousness. In reality the first vows came from a conceptual level. These vows are offered from a deeper level of awareness.

As I sit resting after I have taken my Black Vows, the power of the moment is intense. At the conclusion of proceedings I make a beeline for the bathroom. I can't wait to remove my gnarly beard. As I look in the mirror I notice my face is relaxed and open. My eyes are fresh and alert, and the crow's feet around them are considerably less deep than two months ago. I feel a sense of peace that I thought would never be possible.

The course is coming to an end. When I arrived here I had no interest in being a monk. I just wanted freedom from the chatter. But now I know I want others to experience this. I want to teach Ascension. So for this last month I have been participating in an intensive teacher-training programme.

Maharishi continues teaching us new topics. One evening he uses his hands to illustrate a pipe. "In very simple terms, our nervous system operates like a tube, with energy flowing through it. The energy actually has nothing to do with us, but once we identify the energy with a particular feeling or emotion, we've made it all about us. Once this labelling is in place we effectively close one end of the tube and the energy stops flowing. For example, we may label the energy as sadness and then "Mini-me" starts a cross-examination: 'Oh, I'm feeling sad. Why am I sad? What's causing me to be sad? Why is it happening again? I thought I had dealt with this issue. When will life start getting easy for me?'"

Once this line of enquiry is underway the energy is well and truly trapped in the nervous system, and the story becomes emotional and larger than life. As soon as we stop labelling the energy as an emotion, both ends of the tube are effectively reopened and the energy resumes flowing freely again. Peace is restored. Here is your homework topic for the next 24 hours: assume that any label you use to define an emotion is incorrect. Also, assume that whatever reason you think you are experiencing an emotion right now is completely incorrect."

This is a biggie for me. I'd love to be free of the intensity of emotion. About an hour into my meditation I begin to feel wound up and anxious, a very familiar emotion for me. As soon as I become aware that I'm anxious, I consciously become aware of my body. I realise there's an intense tightness in my solar plexus. As instructed, I stop labelling this tightness as anxiety, and very soon the intensity subsides and peace prevails.

Next Maharishi talks about desire. He explains that desires are a perfectly normal part of life. "There is nothing wrong with having desires. It's holding on to our desires that causes the problems. If you remember the moments in your life when you achieved your desire – they were moments of happiness and joy. But the achievement was not the reason for our sense of fulfilment. Joy was revealed when you stopped thinking about your desire. Have the desire but every time you notice you're caught up thinking about the desire, let it go and see what happens to your experience of life. Contentment is revealed when we stop thinking about our desires."

I remember the moment when I realised the tumour in my head gave me an opportunity to escape from the business. I was without desire for the first time in years and I experienced so much joy.

While I've been here I've been talking on the phone with the board of directors once a month, but in between the calls I barely have a single

thought relating to business. The intriguing thing is that I used to completely identify with being a businessman. Much of my time was consumed
thinking about business-related activities. Now I couldn't care less. I'm
grateful for the life it has given me and the opportunity the management
team have given me to be here on this six-month retreat, but I realise I
no longer has any interest in this business or, for that matter, any other
business. I have the desire to sell the business easily and profitably, but
every time I become aware that I'm thinking about the outcome I let it go
and I remain calm and peaceful.

In a meeting two weeks before the end of my course a new arrival asks,
"Maharishi can you talk about God? I have so much difficulty with the
word."

"Sure. The first recorded name of God was in Sanskrit about 5000 years
ago. Sat-Chit-Ananda. Translated it is Truth, Pure Existence, Consciousness
and Joy. When we are present and aware of the Stillness, absent of movement, we have the purest experience of God. God is the boundless ocean
of love within us all."

The new woman interrupts Maharishi and asks, "What is the difference
between the Stillness and God?"

"The Stillness and The One are other words for God. When we are alert
and attentive to the Stillness there is no sense of an individual separate
from that. There is nothing separate from God. There is only The One. God
is not a concept, nor is it an old man with a beard. We are all a manifestation
of God.

She asks, "What is Heaven?"

"Many great sages, including Christ, taught that the Kingdom of Heaven
is within, and that it is imminent. Or in other words the Kingdom of
Heaven is Now. The Kingdom of Heaven is the experience we have when
we remain attentive to the Stillness now."

In the last meeting of the retreat I ask Maharishi, "With respect to our vow of Brahmacharya and sex, can we have sex when we go back home?"

"Yes, as long as it is not casual and meaningless."

I push it further, "Does that mean we can have casual, meaningful sex?"

"No. You need to be in a loving relationship."

Well, that's clear then.

NINETEEN

I arrive back in New Zealand on 5 November 2006. I've been renting an old house on the shores of Lake Brunner, on the West Coast, for a year or two as a getaway, so I settle back there. My mother lives in Greymouth, half an hour's drive away and I go to see her often. Instantly it's clear I'm getting on much better with her. Loving her as she is and not being judgemental is allowing me to appreciate so much about her. It's easy for me to praise her, and the love between us is very apparent. I've come to see that I created the frustration for myself in the past because I judged her. It's a confirmation to me that if I accept her – or anyone else – fully, if I see them as being perfect just as they are, it allows a much deeper connection to reveal itself.

I'm also so much more accepting of my brothers. After talking about my experiences, my brothers and their wives and several other people I know want to learn to Ascend. Despite my mother telling me, "You've done some weird things in your life, but this monk thing takes the cake," she wants to learn too.

After two weeks I travel to Christchurch to see the management team. The business is going swimmingly. It appears that eliminating the rotting head of the fish has worked wonders. The business has doubled in value since I learnt to meditate 18 months ago. A few days later I get a phone call from an Aussie who is interested in our business. Are we interested in selling? Yes, we are. Magic.

I start socialising with my friends again. Some are intrigued by what I've been up to. Others have insufficient interest even to enquire what I've been doing for the past six months. I tell those who are interested that, in a nutshell, I've just committed myself to being free of the chatter in my head in every moment. Telling them I'm a monk with a Sanskrit name, and have committed my life to helping heal humanity would probably go down like the proverbial lead balloon. I also have another MRI scan of my head to determine if the treatment for the tumour has been successful. The result is everything I could have hoped for. The neuroma is dead.

After about a month on the Coast I realise I would like to live with other monks. One benefit would be having other people to meditate with. The idea of living harmoniously with other people unencumbered by the ego and all its tricks of control and judgement is another draw card, but mostly it will allow me to share my experience and receive feedback from my colleagues – feedback that will identify if I'm holding any subtle, yet limiting, judgements and positions that separate me from the Stillness.

I fly to Auckland to visit the Brightpath Ishaya centre where six monks live together. We go out together on the first night to have a meal and socialise. The following day I convene a strategy meeting. I want to live with them, but half of them are functioning like hippies, and as far as I'm concerned that's nonsense.

I ask them, "What is it you like doing most? What do you see as your individual strengths?"

A young hippy who looks like Christ has been presenting introductory talks. He says, "I love teaching the weekend courses, but I don't feel comfortable giving introductory talks or convening follow-up workshops."

They all share what they are passionate about. Most of them have been doing things they don't particularly enjoy.

I apply my business skills to the problem. There are sufficient individual capabilities to allow the establishment of a robust team. Two of us will focus on introductory talks and follow-up meetings, three will focus on weekend meditation courses, and one will do the administration.

Basically we will all be doing what we are all here to do – follow our passion.

As a group our objective is clear – to help shift consciousness for humanity. I tell them, "I want to move in with you but I want to live like I always have – in abundance. Forget about making money from the teaching. You all need to get jobs so that you're financially independent. And from there we can all teach without any stickiness around money."

The boy who looks like Christ has been trying to augment any income from teaching by busking with his violin outside supermarkets. Two others want to get jobs working in cafes. I respond, "Look, the three of you are intelligent, educated and personable young people. If you are going to work, get a career, not a job. Determine what it is you'd like to do and I'll help you prepare a CV."

While I'm in Auckland I start my introductory talks with a presentation to a small group of people. At the end of the presentation several people are undecided – they probably aren't going to learn. So I say to them, "If you don't feel inspired to learn to Ascend, then I encourage you to learn to meditate using a different technique. If you don't want to do that, then at least do more of what you love doing. We're all attracted to activities that naturally reveal peace and love. Whether it's carving down snow-covered slopes on a set of skis, or reading, or running, or listening to music, or painting, or gardening, or fishing – we're all naturally drawn to that experience of peace."

Within three weeks the Christ lookalike has cut his hair and has a career working for a multinational company as a customer services officer responsible for a large geographical market. The second monk gets a position in human resources recruiting management staff. Another young monk gets a job in an insurance firm. One of the hippies decides that working isn't for him and leaves. We all move into a large modern home near the beach. It has a swimming pool and a stunning garden.

Three months later and I realise how comfortable I am when I introduce myself as a monk. I'm being a bit mischievous because I'm using it as a litmus test. I've noticed people are either intrigued – they want to know more out of curiosity or they are interested in learning to meditate – or they show absolutely no interest at all. One night I'm chatting to a man who must be in his early 60s at a black tie function. Five minutes into the conversation he asks me, "What do you do for crust?"

"I'm a monk."

He steps back two paces as if I've just told him I'm the father of his son. He turns around and reels off to the other side of the gathering. I'm surprised, but I quickly realise he is very confused. Five minutes later he comes back and sidles up to me. "So what's this monk thing all about? Are you a Buddhist?"

"No. I'm an E-shy-ya monk. I teach a relatively unknown meditation technique. There are about 300 of us teaching around the world. Basically, we teach tools that release the mind from thinking."

"Huh. So is it religious?"

"No. We tell people they don't have to believe a word we say because it's an experiential teaching. You know what it's like when you have an experience. You don't need to believe anything, you just *know*. And we teach anyone regardless of their religion. People who have a strong commitment to their faith often continue to practise their faith after they have learnt to Ascend. Ascension doesn't interfere." Pointing to my suit I say, "And clearly I'm not required to wear robes and roman sandals."

The following week we are having our weekly get-together at the house and I say, "I don't know about you guys, but when I'm asked what meditation technique I teach I have trouble telling people that I'm an Ishaya of the Brightpath and that I teach a meditation technique called Ishayas' Ascension. It's a mouthful and it sounds weird."

The others agree.

"Have you ever Googled Ishayas' Ascension?" I ask. "There's a lot of scary stuff out there coming from individuals, as well as groups calling themselves Ishayas."

One of the other monks says, "Yeah, I have. I've even seen Ishayas referred to as a cult."

"*Jeesuz*. Look, if people want to learn to meditate they will Google meditation, not Ascension, so I think we need to use the word *meditation* in our name."

We all agree that we want a name in Australia and New Zealand that allows the teaching to be more accessible, to demystify it and to couch it as a meditation technique. We talk with Maharishi and he gives us the go-ahead. I get in contact with the marketing and advertising people we use in my business to help us develop and promote a new brand for the Brightpath Ishayas. One of the other monks comes up with the name Nowspace, and the creative people come up with the by-line "Meditation for a sweeter life". I stump up $60,000 to fund the rebranding, including a new website, newspaper advertising, public talks and some guerilla marketing ideas tossed in for good measure.

One of the creative guys is nearly as hunched as I used to be. He prepares a series of slogans, and we run a series of large-format advertisements in the Wellington *Dominion Post* and the *New Zealand Herald*: "Now is the winter of my bloody discontent".

During the same week Auckland is about to introduce a new household wheelie-bin dedicated to recycling. We have adhesive stickers printed to apply to the lids of 1000 bins in neighbouring suburbs. Six of us go out one night to place the labels, which declare: "Wrap up your troubles and pop them in the wheelie bin." The labels list the website www.nowspace.co.nz and our phone number.

The next day at 10am I check the messages on the phone. The first eight messages are from aggrieved rate payers, and the ninth message tells me, "This is the Auckland City Council Recycling Manager here. We've received complaints from a large number of customers who are very unhappy that you have placed advertising on Auckland City Council property. If you don't remove the stickers within the next 24 hours we will consider legal action."

Oh dear. That night we go out to remove the labels. We can't budge them. The adhesive is too tough. Shit!

Two months later and the advertising campaign hasn't been effective. The number of people wanting to learn Nowspace meditation has not increased. What to do? Surrender? Let go of any possible expectation? All I know is I want to help shift consciousness. Maybe writing a book could help by shifting the awareness of readers as they read the book?

I decide to go on a road trip through the South Island. Along the way I call in to see Esther. I haven't seen her for 18 months.

Pointing to the gold band on my ring finger, she asks, "Are you married?"

"No, this is a symbol of my commitment to remain present in every moment. Forever."

Her expression suggests that she understands what I mean. She then tells me she's keen to learn to Ascend and she doesn't mind if I teach her.

Three weeks later at 7 o'clock on the Friday night of the weekend course, Esther is part of the group. Although I see the irony in me being Esther's teacher, I feel completely relaxed with her and she too appears to be comfortable. Her partner is here also. I introduce myself as Greg, and tell them I also have a teaching name Mahakala, but I invite them to call me whatever they feel comfortable with.

A monk colleague leads the teaching – I'm in awe of her ability to articulate the teaching. It's another opportunity for me to keep learning.

During the session the next morning I say, "Consider the sky for a moment. It has been there since the beginning of time and it probably will be there at the end of time. It's formless, infinite and unbounded. And it never changes. Little white clouds float by, storm clouds scurry, hurricanes charge through, aircraft, missiles and birds dart across the sky. But the sky couldn't care less. Not for one moment does the sky identify with these movements. How ridiculous would it be if the sky thought it was a cloud or a plane?

Our true nature is just like the sky. The difference between us and the sky is that our consciousness has developed a habit of identifying with the movement of endless thoughts and feelings. As we retrain our awareness to observe the Stillness within, we develop the ability to be uninterested in the thoughts and emotions, and the apparent turbulence of life becomes nothing more than clouds passing."

On Sunday, at the end of the course, I write, "Where in your life are you compromising?" on the whiteboard. I turn to the group and say, "I know it seems incongruous to ask you to think about something when we've been teaching you all weekend to let go of thinking, but acting on this question has the ability to change your life. We don't want you to share the answer with us – just consider it seriously."

August 2007 and it's the New Zealand ski season again. The contract for the sale of the business is completed. Despite the reality of doing a multi-million-dollar deal it's been an effortless dance. I've decided to reward myself for doing the deal with a day heli-skiing. Jonty and Cliffy are joining me.

Not long after arriving at the homestead the helicopter that will take us to the ski area banks to commence its descent. The thump of the blades and the shrill whistle of the jet engine flood the landing zone but it doesn't disturb my peace. We climb in. The pilot gives us headphones and instructs us to fasten our seat belts. The helicopter rises 20 metres above the paddock, then the pilot elevates the tail and lowers the nose.

I look at the others. They are as excited as I am. The machine effortlessly gains altitude, rising up over a series of ravines and ragged ridges and on towards the peak.

As we go higher my attention is drawn across the valley to the marbled ice flow on Mt Aspiring. Above us, at the top of the scrub-covered slope, lies an expansive snow-covered basin. As the helicopter approaches the landing site it's clear the area would be lucky to accommodate a couple of cars. The pilot manoeuvres the chopper down and the skids come to rest on the small snowy platform. One by one we follow the instructions to disembark. Hunched over, we recover our skis and poles from the carry cage mounted on the skids. We move away from the chopper then rest on one knee. The guide gives the thumbs up. As the helicopter rises my body is blasted with snow. I look up briefly and see the undercarriage of the chopper as it peels off to descend into the basin below. It disappears. All that remains is a slight southwest breeze. And silence.

The magnitude of the main divide is accentuated by the crisp, cloudless sky. Wherever I look I see snow-covered slopes dominated by irregular patches of grey shadow and punctuated with smaller scattered outcrops of rock in shades of purple, mustard, charcoal and cobalt blue. We stand in silence. A strong sense of connection permeates everything. Peace and stillness prevail as I experience deep appreciation for this isolated place.

We clip our boots into the ski bindings and the guide leads us off, dropping down a small chute on the west face. Cliffy follows, then me, and finally, Jonty. Keeping the weight of my body over the balls of my feet and my body oriented down the fall line, I carve into and out of each turn. Cliffy, slightly ahead and to the right of me, blasts a plume of loose snow over my path. I move further to the left to avoid the disturbance on the snow surface. The edge of my downhill ski bites into a patch of crusty surface snow, but my thighs work effortlessly to maintain the pressure on the edge. I ski on, fully engaged and at one.

At the end of the day back in our rented house in Wanaka Cliffy suggests we have a joint. I think, why not? I'm interested to explore the Stillness with some drugs on board. Cliffy has a measured toke. I inhale more than my fair share of smoke and soon my consciousness is altered. Quickly I become aware that I need to remain super focused and attentive. Although the experience feels rich and powerful, it's very apparent I have a strong tendency to identify with my thoughts – much, much more than normal. During the next three days it's as if my nervous system is fractured. My ability to remain attentive to the Stillness has diminished. I spend more time than usual meditating to refine my nervous system.

I won't be having another joint in a hurry.

Six months later I call Esther and she tells me that the question I asked about compromise has had a big impact on her. She and her boyfriend decided to terminate their relationship a few weeks after she learnt to meditate. She tells me she is routinely meditating and using the techniques with her eyes open and much has changed in her life as a consequence. She's enjoying living in the Now. She's feeling less stressed and more content with her life, and she's experiencing many magical moments and coincidences. We talk for nearly two hours. It's wonderful. I decide to broach the possibility of us getting back together. Then the unthinkable occurs. We agree to have another go at a relationship. I'm so happy and full of excitement.

We decide to go away for a weekend. On the second night I tell her, "I'm committed to our relationship, but you need to know my primary commitment is to remaining attentive to the Stillness. It's only with that commitment that I will be able to function in a relationship without judgement."

She responds, "Well, that's empowering for me. It takes the pressure off me feeling as though I'm responsible for your happiness. Whenever I've been in a relationship I've always felt responsible for my partner's happiness. It means when I do things I won't have to second guess whether my behaviour will please you or not."

"Great. There's just the practicality of me needing to close my eyes for three hours every day. It won't be an inconvenience for you. I usually meditate for an hour and a half before I have breakfast and again from 4 till about 5.30 in the afternoon."

"That's fine."

"Cool." I feel light and expanded.

A few weeks later I'm co-convening a one-day workshop. In response to a question I say, "Most of us are aware of some synchronicity, but we are unaware of the depth and unbounded nature of the magic flowing around us. We don't notice most of it because we are constantly distracted by the internal chatter. We seldom acknowledge magic even when it's obvious. We downplay the manifestation of a desired outcome by seeing it as 'just a coincidence'. Or we reject what is delivered to us because our judgements suggest there is something wrong with what is provided. The reality is life has always flowed to us – we've never needed to go after life."

After lunch a female participant asks me, "Do you mind me asking you what your own experience of life is like these days?"

"Sure. Life has become an exciting road trip – I don't know what's around the corner, but I'm continuously excited. It's an adventure. I have no interest in leaving Now to consider what could be ahead, and I have absolutely no interest in the past. I still have thoughts, but I don't consciously identify with them."

She says, "But I think the things that have happened in my life are important. I like thinking about the happy moments in my life – it brings me joy. I also believe that everything that has happened has been important to bring me to this point in life."

"Absolutely. Everything that occurs in life brings us to this exact point now. It was all absolutely necessary. However, thinking about it is just a distraction."

She nods thoughtfully.

"It's much more powerful and exciting to be grounded in the present moment. Then life is like flowing down a river at the same velocity as the current. We become the flow surrounded by everything we need, and all we have to do is to choose to use what is provided, or choose not to. Life becomes effortless and we expend minimal energy achieving things. When we start thinking or trying to control things, it's like swimming against the current. And the more we think, or try to control things, the more isolated we become from reality. Living in the thinking mode requires so much more energy than resting in this present moment."

Someone else asks me, "What will happen to my personality if I let go of all this thinking? Will my personality fall away too?"

"I still have a personality," I say, laughing. "I hope. Or maybe I don't?" The others laugh too.

"Because the internal chatter is continual we think it is our personality. But it isn't. Letting go of thinking instantly dissolves the ego and that which remains is our true personality. The moment we identify with a thought is the moment the ego is activated. And for most of us, the identification with thought is endless – the ego is fully engaged. The repressed aspects of our true personality are revealed as the ego falls away."

TWENTY

Maharishi comes to New Zealand to convene a seven-day retreat. On the second night of the retreat he starts the meeting by saying, "Life is continually changing. That's just how it is. The problem is, we have a tendency to resist or try to control the change unfolding in our lives. It's not change itself that causes suffering, it's *resistance* to change."

He explains that our resistance is often based on judgements about the significance of the change. Then he goes on to relate an ancient Taoist parable called "Good news? Bad news? Who knows?" The story goes: Many years ago, a Chinese farmer works hard cultivating and harvesting crops so that he can save money to purchase a horse. After many harvests he searches for and finds the perfect horse for his needs. Not long after he takes ownership of the horse, it escapes its tether and gallops away.

His neighbour commiserates: "Bad news about your horse running off."

The farmer replies, "Good news, bad news, who knows?"

Surprisingly, several weeks later, the horse returns with another horse.

The neighbour, taken aback seeing the two horses, exclaims: "What good news it is that you have your horse back and another one to boot!"

"Good news, bad news, who knows?" replies the farmer. The farmer generously gives the second horse to his son, who after riding the horse for only one day is thrown and badly injures his arm and shoulder.

"Sorry to hear the bad news about your son," says the neighbour.

Predictably, the farmer responds, "Good news, bad news, who knows?"

Within a week, the emperor's men come and take every able-bodied man and youth to fight in a war. The farmer's son is unfit for war duty. Good news, bad news, who knows?

Maharishi concludes, "So if a new or troubling event occurs, rather than being caught up in an angry or fearful response, ask the question, 'Good news? Bad news? Who knows?'"

It's early 2008 and Esther and I have moved in together. I'm living in her new home with her furniture, her art and her dog and I'm socialising with her friends. This is something that I would have struggled with in the past. But now it's as if there are two completely different people engaged in our relationship compared to the first time around. Last time our egos were fully engaged. We were continuously judging each other, trying to control each other, resisting each other's suggestions and trying to dominate one another. Apart from the odd moment, love was always conditional and communication was seldom open. Our true personalities just didn't have a chance to reveal themselves.

But this time we are both finding that our love and appreciation for each other continue to expand. The growth in our relationship continues to be rapid as long as we are willing to discuss issues as soon as they come up. If Esther sees a behaviour of mine that is limiting my experience of life, she tells me. As soon as I become aware of the limitation, I have the opportunity to let go of that pattern of thinking and move forward on an altered tack. Our communication can be direct and forthright, but always it is grounded in love. Rather than the relationship being based on making it all about "me", our relationship is based on giving.

Not long after moving in with Esther I teach her friend Phil to meditate. He has terminal cancer. He is immediately passionate about the peace and comfort it provides. The oncologist treating him comments that he is the calmest patient he has ever had. But within months he passes away.

Some time later his wife calls. "Hi Greg, I'm organising a memorial service for Phil. I was wondering who could give a tribute for him and I immediately thought of you. I know you didn't spend much time together, but he said you and he had a strong connection. He was a Catholic, but in his last days meditation gave him much more than religion ever did. Would you like to give a tribute for him?"

"Absolutely. When are you having the service?"

"On Wellington Cup Day. It was a race meet Phil attended nearly every year for 20 years."

"OK. I'll be there."

I get off the phone and appreciate what a great honour it is to be asked. Everyone will want to celebrate his life.

A few weeks later I'm standing at the cemetery with about 30 people. I know about a dozen of them – most certainly I knew Phil less than any of the others – but I feel comfortable in their presence. Of the people I know, several have prematurely lost someone close to them within the last five years.

I begin, "If you consider the sky for a moment, you'll realise it is unending and eternal. In reality the sky is no different from each of us. We are all eternal. If there was anything Phil would want to say to you right now it would be: 'I love you unconditionally and my love for you is forever. I have no judgements about you, or what you are doing. It's time for you to let go of the grieving and the sense of loss. It's time to move on with your life. You have my full support in everything you do.' "

Looking directly at his wife and two adult children I say, "It's not to suggest you should forget him, or that he will forget you, but rather it's time to get on with what we are all here to do – to live life to the fullest in every moment, to experience unbroken love and happiness."

I'm aware that my speech is having an impact, not just on Phil's family but on many of the other people who have lost loved ones. At the conclusion of the tribute we all choose a horse in a sweepstake for the cup. As the race starts we raise a glass of champagne for Phil.

Life can be a funny old thing. A year later Esther decides to participate in the six-month Mastery of the Self course. I visit her during her course and on my arrival the changes in her are profound. She even looks different. She is light and happy. It is obvious she's having a sweet experience and her passion for the Stillness is no less than my own. After a week at the retreat centre I share with everybody in the evening meeting how my relationship with Esther is going. "Every day there seems to be a new quality, or refinement, to the level of acceptance and appreciation I have for her." Then I ask Maharishi if I can take the eternal Ishaya Vows. He agrees and tells me there will be a vows ceremony the following week.

In the meeting on the night of the vows Maharishi says, "If you had a habit before coming here, such as a habit of pulling wings off flies, and in surrendering you transcend the addiction to that activity, then you have had a profound effect on every other human who is dominated by that same habit. The job of surrendering is not about you – not for one second has it ever been about you. It has always been about transcending that aspect of human consciousness for all. It is a service to humanity."

I know fully the significance of the vows I'm about to take. But the words come as if someone else is delivering them: "From this moment forward, my every thought, feeling and action is surrendered to the will of God and dedicated to the healing of humanity. I will be utterly ruthless; I will master true compassion. I surrender what is left of myself to God . . ."

Once I have completed the vows Maharishi says, "It's such an honour to witness the vows you have given. It is so, so important."

Esther and I go through to the dining room to have a cup of tea and I say to her, "In order to serve humanity I am surrendering all my self-righteous thoughts; my judgemental thoughts; my belligerent, indignant, taking umbrage thoughts; my 'I-wouldn't-do-it-that-way-if-I-were-you' thoughts; my 'Where-is-the respect?' thoughts. I'm letting go of every angst-ridden, melancholic, depressed, and 'I'm-inarticulate' thoughts; the thought that I need to drink heavily or smoke marijuana to experience peace and happiness. The 'I'm-unlovable' thoughts, the frustrated thoughts. The 'I'm-the-most-uncoordinated-person-I-know' thoughts; the resisting and rejecting thoughts; the doubting someone else's capability, as well as doubting my ability, thoughts. Added to that there are the obsessive thoughts about falling in love with someone other than the one I'm with. I am surrendering those too."

She raises her eyebrows and adds, "I'm surrendering some of those too, plus my own favourites: doubt, lack of trust, unworthiness of love, fear of losing all my money, I'm not good enough, controlling, planning. And needing to do everything and do it perfectly. All of them, I surrender for the good of humanity."

Esther and I are sitting on the deck of the new house I had built while she was away on her six-month retreat. It is in the foothills of the Southern Alps, a location that is isolated and stunningly beautiful, yet only an hour and a half's drive from Christchurch. She has returned home to live with me and she too is now a monk. She says, "Has it ever occurred to you that I woke you up when I ended our relationship and that drove you to Ascension. Then you returned to wake me up?"

I laugh. "Yeah, I guess that's what happened."

Esther says, "I would never have predicted that I'd be a monk, let alone a monk in a relationship with another monk."

"Bizarre, eh?"

"I always thought we were soul mates. I just knew we had to find freedom from our judgements about each other. Otherwise it wasn't viable for us to be together."

"I know."

"I had a strong sense we'd get back together. But I thought it would've taken about 20 years, not three."

I say with a sense of ironic satisfaction, "I thank you for causing me so much grief that I had no alternative but to find my path."

As our conversation continues, my awareness is drawn to the white patches of snow on the mountains behind our home. The pyramid shape of the most prominent mountain draws my eyes upwards. Tubes of cloud dominate the sky like powerful giant fingers. Beyond the clouds lies the vast endlessness and my attention is drawn deeper into the infinite. I move my attention to the depth of colour in the beech trees in our Japanese garden. Deep peace and attentiveness prevail. I remain supremely attentive to the Stillness. For a brief moment I bathe in the satisfaction at the ongoing perfection of my life.

EPILOGUE

If you are looking for a sweeter experience of life have a look at the website www.boundless.info sometime. Some mates and I have cobbled together a few videos. Each clip focuses on one of the clues contained within this book.

ACKNOWLEDGEMENTS

Many people shared my journey in life and it's quite possible that every one of them will have had a different subjective experience of the events I've related. The story is based on actual events, but my memory and interpretation of these events might well be distorted. It's what Mini-me was good at. I have also deliberately manipulated some scenes to give the story a better flow.

Some characters are real but I have changed their names to protect their privacy. Jonty, Clifford, Lukhum, Vlad and Merv are all composite people – they represent many friends and colleagues. For example, the real Merv would never biff a glass of vodka over his shoulder, but he would always be quick to say, "Don't let the truth get in the way of a good story." These characters were an integral aspect of my journey, but some of their behaviour patterns exist only as a reflection of my own.

To achieve an adequate tension in the story many important people have not been included. Some events have been subtly changed and embellished and in some situations the sequence of my life has been altered. I learnt so much from so many people – people who provided me with opportunities or who offered friendship and more than a few laughs. In particular I thank the following for playing their significant role in my life: Monica for her support throughout my prolonged period of unsatisfactory behavior, my family, those boys (men) who are the essence of Jonty, Cliffy and Merv. But especially Esther, for helping me to wake up, and for walking this journey together with me. Also thanks to my dear friends Karen, Cath, June and Cat, who have enthusiastically encouraged me during this project. Thanks to the accomplished authors Rebekah Palmer and Charlotte Randall for knocking this tome into shape. The latter made a big impact on the structure and the pace of the story. Thanks to Sue Reidy for polishing the final edit, and to Geoff Walker for his guidance, and to the capable women at Mary Egan Publishing who created this physical book. Thanks to Robbie Burton at Craig Potton Publishing for having the courage to distribute the book.

The teaching communicated here is the teaching of the One as taught by the Ishayas of the Brightpath. It is not the teaching of Greg Hopkinson. My particular flavour of teaching has been inspired by so many of my monk mates, especially those I regularly spend time with. Thanks for all I have learnt from you and good on you for continuing to remind me to let go. But, most significantly, thanks to my teacher Maharishi Krishnananda Ishaya, for his on-going guidance and commitment to being my teacher, and his desire to give consciousness a good nudge. The Buddha said something like, "It truly is a lucky person who finds their spiritual teacher in life."

I also acknowledge you, the reader, for purchasing this book and reading it.

30490503R00155

Made in the USA
Charleston, SC
17 June 2014